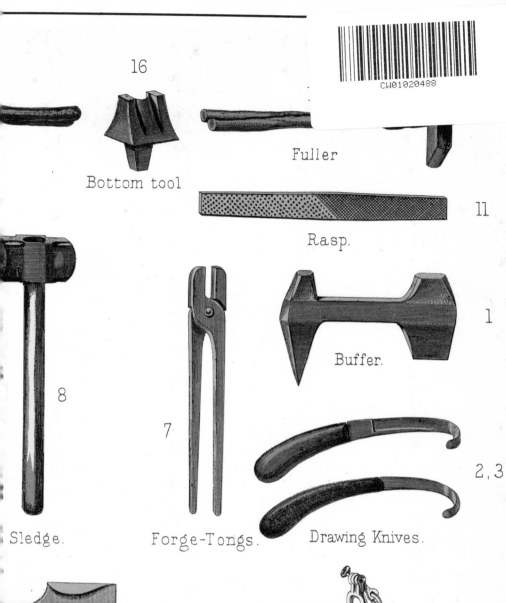

16

Bottom tool

Fuller

11

Rasp.

8

7

1

Buffer.

2, 3

Sledge.

Forge-Tongs.

Drawing Knives.

ttress

A

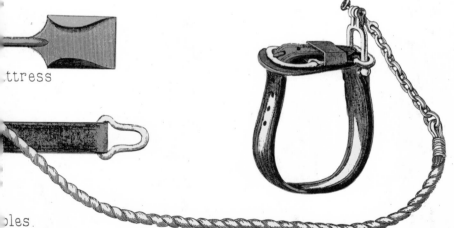

les.

The Farrier and His Craft

VI ET VIRTUTE

Mr K Thomas
Lea Farm
Lea Road
Rugeley
Staffordshire
WS15 3NT

The Farrier and His Craft

The History of the Worshipful Company of Farriers

Leslie B. Prince, CBE
Master 1955–56

Foreword by
HRH The Princess Anne
Mrs Mark Phillips, GCVO

J.A. ALLEN
LONDON · NEW YORK

British Library Cataloguing in Publication Data

Prince, Leslie B.
  The Farrier and his Craft
  Worshipful Company of Farriers – History
  I. Title
  338.632   HD 6461.   H6
  ISBN 085131 353 1

Published in 1980 by
J.A. Allen and Company Limited
1 Lower Grosvenor Place
London SW1W 0EL

Typeset by Inforum Ltd., Portsmouth
in 11 on 12 point Palatino
Printed in Hong Kong by Dah Hua Printing Press Co., Ltd.

Designed by Jonathan Gill-Skelton

DEDICATED to my dear wife Norah

Contents

Acknowledgements

The Author has elsewhere thanked Her Royal Highness The Princess Anne Mrs. Mark Phillips for contributing the Foreword. Many others, too numerous to mention in toto, have helped to greater or lesser degrees, some of whom are mentioned in the text, but particular acknowledgment must be paid to:

Franklin E. Birch, the learned Clerk

Miss Betty Masters, BA, FSA, Deputy Keeper of the Records of Guildhall

Sir Joseph Hollam, Deputy Governor of the Bank of England

Edgar Harborne

Derrick E.L. Parsons of J.A. Allen & Co. Ltd.

George Gould, CBE, Chairman of the Council of the Royal Veterinary College

A.R.W. Porter, Royal College of Veterinary Surgeons

David Tucker for his work in connection with illustrations

To the many Past Masters of the Company, some of whom have been mentioned, but particularly to Sir Hugh Linstead, Brigadier Clabby and Dorian Williams, and to the Senior Past Master George Garnham for the support and encouragement he has given me during a difficult period.

To the indefatigable work of my Secretary, Helen Botting, in assisting me throughout in typing and photostating documents and with the voluminous Index; and to Sue Whitaker, Sheila Mann, David Sinkins, Gerwin Davis and Fay Kingsford for their help in many ways in the preparation of this book.

Finally, to my Editor, John Kennedy Melling, whose unlimited patience has guided an enthusiastic amateur in writing his first book by spending so many evenings and eating so many dinners over a period of eighteen months, and who I am pleased to say has become a member of the Company.

LESLIE B. PRINCE
November 1979.

In writing this Foreword, I hope I will be forgiven for making it sound more like a Foreword to the author, but this history of the Worshipful Company of Farriers has been a real labour of love by Mr Leslie Prince and we in the Company owe him our thanks for all his work on our behalf over many years. Mr Prince joined the livery of the Company in 1936 - was elected to the Court in 1946 and was Master of the Company from 1955-56. As well as the Company he has been deeply concerned with the life of the City and became a member of the Court of Common Council for Bishopsgate Ward in 1950, since then he took his place as Ward Deputy in 1970 and was Chief Commoner in 1971 as well as having been Sheriff to the City 1954-55. His continuous service to the City was rewarded in 1973 when he was awarded the C.B.E. But Mr Prince is first and foremost a Farrier and in this book he has recorded all the achievements of the Company with humour and pride as the Company is one of the few Guilds which is still totally involved in the Craft for which it was formed as a fellowship in 1356 and although the horse is no longer the main form of power and transport, it still holds a place as one of man's best friends with ever widening scope for giving many people a lot of pleasure. That its welfare is still the concern of the Company is very obvious, the Farriers (Registration) Act of 1975 is almost completely the result of lobbying from the Company.

We think we have a Company to be proud of, I know Mr Prince is convinced of it and I hope this book will help, as well as inform, many people who are interested in the horse as well as the Company and the City.

Anne.

Introduction

7th October 1830
Mr. John Callender of No. 9 Barbican, one of the Livery of the Company, attended the Court and delivered the following Memorial on behalf of himself and the other (thirteen) Liverymen whose names are subscribed thereto, which Memorial was read by the Clerk and is as follows, viz:

To the Master, Wardens, and Assistants of the Worshipful Company of Farriers.
'Gentn.
We the undersigned Liverymen of the Company of Farriers being wholly ignorant of the Constitution, Bye-Laws, and the Property, Gifts, Charities, Rights, Privileges and Immunities of the Guild and Fraternity of which we are members; we most respectfully request you will afford us an opportunity to inspect the Charter by which the Company is incorporated and all and every Rule and Order in any way connected with its government.'
(Here follow the 14 names)

Mr. Callender was then informed by the Master that the Court would take the said Memorial into consideration.

6th January 1831
It was resolved that if the Gentlemen who signed the Memorial will appoint any three of their Body for that purpose the Court will at any time which may be convenient allow them the inspection of the Charter and Bye-Laws of the Company.

Almost one hundred and fifty years ago it will be seen that the Liverymen of the Company of Farriers were wholly ignorant of the affairs of the Company.

In 1980 no Liveryman of the Company can plead such ignorance as they have been supplied with a copy of the History of the Company entitled 'The Farriers of London' compiled by Leonard C.F. Robson, Clerk of the Company, which was printed for private circulation in 1949, with my Supplementary History from 1949–1972 and The 'Record' published annually from 1949. Included in the Supplementary History were Chapters on the Registration Committee compiled by Dr. W.R. Wooldrige, MSc DVSc FRCVS FRICS (1951–61) and Mr. Alec Hobson, CVO (1962–72).

This present volume incorporates more conveniently these three sources of information, not all readily available, bringing the story to 1979, and is designed to appeal to Liverymen present and future of the Farriers Company, to working Farriers, and to those interested in our City, our traditions, our countryside and above all in that noble animal the Horse, which our Company has been privileged to help for six centuries.

Naturally, it is not possible to include a full account of the rights and privileges of Liverymen or the rise of crafts guilds in the City of London, although my memorandum on 'The Rights of the Liveryman' and Professor F.R. Bell in his paper on 'The days of the Farriers' have dealt with the subject (see Appendices). Those readers who wish to learn more about the Guilds and Liveries are recommended to read the book 'Discovering London's Guilds and Liveries', the author of which is John Kennedy Melling who has kindly acted as Editor of this volume.

This book has been a labour of love. I have chosen these words for both are true. I had thought of entitling this book 'What to Leave Out' for in reading Minutes covering three hundred years it would have been tempting to include so many of the domestic events which happened at the Court Meetings. With the experience of over forty years as a committee man in the City of London and elsewhere, no one appreciated more than I the many thousands of Resolutions and Amendments which appeared on the pages of the Minute Books of three centuries. Thus Labour indeed it was and it was also of Love. Over thirty years of attending Court Meetings and whilst 'never having shod a horse' no one could fail to be more enthusiastic and full of admiration for the work done by my colleagues who year by year became Masters of the Company. Asked the dominant feature that had pervaded throughout the Company's History, I, would without a moment's hesitation say 'FINANCE' – or the lack of it – for the Company never had any money. It never had any endowments, never able to purchase a permanent Hall or property of any kind, and throughout its history the 'relentless pursuit of riches' by appeal after appeal, enables readers to see that all its endeavours throughout the centuries and especially during the last 90 years have been frustrated by lack of funds. Today with the word 'inflation' (see Appendix 'Value for Money') being part of the World's vocabulary, it is perhaps not so unusual to hear that this or that institution is appealing for this or that object, but in the nineteenth and the early part of the twentieth century, Livery companies were looked upon as the source of wealth from whom everyone expected large donations, and even today those not associated with the City will always start the appeal list – 'Livery Companies of the City of London'.

CHAPTER 1

History

The History of the Company is really divided into four periods:

1   From 1356 when the Farriers in the City were called together by the Mayor of the City of London and first established as a Fellowship until 1674, during which years it was the endeavour of the Company to look after the Trade in the Area, being 'the Cities of London and Westminster or within the seven miles thereof'.

2   From 1674, the date of the Charter, by Letters Patent under the Privy Seal to 1890 when the Company, together with the Royal Agricultural Society and the Royal Society of Veterinary Surgeons, began a Scheme for the Examination and Registration of Shoeing Smiths Nationally.

3   From 1890 to 1975, the date of the Farriers Act.

4   From 1975 to date of publication.

As regards the first two hundred years' activities little is known for practically all the Company's records were lost in the 'Lamentable Accident of Fire in 1666' and, the earliest Minute Book now extant begins in 1719 as will be explained, matters concerning this period have been obtained from the Corporation of London's records. The period 1674 to 1890 is fully Minuted and examples of interest have been extracted. From 1890 to 1975 the history of the Company has been obtained from the Court Minutes and from the Minutes of the Registration Committee which was formed in 1890. Lastly, the present activities since the 1975 Farriers Act have been described from current Minute Books of the Court of the Craft Committee (the new name of the Registration Committee) and the Farriers Registration Council set up by the Company in accordance with the 1975 Act.

An attempt has been made to reproduce some examples from the Court Minutes into various categories, viz: those concerned with Trade and the Craft of Farriery, with Civic matters, reference to the Lord Mayors and Court of Aldermen, reference to the Registration of Farriers, and finally to the domestic activities of the Masters, Wardens and Court of Assistants, details of elections of Masters and their biographies, their disputes, their arrangements for Livery dinners, Court luncheons and some breakfasts.

In its early days the Company was charged with the duty of safeguarding the horse and every farrier and shoesmith was expected to register with the Company, pay its dues, and thus there should have been a sound basis upon which to build its fortune. But from the beginning this was not so. There are constant references to an appeal to the various associations connected with the horse and readers will come across these in this volume. Perhaps the best example is when in 1890 the Company, together with the Royal Agricultural Society, had a meeting at the Mansion House with the Lord Mayor in the Chair when the scheme for the Examination and registration of Shoeing Smiths was evolved – a very high point in the history of the Company. The Registration Committee was formed, moneys were collected and promises were made to keep the Committee viable, but eighteen years later it had completely run out of money. The Company itself could ill afford to subsidise it to the extent of £100 per annum and so on and so forth. This volume will contain many references to its lack of finance. Nevertheless, for over 600 years the Worshipful Company of Farriers has existed and has reached its High Water Mark, with the great challenge to the Farriers Registration Council established by the Farriers (Registration) Act 1975.

The Author began his researches by discussing the earlier history of the Company with Miss Betty Masters BA FSA, the Deputy Keeper of the Records at Guildhall and obtained from her the Ordinances of the Farriers and much information which allowed him to search the references in the records and at least able to give some extracts about the Company from 1356–1692. In 1692 the Company was recorded by the Court of Aldermen as having been in existence since 1356 as Marshalls of the City of London. The medieval Latin Word list gives 'marescalcia' and the variants as medieval Latin for 'stable', stabling, farriery and 'marescallus' for farrier. The Ordinances of 1356 in French refer to 'marchalcie' and 'marechals' with a Latin marginal annotation 'mareschalcie'. Miss Masters is sure that these terms should not be rendered as 'marshalls' and H.T. Riley, the translator of the Ordinances, has not so translated them. Accordingly, whilst the word 'Marshals' has been mentioned in the description of the Six Hundredth Anniversary Banquet and elsewhere, his further researches mentioned above should perhaps have read . . . Fellowship by the name of Farriers of the City of London.

The Blacksmith and the Farrier are so closely connected that the 'man in the street,' if there is such a person, would know of a Blacksmith but might be puzzled by the word 'Farrier'. To the Author's knowledge it is sometimes thought that the word Farrier is a 'Furrier' and it was embarrassing to the Author to have to explain that his Company looked after horses shoes and not his lady's fur coat!

However, when discussing Shoeing it must be borne in mind the old definition that a man who works iron at a forge is a Blacksmith and a man who shoes horses is a Farrier. Thus, although all Farriers are therefore Blacksmiths, not all Blacksmiths are Farriers. The word 'smith' is derived from the old Saxon words 'to smite', while the Norman word for 'smith' was a 'ferrier', a worker in iron, and it is this word that has become associated with those in general charge and care of horses. Nevertheless, as with the tyring process, the shoeing of horses is part and parcel of the Blacksmith's craft.

The London Company of Blacksmiths was formed in the 13th Century, whilst a hundred years later there existed the Fraternity of St. Eloy. The Blacksmiths Company was formed in 1372 and on amalgamation with the Spurriers, the makers of spurs, was chartered in 1571 and are number 40 in the order of precedence of Livery Companies. The Worshipful Company of Farriers received its Charter in 1674 and are number 55. Today the Blacksmiths Company and the Farriers Company use the Hall of the Innholders in College Street in the City of London for their Court meetings. They share the same Patron Saint, St. Eloy, or Eloie or Loye (see page 48). The National Master Farriers and Blacksmiths, which will be referred to elsewhere, have their headquarters at Wakefield in Yorkshire.

To begin with the Company's Records, some of which have been perused, some of which do not appear to be amongst the archives. It must be remembered, and a future reference will be found, that the Company has never had a hall and consequently every scrap of paper Minute books and other documents have been passed from Clerk to Clerk over the last three hundred years. The Guildhall library contains the Minute books only from 1719–1962, a copy of Robson's History and the Author's supplement, 1949–1972, which have been the source of all the later information contained in this publication. (The Calender of Documents, 1356–1972 at the Guildhall Library are shown in Appendix.)

It has been mentioned that the Author discussed the earlier History with Miss Betty Masters, and he is greatly indebted to her for her help and assistance. From a search of the references in the records of the Corporation of London City's Letter Books, which were memoranda books of Civic Proceedings and events which pre-date the actual surviving Minutes of Courts of Aldermen and Common Council – they are called 'Letter Books' because they are distinguished by letters of the alphabet – the books from 1275–1495 (A–L) have been published in calendar of precis form and they include the Ordinances of 1356.

After 1495, the information comes mainly from the Repertories (ie proceedings) of the Court of Aldermen, occasionally from the Journals (proceedings) of the Common Council. These extracts, a selection from a considerable quantity traced by Miss Masters, are designed to show the drama and humour of those days, eschewing some of the more mundane administrative matters, and the continual frictions between the Companies, which the City had patiently to decide!

Company of Farriers

10th December 1356

It was ordained by the Mayor, Aldermen, and good men of the Mistery of Farriers that if any one of the said mistery commits a trespass in the future, he shall on his first conviction by the Wardens of the Mistery pay the Chamber of the Guildhall 40d; on his second, half a mark (6s. 8d.) his third, 13s. 4d; and on his fourth, abjure the mistery.

Master Richard de Hertelee and John de Oxon, farriers, elected and sworn to survey the mistery etc.

(Calendar of Letter Book G p.78)

The Ordinances of the Mistery of Farriery submitted to Henry Pykard, the Mayor, the Aldermen, 1356 (the ordinances are set out in the City's Letter Book G at this point but a marginal note refers to a subsequent re-entry with additions in 1364. This was only the second occasion 'when Masters were so titled in the City as governing a Guild or Mistery, the previous time being 9 years earlier when the 4 "Masters" of the Mercers were described in this same context.'

Henry Smythe de Holbourne, Roger Smythe de Holbourne, Robert Smythe de Holbourne, Thomas Smythe de Castebaynard, Walter Smythe, Edward Smythe, John Suttone, and William Rondolf convicted once of false work.

(Calender of Letter Book G p.82)

A proclamation, temp. Stephen Cavendisshe. Mayor (1362–3) concerning the redress of grievances due to overcharging by many kinds of workmen and labourers, contains *inter alia* a provision that farriers take no more than they were wont etc.

(Calender of Letter Book G p.150)

The former Ordinances of 1356 were recited with an addition that because in the said articles all the grievances of their trade were not set forth, the good folk of the said Aldermen on 16 August 1364 for an addition to the articles, which the Mayor and Aldermen agreed.

And the farriers chose Richard de Westminster and John Beverle, farriers, to govern their trade and to present defaults to the Mayor and Aldermen and they were sworn accordingly.

24th December 1372

Proclamation made that, *inter alia*, no farrier within the franchise of the City take for the shooeing of a horse with a shoe of eight nails and above more than 2d., and for a shoe of less than eight nails more than 1½d., and for removing a shoe more than ½d., on pain of imprisonment and a fine at the discretion of the Mayor and Aldermen.

(Calender of Letter Book G p.303)

1st June 1431

Precept issued by Nicholas Wortone, the Mayor, and the Aldermen for certain unspecified reasons, to the Sheriffs and their officers, to abstain in future from summoning any ironmongers called horse farriers to serve on juries etc. except in cases of urgent necessity.

(Calender of Letter Book K p.121)

9th May 1609

Court of Aldermen. Ordered that the Chamberlain and the Comptroller of the Chamber shall hear and examine the causes in difference between the Companies of Farriers and Painterstainers using the trade of a farrier, and to end the same or to report.

(Repertory 29 f28)

24th July 1617

Court of Aldermen. The Committee reported upon the above petition that the Farriers have been an ancient brotherhood and are now poor and decayed and that of late they have purchased a Hall by which means they have not only disbursed that small stock they had and such sums as they have collected by contribution of the able men of their Company but are become much indebted not having any revenue at all whereby to pay the said debt. The committee recommended that they should have the benefit of so many persons to be made free of this City by redemption in their Company as the Court of Aldermen should think fit. Such persons to be farriers by profession and Englishmen born, and to be first presented and allowed of by the Court of Aldermen and to pay to the City's use 6s. 8d. each, and to be bound with sureties that none shall keep victualling or sell ale, beer or tobacco, and that none shall set up or keep any forge or farriers' shop within the liberties of the City save in places convenient and fit for men of that trade without annoyance to their neighbours.

The Committee further reported that the Wardens of the Company promised to pay such sums towards the plantation in Ireland as the Court of Aldermen should think fit and all other charges to be levied upon them in the future.

Report read and recommended to the next Common Council. (No reference traced in next Common Council)

(Repertory 33 f150–150b)

28th February 1628
Court of Aldermen. The Committee reported that the Company is of long continuance but of late much decayed, the most apparant causes being the late visitation of sickness (the Plague of 1625) which the Farriers allege 'swept away' most of the ablest and expert in their trade, and the mixture of those who are free of other Companies in the use of their art 'whereby multitude of prentices are brought upp and noe good order used in ye government of them'. The committee recommended that by Act of Common Council 12 men expert farriers be admitted into the Company by redemption for the better strengthening and assisting of the Company, being first severally presented to the Court of Aldermen and paying to the City's use the usual fine for redemptioners. And also and again by Act of Common Council that henceforth all persons using the art of a farrier within the City shall bind all apprentices unto a freeman of the Company who shall forthwith turn the said apprentice over unto his master that first took him to remain until the expiration of his terms and then to be admitted into the Company of Farriers. Report approved and to be recommended to the next Common Council.

(Repertory 42 ff106–106b)

25th September 1690
Court of Aldermen. Petition of the Company of Farriers to be granted Livery. Search to be made whether they ever had a livery (as they pretend) and when and how they came to be deprived thereof.

(Repertory 95 f166)

23rd June 1692
Court of Aldermen. They also found that by the oath of George Daggett, late clerk of the said Company, that most of the said Company's books and records were burnt in the dreadful fire of 1666 and that but three books and some loose papers relating to

the said Company were then preserved by one of which it doth appear that in the year 1632 and every year since successively they have called persons on their Livery who have paid fines to the Company upon that account in like manner as other Livery Companies of the City did. They also found by the said book that they had attended the solemnities of Lord Mayor's Day and other public festivals.

The Report also stated; 'Wee do also find in the 12th year of King Charles the Second (1661 approx) that all Livery Companies of this Citty were rated to a poll which were names in the Act of Parliament amongst which the Company of Farriers is named. And it doth also further appeare unto us by the oath of the said Mr. Daggett that the ancients of the said Company have always reputed themselves to be one of the Livery Companies of this citty. We have made enquiry when they first claimed a Livery but cannot find any grant in any of the citties bookes concerning the same to which they answer that severall other Companies who do now claime and are admitted and allowed to have Liverys as the Curriers, Plaisteres, Masons, Founders and others have no order or constitution for the same from this Court as far as doth "appear to us from the said bookes." Upon the whole matter it is our humble opinion that the said Company hath sufficient grounds to pray the favour of this Court to re-establish them a convenient Livery according to their humble petition that all questions about the same which have been occasioned by the burning of their bookes and papers may be putt to an end all which notwithstanding wee submitt to the wisdom of this Honourable Court.'

The Company's Records

An old Vellum Book now containing twenty-seven leaves about $8\frac{1}{2} \times 12\frac{1}{2}$ inches. Some pages are missing, having been cut out. It was re-bound at some comparatively recent date, as the insides of the covers are marbled paper.'

As the pages all seem to have been folded down the middle, in many cases to the great detriment of the contents, it would appear likely that for some considerable period the leaves were unbound. The writing is in some places very much rubbed. The contents are copies of various documents written in black letters and various scripts, in English, Latin and Old French. A kalendar showing Saints' Days, Domenical Letters etc., written in black, red and blue, occupies six pages.

The Documents, of the 16th and 17th centuries, relate not only to the Farriers' Company, but also to the defunct Company of Spurriers and to the Blacksmiths Company. There are also mentions of the Guilds of St. Loye and of St. Katherine the Holy Virgin.

There seems to be no doubt that the book has been in the possession of the Farriers Company for many years as in the Inventory at Mid-summer 1768 there appears: 'An old book beginning 1612 with an Almanach'. The date given is, however, misleading, because the book contains copies of documents of an earlier date.

It would appear possible that this is one of the three books mentioned by George Daggett (Clerk 1675) in his evidence at the time of the granting of the Company's Charter as having escaped 'the dreadful fire in anno 1666'.

Minute Books

The contents of these are by no means as informative as one could wish. One often finds a certain matter suggested, or even re-solved, but with no later reference as to whether it was carried into effect. Sometimes one can glean from the Audit Books that the resolutions were not carried out. Much regarding the trans-actions of the Court cannot have been recorded, but, despite everything, these old records are of great interest and, especially from the earlier volumes, one can imagine a good deal of the atmosphere surrounding the meetings of the Court

There are ten volumes, bound in vellum, with brass clasps; the earlier ones have been re-bound:

Vol 1 1718/19–1747	Vol 4 1776–1806	Vol 7 1890–1916
Vol 2 1747–1760	Vol 5 1806–1847	Vol 8 1917–1943
Vol 3 1760–1776	Vol 6 1847–1890	Vol 9 1943–1962
		Vol 10 1962–

The Charter Book

This Book was bought in 1674 at a cost of eight shillings. The copying of the Charter and By-Laws therein cost £2. 0s. 0d. It has been re-bound. It includes inter-alia; the Charter and By-Laws, the evidence of George Daggett concerning the Company at the time of the Great Fire in 1666 (see supra) and the Petition to the Lord Mayor and Aldermen for the re-establishing of the Livery and documents relating thereto.

Perhaps we should begin by explaining that the Farriers Livery Company elects annually a Master and three Wardens by the Court on MIDSUMMER DAY, being the Feast of the Nativity of St. John the Baptist, and they are installed at the Quarterly Court next following. These Courts normally meet in June, September, December and March. The Court consists of the Master, the Upper, Middle and Renter Wardens and not less than ten or more than twenty Assistants. It must be pointed out that there are 92 Livery Companies and each has its own traditional pattern. Gen-erally, each Company has a Master, not always described as such, some are known as Prime Wardens, and in the case of the Weavers Company as Upper Bailiff and, two, three or four Wardens of varying titles.

A list of the Company's Masters from 1673/4–1978/9 and biographies of Masters appears elsewhere. There are no records of earlier Masters before 1673 other than the reference in 1364 that the 'Farriers chose Richard de Westminster and John Beverle Farriers to govern their trade'. Whether he was known as Master is not known. In the Charter granted 1674 is a mention of Gregory Costen, the first Master to hold office until Midsummer Day 1674, and thereafter Andrew Snape (who was Serjeant-Farrier to King Charles II). It is interesting to note that on 25th June 1929, Miss Moore Brabazon presented to the Company an Engraving of Andrew Snape, which appears in the list of Gifts, but unfortunately is not in the list of Possessions of the Company.

It is clear from the Court of Aldermen's Minutes of 1617 that the Company was in great financial straits and continued over the many centuries to have no endowment of any kind.

There are some grounds for believing that the Company at one time had a hall just off Aldersgate Street, called Trinity Hall, formerly the Common Hall of the dissolved Fraternity of the Holy Trinity in the Parish of St. Botolph Without. In 1613 the Company leased some rooms to their Clerk, Robert Glover, who, in return, agreed to assist in matters financial. In 1760 the lower floor of Trinity Hall, near the North East corner of Little Britain, was a coffee house – the upper floor a non-jurors place of worship. There is, however, no mention of the hall in any of the records now in the Company's possession.

When the Author of this history was admitted to the Livery in January 1936 he was received in a sitting room at the Great Eastern Hotel, Liverpool Street, with no Court Luncheon to follow!

To return to the history from 1719, it will be clear that matters referred to in the Minute Books (the only source of information) must be of a very domestic nature. Each year the Master and Wardens have been elected, carrying on the activities of the Company. There are many references to the behaviour of members of the Company and of the Court – many references to persons being in default and 'presentation as the Law directs'. There are references to the fact that 'No Master or other person do send any victuals or wine for the table only the Roome without Leave of the Master for the time being. Nor any person to Dine without the Master's Leave'.

The Court on the 24th June in each year, according to the Charter, was required to take an Inventory of the Company's Possessions, of which the following is an example:

The Inventory 1786 – 24th June
An old book beginning 1612 with an Almanach
The Audit Book, 24th June 1726, ending 7th July 1768
An Audit Book, 7th July 1768
Minute Book, 26th January 1718, ending 6th November 1747

The Inventory
Minute Book 24th Nov 1747 Ending 3rd July 1760
Minute Book 24th July 1760 Ending 6th June 1776
Minute Book 24th June 1776
An Apprentice Book Aug 1619 Ending 1st June 1744
An Apprentice Book 24th June 1744
A Vellum Orphan Book for Apprentices for the
Chamberlain's ffine 24th June 1694
A Book of the Charter Bye-Laws Councils Opinions etc etc
An Admission Book for Freemen with Stamps beginning 21st Jany
  1755
An Assistant Book
Livery and Steward Book
Yeomanry Book
Rough Minute Book beginning 1st January 1785
A Copy of the Charter examined at the Rolls
The Bye-Laws wrote on Parchment with 3 large Seals
2 Bags
Scales and Weights for Gold
Copper Plate Engravings
Clerks Gown
Beadles Gown
A Bible dated 1780
Two small Copper Plates of the Company's Arms
One ditto in Wood
Copper Plate for Receipts
Copper Plate for Summons's
The Beadle's Staff
A Desk
A Silver Cup
A Hammer dated 1779 on it
A Large Chair with a Cover and Footstool
The Pedigree
The Companys Arms
An Ivory Seal
A Chest with the Arms of the Company to keep the Books in
A Livery Gown
A Silver Seal
A Box for the Pedigree
The Poors Box.

At the Beadle's House:
10 Caps
10 Jackets
1 Long Chest with 2 Locks and Keys

1 Long Chest with 3 Locks and Keys
2 Small Streamers
Companys Banner
Citys Banner
Long Streamer
Kings Streamer
12 Whifflers Staves
1 Pole for the Long Streamer
12 for Banners – 2 for long and 10 shorter
The Die for the Medals

The Minutes contain many references to the Company's attendance at the Lord Mayor's Day – which was always held on the 9th November until the year 1958.

The Procession or Show was held in the morning and the Banquet in the evening of the same day. Since 1959 the Lord Mayor's Show is held on the 2nd Saturday in November and the Banquet on the following Monday. This change which emanated from the constant complaints from the public, and through the Press, of traffic delays on a week day and a plea for a Saturday show for the benefit of the children who could only attend on a Saturday. In the author's opinion, when he was one of the Queen's Sheriffs, in 1954 a sensible decision was made, for to hold both the Show and the Banquet on the same day was indeed 'A Hard Day's Night'.

The Farriers, like all other Livery Companies, each year had long discussions as to whether they would support the procession.

18th October 1733
Ordered that this Company do Walk in Procession on the next Lord Mayors Day and that they be Marshalled and do March in the following Manner.

1st	The Staffmen	6thly	The Great Standard
2	The Whifflers	7	The two Pendants abreast
3	The City Banner	8	The Musick
4	The King's Banner	9	The Beadle
5	The Company's Banner	10	The Master etc., according to seniority.

And that the said Company do in their Procession Walk and Pass through several Streets passages and places following. That is to say;

That the said Company do meet at the Crown Tavern at Cripplegate by nine of the Clock in the morning to Breakfast and that about Eleven they do proceed from thence through Cripplegate, down London Wall, up Coleman Street, along Lothbury, up Bartholomew Lane, through the Royal Exchange, down Cornhill, along the Poultry, through Cheapside, round St Paul's Church, down Ludgate Street, along Ditchside, up Snow Hill and there to stop at Mr. Burts to drink a Glass of Wine and then proceed along Newgate Street and Cheapside, down King Street and Aldermanbury and to the Crown Tavern at Cripplegate to Dinner.

Ordered that there be provided for the Company's Breakfast One Large Sirloine of Beef.

And for their Dinner Twenty-four ffowles, four Hams, four Turkeys, four Chines and six Dishes of Tarts.

Ordered that the Staffmen Whifflers etc (except the two that hold up the Standard Table) be allowed six pence each for Breakfast if they come by Nine of the Clock.

And that they have provided for their Dinner a Leg of Veal Bacon and Greens and a Shoulder of Mutton. And that each Man shall be allowed one shilling for Drink.

That they do Dine at the Widow Rogers at Red Cross in Red Cross Street.

Ordered that the eight Supporters of the Colours be allowed Two Shillings and Six Pence each

In 1734 it was much the same as the previous year but the costs of it all was given as follows:'

Paid Mr. Dean for this day	18	18	0
Paid to the Musick	6	6	0
To the Standard Bearers	1	7	6
Expended upon the March	–	6	–
Paid the Pastrycook's Bill	3	0	0
Paid to Mr. Clark for Ribbons	3	12	0
To Mr. Ingram for Gloves	1	19	8
Paid at Mr. Cowper's as by Bill	2	6	6
Paid the Poulterer's Bill	3	0	0
Paid for Beef	1	7	5
ffor Hams	1	5	5
ffor Bacon and Chines		16	0
	£44	4	6

Music was also provided and of course food and wine, for here follows an Order of the Court in the same Minute:

'Ordered that the Musick to be provided against the next Lord Mayors Day consist of two French Horns, Three Hautboys' (to-day's oboes), 'a Trumpet or Bassoon and a Tabor and Pipe and that the Musick have Favours.'

Mr. Thomas Clark agreed to provide and furnish the Company against the next Lord Mayors Day with Ribbons and Gloves as follows:

'Blew and White Ribbon at Six pence per yard to be made up into Favours and Scarffs ffour dozen of Gloves, pointed with Tops at one Shilling per pair.'

'Ordered that there be provided for the Company's Breakfast one Large Sirloin of Roast Beef.

And for their Dinner Twentyone Fowls boiled and roasted with Greens ffour Hams not exceeding Eighteen pounds each ffour Geese three Apple Pyes and three Marrow Puddings Ordered that there be sent to the Strand on Lord Mayors Day Two Dozen of Rolls and Two Dozen of Biscuits and one Dozen of Mountain one Dozen of Lisbon or White Port and one Dozen of Red Port Ordered that the Supporters and Staffmen have provided for their Dinner a Large Leg of Veal Bacon and Greens and that each Man shall be allowed one Shilling for Drink. And that they Dine at Mr. William Gogneys at the Coopers Arms in Golden Lane.'

It should be noted that the Supporters and Staffmen had not been overlooked.

17th October 1740

Upon a Motion being made and the question put whether this Company do walk on the next Lord Mayor's Day it was carried in the Negative.

And also whether a Dinner be provided for the same Day and it was carried in the Negative.

1742

Obviously this extravagance, having regard to the Company's financial situation, was fully discussed and at a Court Meeting in October 1742 the following Resolution was passed:

'Agreed and ordered that the Company Do not Walk on the next Lord Mayor's Day nor provide any Dinner.'

5th November 1761

This also happened in other years. However, in 1761 it was decided that the Walk and Dinner on Lord Mayor's Day should be resumed.

The Minutes of that date contain not only the details of the Show and the Procession and the Dinner to follow, but also contain details of the Writ against a Mr. James Gregory of Alresford in Hampshire who was required to serve the Office of Steward of the Company to which he was elected on Midsummer 1761 and who was charged with his Share or one Third of the expenses of the Dinner on Lord Mayor's Day. On September 12th 1761 Counsel's Opinion had stated 'That Mr. Gregory is not exempted from serving this office' on the strength of his 1733 Certificate obtained when he left his trade in 1759 to purchase a place as one of His Majesty's Yeomen. Accordingly, the Writ was served in 1762, but in June 1764 the Attorney General's letter to the Company of a contrary opinion was read and recorded in full in the Minutes. The letter, in short, stated that the King by his Order in Council dated 13th January 1761

'Declared his pleasure to be that all his Servants in Ordinary with fee should enjoy their Ancient privileges. And in regard to their constant Attendance upon his Majesty should be exempted from bearing Public offices, on serving on Juries, or Inquests Watch or Ward, and should not be subject to any Mulct or ffine for not submitting thereto.'

It appears that Mr. Gregory, as a member of His Majesty's Guard, was exempt from the Company. It was obviously assumed that any member of a Livery Company was in Public Office. There is no further reference to be found on the matter and presumably the Attorney General's letter was acceded to. As regards the share of the cost of the Dinner on the Lord Mayor's Day, this was presumably written off as a bad debt. Needless to say, the list of Past Masters of the Company does not include the name of Mr. James Gregory.

5th November 1761

The arrangements for the day were also carefully planned. 'Ordered that the Company do meet at the White Horse Cripplegate by Nine of the Clock in the morning to Breakfast and that about Eleven they do proceed from thence through Wood Street into Cheapside from thence round Saint Pauls Church Yard down Ludgate Street and to their Stand on Ludgate Hill and that the Company do return the same way to Dinner.'

Only two references can be found in the Minutes since 1761 when it was decided to resume the practice of supporting the Lord Mayor and on 9th November 1793 a reference that 'Dinners usually provided on the Quarterly Courts held in January, April and October each year be discontinued until the further Order of the Court', implying that the financial situation of the Company was again in question.

It would be tedious to make mention of the decisions of the Court year by year – as to whether the Company supported the Procession – it depended on two conditions (a) the condition of the Colours etc. and (b) finance. In fact, very few references to the Procession could be found.

1837

However, on 25th October 1837 'The Master laid before the Court a Circular Letter he had received from Mr. Woodthorpe, the Town Clerk of the City of London by direction of a Committee of Aldermen suggesting the expediency and propriety of the Company taking up their ancient and accustomed standings with their Flags and Banners on Lord Mayor's Day next when the Queen (Victoria) will pass through the City to Guildhall.'

'The Clerk reported that he had made several applications to Mr. Woodthorpe and had also attended the Committee of Aldermen in order to obtain full information as to the facilities and accommodation which would be furnished to the several Companies or to such of them as might chuse to attend. That the result of such enquiries was that no Stands would be permitted to be set up in the streats and therefore no accommodation could be afforded by the City Authorities beyond the protection of the Police.

'The Court then proceeded to consider and discuss the subject and having examined the Colours etc, which are too bad to be repaired: considering also that the expenses of the Measure would be considerable and such as the Company is not in a condition to incur and considering also the inconvenience of standing in the open Street without any protection.'

It was moved and seconded and the question being put was carried unanimously in the Affirmative.

'That it is not under all the circumstances expedient for the Company to go out on Lord Mayor's Day. And Ordered that the Clerk write a letter to Mr. Woodthrope to that effect accordingly.'

We do not know the date of the Circular Letter, but as it was put before the Court only fifteen days before the Lord Mayor's Day and having regard to the financial points, it is not surprising at the decision the Court took. The City Corporation had learnt their lesson in its giving of Notice of future events, for discussions for the 1977 Jubilee were in hand during the writing of this volume.

One final reference to the Lord Mayor's Day which may be of interest to the reader, for it concerns the Company:

9th November 1872
'Mr. Thomas White a Liveryman of this Company (since 1848) having been elected an Alderman of the City of London and one of the Sheriffs of London and Middlesex (the Court wished to offer congratulations and to entertain him at Dinner at an early date).'

1876
Four years later the Clerk reported that Alderman Sir Thomas White had been elected Lord Mayor of London and on the 13th October it was recorded that a sum not exceeding £100 should be expended in representing the Company in the procession on Lord Mayor's Day. But on 30th October the Clerk reported that Sir Thomas White had excluded the Company (of which he was a member) which had been invited to attend the procession on the 9th November from the usual proceedings on the 8th (presumably the SILENT CEREMONY which takes place on the day previous to the admission of the Lord Mayor taking up Office) whereupon it was proposed . . . That the resolution of the Court of the 13th October be rescinded the Court feeling that after the above statement of their Clerk they could not pass over the slight put upon

their Company by the Lord Mayor elect.

However, on 6th November the Lord Mayor elect wrote to the Clerk that he had given no such instructions and consequently the Resolution of 30th October was rescinded and the original resolution of the 13th should stand – proceedings to be taken at once for the representation of the Company on the 9th November. So, All's Well that ends well! Alderman Sir Thomas White was the only member of the Company to become Lord Mayor other than Sir Francis Cokayne. It is interesting to note that Francis Cokayne, Alderman of Cornhill Ward 1744–67, was a member of the Company, Master 1741–42, but on becoming Lord Mayor Elect, he was translated on 9th October 1750 to the Vintners Company. It had been customary prior to 1742 for Lord Mayors to be members of one of the Great Twelve, by translation if necessary. Alderman Willimott, Lord Mayor 1742–43, did not leave his parent Company, the Coopers, and Cokayne was one of the very few Lord Mayors thereafter who observed the old practice.

There have been nine members of the Company who have held the office of Sheriff of London:

1745–6	Francis Cokayne	Lord Mayor 1750–51, Master 1741–42
1872–3	Alderman Thomas White	Lord Mayor 1876–77
1874–5	James Shaw	Master 1878–79
1878–9	*George Burt	Master 1888–89
1895–6	John Robert Cooper	Master 1881–82, 1895–96, 1903–04
1927–8	Sir Frederick Daniel Green	Master 1930–31
1917–8	*George Rowland Blades (later Lord Ebbisham)	Lord Mayor 1926–27
1954–5	Leslie Barnett Prince	Master 1955–56
1957–8	*Samuel Richard Walker	Master 1954–55

*George Burt	Mother Company Glass Sellers
*George Rowland Blades	Mother Company Gardeners
*Samuel Richard Walker	Mother Company Founders

The office of Sheriff is of great antiquity. It was in existence before the Norman Conquest and the names of some of London's Sheriffs from Circa 1030 AD have been traced. There is even a record of Sheriffs in the reign of King Alfred. The annual election of two Sheriffs by the citizens was granted or confirmed by Royal Charter of King John in 1199 and more than 1,500 men have served this High Office since that date.

It has been possible to trace twenty-five member of the Company who have been members of the Court of Common Council in the 18th, 19th and 20th centuries of whom seven still remain members.

Members of the Company who have been members of the Court of Common Council 1757–1979

	Ward	Date of Admission	Dates on Common Council
Geoffrey Wilson	Vintry		1757–93 Deputy 1773–93
George Hudson	Castle Baynard		1788
James Brooks	Vintry		1798–10 Deputy 1808–10
John Dunkin	Aldersgate		1800–05
George Turner	Farringdon Without		1821–24 (Master 1814–15)
David William Witton	Aldgate		1827–35 (Master 1836–37)
William Blanch	Bridge		1868–79
Clifton Tollit	Cheap	1903	1932–62
Herbert Roper Barrett	Lime Street	1916	1910–43 Deputy 1941–43 (Master 1921–22, 1933–34)
George Allison-Beer	Cordwainer	1920	1942–74 Deputy 1955–74 (Master 1959–60)
William Newcome Wright	Bishopsgate	1931	1928–63 Deputy 1950–53 (Master 1947–48)
Cyprian Whiteley	Cordwainer	1932	1937–55 (Master 1946–47)
Leslie Prince	Bishopsgate	1936	1950– Deputy 1970– (Master 1955–56)
Walter Rose	Castle Baynard	1942	1945–61 (Master 1945–46)
Samuel Walker	Bread Street	1943	1937–76 Deputy 1951–76 (Master 1954–55)
Walter Loweth	Bishopsgate	1948	1946–68
Hemsley Miller	Cordwainer	1950	1952–63
Hugh Brewer	Langbourne	1953	1970– Deputy 1976–
Charles McCauley	Bread Street	1958	1957–
Harvey Dean	Cordwainer	1959	1958–76
Reginald Willard	Bishopsgate	1964	1970–75
Thomas Fripp	Cripplegate Within	1965	1976–
Geoffrey Lawson	Portsoken	1972	1971–
Arthur Brian Wilson	Aldersgate	1973	1960– Deputy 1974–
Henry Spurrier	Dowgate	1977	1970–73 1974–

The Author, by describing the Company's activities with the Lord Mayor and Sheriffs, has possibly left the reader with the impression that the Company does not appear to have had much regard to the farriery trade during the period from the date of its Royal Charter granted in 1674 for the next seventy years for the Court Minutes contain references only to procedural matters dealing with its own domestic affairs and as has been seen, arrangements for dinners, Lord Mayor's processions, fines for non-attendances, etc. It was not till 1749 that the trade was mentioned when the following Minute appeared:

'A Motion was made and the Question put whether the Opinion of John Brown Esqre Councellor at Law of Lincolns Inn be taken with regard to this Company compelling all persons useing the Trade of a Farrier in London or Westminster or Seven Miles Distant to be admitted Members hereof'.

17

As has been explained, the origin of the Company was the damage done by inexpert and unskilled persons in the trade of Farriers, when 49 named persons and all others that professed the Trade, Art or Mistery of a Farrier had used the same by the space of three years last passed within London and Westminster and seven miles thereof and all others that should thereafter exercise the same and should have served as apprentices within those limits for seven years should be one Body Politique and Corporate in the name of the Master, Wardens, Assistants and Commonalty of the Farryers of London with perpetual succession capable of holding land not exceeding the yearly value of £100 besides their Hall and all things personal to any amount with power to sell and deal with the said land as fully as any other subject and to sue and be sued in respect thereof.

In June 1749 when it was 'Ordered that the Clerk do prepare a New Bye Law inflicting a penalty on Persons (residing within London or Westminster or Seven Miles Distant) useing the Farriers Trade not being free of the Company and refusing to become Members thereof and pay Quarteridge to the Company and bind their Apprentices with them. And that the same be laid before this Court on the next Audit day.'

Notwithstanding the new Bye Law, in January 1765, eight years later, it was decided by the Court to obtain an Act to oblige all persons who shall use or Exercise the Trade of a 'ffarrier' within the City of London of Liberties thereof to take up their 'ffreedoms' of this Company. And that the present Master and Wardens Mr. Richard Stratton, Mr. David Rice and Mr. William Wackett or any 'ffive' of them be a Committee to make such an Application and to Endeavour to obtain such Act of Common Council in such manner as they shall think proper.

In November 1757 the Committee met and Attended the Committee of the Court of Common Council at Guildhall on the Company's Petition referred to their examination, when the Same was heard and is Reported to the Court of Common Council. And on the 12th December 1758 the Act of Common Council for the regulation of the Company was duly passed into a Law.

Following the Act again there are numerous references to take up the Livery of which the following is a typical example:

9th November 1759

'Mr. Maddock Jones being summoned to take up his Livery this day appeared, and was Elected into the Livery but he refused to accept the same. And it is Ordered that the Clerk do acquaint him therewith and that he be summoned to the first Thursday in the next month and in default of his Appearing on that Day that he be prosecuted for his Refusal.'

5th December

'Mr. Maddock Jones . . . appeared and it is ordered that he should make oath in Writing before the Lord Mayor or sitting Alderman at Guildhall relating to his Circumstances and Lay the same before the Master.'

From 1762 it appears that the Court became more active and that more interest was being displayed for there were references to the 'trade' in addition to the usual references to 'Dining and Wining' for in that year a Committee was appointed to look into the Charter and Bye-Laws of the Company and to examine what Amendments may be necessary to be made therein And that the Committee do consist of Seven and that the Master, the Upper and Middle Wardens and Four Assistants (names all mentioned) be the Committee and that any ffive of them shall be a Quorum and that they Report their Proceedings to a General Court of this Company.' And in that year the first reference to 'fforeign ffarriers' appears and many extracts show that the Court is following Farriery very seriously: for in September the following letter appears:

(The Clerk having been ordered by the Committee to write to several Master Farriers not free from the Company).

'Sir,

I am directed by the Master and Wardens of the Farriers Company to acquaint you that by Virtue of a Royal Charter granted the Company by King Charles the 2nd No person (not being made free of the Farriers Company) can Exercise the Trade of a Farrier in the Cities of London and Westminster or within Seven Miles thereof without being liable to a Prosecution by Law; this is to require you forthwith to be made free of the said Company, otherwise the Company are determined to put their Laws in Execution.

I am, Sir
Your humble Servt

Sam Coates – Clerk of the Company.

St Thomas Apostles
near Bow Lane, Cheapside.

NOTE: This is done at the request of Several Noblemen and Gentlemen of the First Distinction who have suffered by the Ignorance of unskilled Quacks who assume to themselves the name of Farriers.'

In the following October (1762) no fewer than 12 farriers were made free of the Company and 9 more at the November meeting.

The Committee appointed in October 1762 to look into the

Charter & Bye Laws of the Company reported, among other matters, that the Company had power to 'Compel fforeign Farriers Exercising the Trade within Seven Miles of the Cities of London & Westminster to take up their Freedom of the Company' and many had done so. It appears that the Committee had no power to prosecute any 'fforeign Farriers for their Refusal' It was ordered that the Committee have power to prosecute'.

It is not clear from the above report as to how this power was bestowed on the Committee by the Court of the Company. In any event, in the following month, the Clerk was ordered to write a letter to Mr. George Shaw (presumably a Solicitor) 'to acquaint him' that 'it is the Resolution of this Committee to commence a Prosecution against John Wisdom of Park Lane Hyde Park Corner for Carrying on the Trade of a Farrier upon proper and Sufficient Evidence being produced to prove and Support the prosecution; and that the person who was expected did not attend the Committee to give his Information in the Affair', also the Clerk was ordered to bring an Action in the name of the Company against John Coles of Southwark Farrier for exercising his Trade not being free of the Company.

A month later, the following Minute appeared 'Resolved that the Prosecution to be Commenced against John Wisdom be by Indictment or Information under the Statute of Queen Elizabeth and not by Action in the Name of the Company Provided that proper and sufficient Evidence be produced to prove and support the prosecution. And it is ordered that the Clerk do take care to Carry on the prosecution accordingly' and three months later 'The Clerk acquainted the Committee that John Wisdom against whom a Prosecution has been Commenced had made Application to him with his Attorney to Compromise the Suit and had submitted to shut up his Shop and Quit the Trade. Therefore It is Ordered that the Clerk do settle and finish the Suit with the Attorney in a proper manner'.

It seems that the prosecution was having an effect for in the same year many Master Farriers at Westminster were prepared to contribute with 'sums of Money' for 'Renewing and Strengthening' the Charter for the purpose of bringing Prosecutions. There must, however, have been some doubt as to whether the Company had the power to prosecute for a case was 'Laid before the Solicitor General for his opinion'. Whilst the Minutes do not make any reference to this opinion, the Company was continually commencing prosecutions.

A further Minute shows that

'A prosecution be commenced against (William Howard) under the Statute of Queen Elizabeth in the name of "ffrancis Butler the Beadle"'

20

and that the Clerk carry on the prosecution accordingly.

Finance, as will be seen in the Chapter entitled 'Relentless pursuit of Riches' was fundamental in the Company's activities. Its income came only from Quarterages – four shillings per annum from Liverymen – and Fines for Stewards and elevation to the Court. Elsewhere will be found some examples of the difficulties the Company had in collecting the sums of money from members.

These financial straits did not permit of any unnecessary payments, as shown by the Minute of 9th November 1764 – 'Ordered that the Caveat Money Yearly paid to Mr. Crumpe of the Chamberlains Office be discontinued from Lady Day last.' In fact, the Chamberlain's Court did not receive very many voluntary payments from the Company! But when, some thirty-four years later, in 1798 'The Clerk laid before the Court a letter from the Chamberlain of London, requesting payment of the arrears of the Orphans fees on binding apprentices to this Company Whereupon Ordered that the same be paid accordingly.' 'Fforeign ffarriers were still exercising the Company for again in 1765 appears a Minute –'

'At this Court the Affair of the fforeign ffarriers was taken into Consideration according to the Charter of the Company. It is Resolved and Ordered by this Court that it be left to the Discretion of the Master to take the Opinion of any one or more Councel in the Law on that point of the Charter and Whether on failure or Defect in that Point the Whole Charter will be forfeited? And that the Master may be at Liberty to give such ffees to Councel as he shall think proper'.

When, a week later, the opinion of Mr. Warren was obtained and read to the Court, consideration thereof was deferred to another meeting. Curiously, there is no further reference in the Minutes to the opinion and, even more curious, the words 'Fforeign Ffarriers' never appear in any subsequent Minutes – so much for the 'Affair'.

The Court appears to have had no hesitation in obtaining opinions, perhaps the members preferred professional advice, the fees were not onerous, for the following Minutes now appear – and for the first time the expression 'Honorary Freeman' appears, with no definite explanation as to who was an Honorary Freeman (although in a Minute in 1769 'Honorary Freemen of this Company living at a Distance in the country' could indicate what is known today as a 'country member'):

'The Case drawn up by the Clerk pursuant to the order of the Committee relating to the payment of the Quarteridge (by Several of the Honorary Freemen of the Company) was read to this Court And It is ordered that the same be Laid before the Recorder of the

21

City for his opinion thereon And that the Clerk do give him a ffee of Two Guineas therewith' and, a month later, the opinion was set out in full as follows:

'The Committee Reported to this Court a Case and the opinion of James Eyre Esqre the Recorder of this City thereon relating to the Holding of Quarter Courts for payment of the Quarteridge due, and for other Business relating to the Company, which Case and Opinion was now read to this Court. And it is Resolved and Ordered that for the future there shall be Four Quarter Courts held by the Master Wardens and Assistants at the Half Moon Tavern in Cheapside which Quarter Courts are agreed and ordered to be held on the first Thursday in January the first Thursday in April the first Thursday in July and the first Thursday in October in every year. Yearly pursuant to the tenth Bye Law made for that purpose And it is further Ordered that the Monthly Courts kept at Guildhall Coffee House shall Cease for the future and whatever Business may be wanted to be done by any Member of this Company between the Quarter Courts may be Transacted by the Clerk paying him his ffee of Three Shillings and four pence for his Attendance thereon And it is further Ordered that every Member of the Court of Assistants shall attend in his Gown at ever General Court Day as well as the Quarter Court Days and that every Member of the Court of Assistants as well as the other Members of the Company shall forfeit and pay the Sum or Penalty of Three Shillings and four pence for their Non Attendance at the said Courts pursuant to the first Bye Law of this Company unless a reasonable Excuse be given to and allowed by the said Courts, And that the same be mentioned at the bottom of the summons's to the several Assistants and likewise that they shall Attend in their Gowns on the next Lord Mayor's Day and all other Court Days for the future.

Ordered that the Beadle of the Company Shall always attend the Court of Assistants in his Gown and Staff.

Ordered that Mr. Butler, the Beadle, be allowed a pair of Leather Breeches of the price of One Pound Seven Shillings.

Ordered that all the Honorary Members as well as others Members of the Company owing any Quarteridge at Lady Day last be summoned to Appear at the next Quarter Court to discharge the Same.'

At least the Court was laying down the procedure and later in the same year 1765 the Clerk laid before the Court an Abstract of the Act of Common Council relating to the Company. It was ordered that 500 of the same be printed with the Company's Arms engraved on the top and shall be Distributed by the Beadle of the Company to the Several Farriers of this City and the Liberties thereof not being ffreemen of this Company.

Perhaps one more reference to a prosecution and costs; in 1767

'The proceedings in the prosecution against Mr. William Osmer being Laid before this Court. And that he hath procured a Rule of the Court of King's Bench for a Special Jury on the Tryal of the Cause Whereby the expence must be greater than at first intended It is Ordered that the Master have power to sell out the sum of 25£ South Sea Annuities (if necessary) out of the Company's Stock to support the Expence of the Tryal'.

and with rather a dramatic anticlimax in the following April –

'The Master represented to this Court that the Tryal of Mr. William Osmer came on in the Court of King's Bench at Westminster Hall before a Special Jury at the Sittings after the Last Term, and for want of sufficient evidence the Company were Non Suited'

Incidentally, Mr. Osmer was a 'fforeign ffarier'.

Readers may have found the above extracts of esoteric interest but the Story of the Company is the maintenance of the control of the Trade. It must be borne in mind that the procedural election of Assistants to the Court, the annual election of wardens, the election of the Master and the annual accounts were an intrinsic and necessary part of Company life. Naturally the Lord Mayor's Day was being celebrated and the 'dining and wining' was all part of being a Liveryman; but these matters are dealt with elsewhere in the book.

To slip decades in 600 years would appear of miniscule importance but it is hard to know 'what to leave out' after all Robson's History, to which reference has been made, was filled with extracts year by year, even month by month, and the object of this book, as explained in the Introduction, is 'The Story of the Company – how it started in 1356' but it is difficult to do so without references to such extracts chronologically.

6th July 1775

So to continue. In 1775 the Minutes record:

'Ordered that No Children be admitted to Dine with the Company on Lord Mayor's Day, or on any other Day. And that Notice hereof be given of the same on every Summons of the next Lord Mayor's Day'.

As will be seen elsewhere, in 1957 the Lord Mayor's Day was altered for the future from the 9th November to the second Saturday in November in order that the children should view the procession, but not even today would the Liverymen take children to 'lunch or dine' with the Company.

In 1776 appeared –

'Ordered that No Roman Catholic shall be admitted into the Court of Assistants of this Company for the future'.

A Goblet was purchased for the use of the Company with the names of the Master (Henry Brooks) and Wardens inscribed thereon, and it was placed in the care of the Immediate Past Master (Charles Bartrum).

A Silver Cup, 1778

This Cup is engraved with the Company's Arms and is without a contemporary cover.

In the Inventory of the Company's possessions given in the early Audit Books for many years appears 'A Silver Salt', Later, in a very full Inventory for the year 1768 appears 'A Silver Cup.' In 1776 a Minute dated November 9th says: 'An old piece of silver plate . . . was produced to the Court and ordered to be melted and sold, and a goblet purchased for the use of the Company'. This old piece of plate was probably the 'Silver Salt' and the reference to 'A Silver Cup' in 1768 may have been a mistake.

The matter is again referred to in a Minute of April 2nd 1778, as follows: 'The produce of the Old Piece of Silver Plate . . . with a free gift of Ten Shillings and Sixpence from several of the Court of Assistants was directed to be laid out in the purchase of a Two-handled Silver Cup to contain about two quarts . . . and if the charge of the Cup shall exceed the amount of the old silver and the voluntary subscriptions . . . it is ordered the deficiency shall be paid out of the Company's stock.'

A Minute of June 24th 1778 shows the transactions:

	£	s	d
Sale of old Silver, 31 oz. 4 dwt. at 5s. 8d.	8	16	8
Contributions by the Court of Assistants	8	7	6
Cash paid from the Company's Funds	–	5	10
	£17	10	0
The New Cup. 43 oz. 14 dwt. at 7s. 9d.	£16	18	0
Engraving the Arms of the Company	–	12	0
	£17	10	0

The Valuation of this piece made in 1974 was £650.

In 1787 the Court was having trouble with Freemen who refused to take the Livery to which they had been elected and were repeatedly Summoned, amongst them John Prince who, according to the Minutes of October, twice attended the Court and 'treated the Whole Court of Assistants present with indecency'. He was allowed until the following April to take up his Livery or he would be sued. Fortunately, at the Court held in April 1788, he was admitted to the Livery of the Company, was sworn and paid the sum of Five Pounds.

Eleven years later the Reverend John Prince of Sion College London Wall was admitted into the Company and appears to have been the first Clerical Liveryman.

Back to 1776, Francis Blackbeard appeared and refused to take the Livery to which he had been repeatedly Summoned and he was 'ordered to be sued forthwith to Compel him so to do'. He too later was admitted, having paid the cost of the Suit against him and the Five Pounds admission fee. He was an employee at the Bank of England.

All during this period the Company was doing its utmost to attract farriers to join the Company. Several Master Farriers of Westminster demanded that the Charter of the Company be read. It was not thought proper to read the Charter to those gentlemen out of the City but that it could be read at a Court to be Summoned for that purpose at the George & Vulture in Cornhill. Naturally, this involved further Opinion from Counsel at the request of the Farriers of Westminster on parts adjacent. The several Opinions were read to the Master Farriers and the Clerk was ordered to enter such opinions in 'Some Book belonging to the Company'.

It will be seen that there was nothing easy in being a member of the Court for time after time the Law was involved. In July 1777 –

'Edward Carpenter having been Served with Process for Not taking the Livery of the Company having been Elected thereto. Appeared & produced to the Court an Opinion of the Court of Aldermen that he was Not Eligible thereto, in Consequence of a By Law of the Court of Aldermen in the Year 1697. Which Determination he declared his intention to Abide by. And such a Precedent being deemed very detrimental to this Company, the following gentlemen were appointed to a Committee to procure the best information as to the Validity of it And to make a Report of their Proceedings herein to the Next Court.'

Naturally the Minutes of the next Court nor of any other Court refer to Edward Carpenter so nothing is known of what happened to obviously an important precedent.

Again, what happened following the advertisement in the Morning Chronicle denying Joseph Lewis who polled as a Liveryman of the Farriers Company at the Election for a Chamberlain in 1777 (Benjamin Hopkins) to be on their Livery or free of that Company.

A domestic happening in 1791 – 'an Assistant of the Company had not attended in his place for eight years, not paid his quarteridge during that time and wholly resided in Norfolk and that he had treated the Court with contempt in not answering several letters – Resolved that Mr. John Banwell be now expelled' – whereupon the Master declared a Vacancy.

The Nineteenth Century
The new Century opened with the usual domestic matters and in

1803 it was 'Resolved that a handsome Livery Gown and Hood be provided at the expence of the Company to be worn by the Master as a Mark of Distinction and respect on the several Court days. And Resolved that the Company's Chair be placed for the Master's use in the room where the Court meets to do business'

All fines were increased – being excused the office of Steward raised from £5 to £10. The fee of 2/6d which is taken for the Poor to be increased to 5/–d. To be a member of the Court was raised to £10.

In 1804 a fee of 1/–d be paid by every member of the Court who attends without wearing his Medal – such fines for the use of the Poor.

In 1811 – It was Resolved that in future the names be called at precisely one o'clock on every Court Day and that every Gentleman who shall be absent when his name is called shall be fined. Today the Court meets at 11.30 a.m. or 5.0 pm. – certainly not at one o'clock – although the Court of Common Council still meets at one o'clock, but with no fines for absence!

In 1817 that Court be summoned to meet at two o'clock instead of one, and that the Court dine at four instead of three. The fashionable dining hour changed more quickly in towns than in the country, in aristocratic circles than in working classes, and luncheon had not yet achieved its present dominance through the influence of gentlemen's Clubs. In fact, in November of that year the Court did not dine on account of the recent melancholy death of Her Royal Highness The Princess Charlotte, of unhappy childhood, with warring parents, brief but happy marriage and whose death changed completely the royal succession.

The matter of fines occurs throughout the next 175 years. Constant references appear in the Minutes – protests from members of the Court.

(The Author has many memories of such protests, Resolutions amendments and finally in 1979 it was decided to amend the ordinances whereby there would be no fines for absences from the Court but for a member to attend not wearing his badge be fined 15p which goes into the poor box.)

It was curious to find that in 1800 the Clerk was of the opinion that the Court had no power to increase fees without first making a new Bye-Law for the purpose and having the same duly allowed and confirmed according to the directions of the Act of Parliament in the reign of King Henry VII, and following that opinion it was Resolved unanimously that no alteration be made at present in the Fines and Fees of the Company.

There have been so many references to alterations in Fines and Fees since 1800 – whether the Bye-Laws have been 'duly allowed and confirmed' it is difficult to ascertain – but from what appears, the Bye-Laws take account of the existing position whenever they are printed.

What is typical of the Company is the Minute:

'Resolved that the Fines of the Court for the year now ending be collected and spent on Lord Mayor's day'.

As has been said, the Minutes of the Company are the only record of events and as Robson found out and the Author has confirmed, it is regrettable that the Minute Books are not more informative. So many matters have been raised but not always followed up. Nowhere was found the expression 'Arising out of the Minutes' – also, until Robson's Clerkship in 1942, were items indexed. However, it is hoped that the many extracts included in this book can be followed.

An example of elegant English of the period is a letter from Sir James Shaw, Bart. one of the Members of Parliament for the City of London:

'To the Masters, Wardens, Court of Assistants and Livery of the Worshipful Company of Farriers

America Square
24th Nov. 1812

Gentlemen,

On the opening of the Second Parliament in which I had the honour to be one of your representatives, I did myself the pleasure to address a Letter to your most Respectable Company to say that you could not do me a greater favour than to put in my power to serve you in conjunction with my Worthy Colleagues by the transaction of any business you might have occasion to solicit in the House of Commons. This declaration I beg now to confirm and repeat at the commencement of the third Parliament to which the great goodness of the Livery of London has raised me, as one of their Representatives, and to assure you with all the sincerity of truth that my gratitude is as unbounded as your friendship has been remarkable for its constancy and kindness.

With the greatest consideration
I have the honour to be Gentlemen
Your most faithful and most devoted servant
JAS. SHAW'

There is no mention as to whether this letter was sent to every Livery Company.

In 1814 it was reported that –

'Mr. John French who owes seven years Quarterage attended and stated that he had been a prisoner in France for nearly the whole Time and was now in very indigent circumstances and therefore unable to pay his quarterage; which matter being taken into consideration It . . . was carried unanimously in the affirmative That Mr. French be excused his Arrears'.

It will be remembered that the Company's Minute Books were lost in the Great Fire of 1666. The first Minute available was 26th January 1712, so, when in 1816, a member of the Court presented to the Court a Paper purporting to be an Original and signed by the City Town Clerk William Rix dated 27th July 1697. It showed that members of the Livery Companies, both Major and Minor, had to be men of standing – also a confirmation of the word 'Livery' – meaning Clothing.

9th November 1816

'Clarke Major
    'Martis xvij die July 1697 Annoq. R, Rex Willi.
    Tertij Anglise Xc.'

This Court being highly sensible that several persons free of the companyes of this citie (amongst others) are called upon the Liveryes of their respective companyes who have neither Estates nor Abilities to take the Cloathing upon them which proceedings tends not onely to ye Impoverishment of them and their famelyes, but is also at Last a charge & burthen to the companyes to which they belong. It is now Ordered for the future that noe persons be called to take upon them the Cloathing of any of the Twelve Companyes unless they have an Estate of a thousand pounds and that noe persons be called to take upon them ye cloathing of any of the Inferiour Companyes unless they have an Estate of Five hundred Pounds.

A true copy taken out of the
Book Reportory Clarke No.101,
in the Town Clerk's Office,
Guildhall, London'

    WILLIAM RIX'

Whilst all Liverymen are conscious of the importance of the twelve great companies nevertheless today they may not appreciate the expression 'inferior'!

In 1820 a letter was received from the Secretary to the Commissioners of Charities requesting to be furnished with a Statement of all Charities under the management of the Company with full details of the name of the donor, date and nature of the benefactor, the annual amount and for what purpose it is now applied.

This letter was answered and it could not have taken long to compose as the only Charitable Gift was that of Mr. John Sowle arising out of his Will dated 28th March 1572, the Company being entitled to an amount of 13/4d. charged upon property in West Smithfield and payable by the Church Wardens of the Parish of St. Sepulchre, Holborn. (see page 179)

6th April 1826
In 1826 a Petition was received from the Company of Tobacco
Pipe Makers stating that 'having incurred various large legal
expences in several Actions at Law to support the chartered rights
which expences they were unable to pay and therefore requesting
that this Court will grant them some pecuniary assistance on the
occasion was received and read'. (This was the second of three
tobacco pipe makers companies). It does not state whether any
contribution was received but 'received' is very like the expression 'laid on the table'. In applying to the Farriers for money
showed more optimism than foresight!

4th October 1827
In the following year 1827 –

> 'Read a letter from the Revd. H.J. Watkins addressed to the Court; &
> accompanied by a Book lately written by Mr. Watkins containing
> admonitions and Instructions for Apprentices & which Book has been
> adopted by several of the City Companies.
>   And it appearing to the Court that the Book is a very fit and proper
> one for the intended purposes, Resolved that Mr. Lacy, one of the
> Wardens, be requested to purchase one hundred copies of Mr. Wat-
> kins book against the next Court'.

In 1829 the following Minute –

> 'A letter from Edward Calgas in nomination for Livery was read
> stating that he was prevented attending by having fallen from a Stage
> Coach. Ordered that Mr. Calgas be passed over for the present'.

Somewhat unfortunate phraseology for this applicant with his
intriguing fall from public transport.
In 1832 the Clerk laid before the Court a Precept he had received
from the Sheriffs of London requiring him to return pursuant to
the directions of the Reform Bill an Alphabetical List under his
hand together with two printed copies of all such Freemen of this
Company as are Liverymen of the Company entitled to vote for
Members of Parliament according to the form of a Schedule
annexed to the Act. This practice still exists and enables the
Secondary to prepare the Livery List each year.
It was also in 1832 that a Freeman. Thos. Godsell, Senr., paid
up his quarterage amounting to £4. 13s 4d, being 35 years at 2s 8d
per annum.

In 1833 the Clerks of the Livery Companies were obviously
concerned as to 'the measures that could be adopted against
persons refusing or neglecting to take up their Freedom and
found that where a person was free of the City the City would not
take any measures against him although he was exercising various Trades in the City without being free of the various Com-

panies. That where a person carried on a Trade in the City without being free of the City any individual might after summoning him before the Chamberlain takes measures against him in the Name of the City, but at his own expence. That where a person not free of the City had his place of Business without the City but actually did Business in the City he might be proceeded against in the way before mentioned but that where he merely came into the City to fetch Work and took it to his Premises without the City and did it there he could not be proceeded against in the Name of the City but could only be sued under the Bye Laws of the Company'. This advice had been given to them by the Lord Mayor's Court Office.

In 1843 the question of regulating Elections in the City of London when a Special Court was held 'To consider a report made to the Common Council recommending an Application to Parliament to amend the Act of the 11th George the 1st. for regulating elections in the City of London.

The report was now read and the subject matter thereof debated. After which it was moved by Mr. William Coates seconded by Mr. D.W. Witton and Unanimously Resolved with one dissentient That this Court having read the Recommendation and Report and having considered the same Clause by Clause, are disposed without committing themselves to the details, to take a favourable view of the Object of the proposed Measure. And for the present were willing to leave the Matter to the mature consideration of the Corporation of London'.

In 1846 the Court was much concerned with the state of the Company and a Special Committee was formed –

'To take legal steps against persons infringing the Charter.
To compel persons to take up their Freedom.
To enforce the payment of Quarterage.
To summon Freemen to take up their Livery.
To state who are eligible to serve as Stewards. And that they report their proceedings to the next Court'

The Committee reported 'at great length', the main points being as follows:

'We have investigated the rights and privileges conferred upon this Company by the original Order by which the Company was founded in 1356, The Charter of Incorporation, The Bye Laws, And the Act of Common Council of 12 December 1758. And have made enquiries of the Chamberlain, The City Solicitor and the Town Clerk of London.

We have called upon certain Farriers not free of the Company to take up their Freedom. And we recommend that should they refuse to attend or be sworn to the freedom a summons from the Chamberlain be obtained against them.

30

Certain persons have been summoned to this Court to pay their Quarterage but we recommend to the Court that if they do not pay they shall be fined pursuant to the tenth Bye Law and a summons before the Chamberlain obtained against them.

Certain Freemen have been summoned to attend the Court and take up their Livery. If they do not do so after being summoned twice the forfeit of £10 inflicted by the sixth Bye Law shall be enforced.

The 7th Bye Law has not of late years been sufficiently acted on. And therefore we recommend that every year yearly the Court shall elect and choose 3 fit persons being of the Livery to be Stewards. And that every person or persons so elected Stewards that shall refuse to hold and execute the same place shall forfeit and pay the sum of £20. Your Committee however do not hereby mean to interfere with the fine respectively of £8 or £10 which is now generally imposed not with the power of the Court under the 25th Bye Law to mitigate or wholly remit such fine if the person or persons elected steward offers a reasonable excuse'.

Further reference to Stewards will be found elsewhere.

The first reference to the Royal College of Veterinary Surgeons appeared in the minutes of a Committee Meeting of that Council on 9th February 1848 as follows:

'I have the pleasure of informing you that a Committee has been appointed by the Council of the Royal College of Veterinary Surgeons to confer with the Company of Farriers and to ascertain if any steps can be taken for the advantage of both parties'.

However, there is no evidence that this Committee met or reported back to the Council. A possible explanation is that a short time after the Committee was formed, one of its members, William Ernes, was served with a Summons by the Farriers Company 'for practising within their alleged jurisdiction' and that the R.C.V.S. decided to resist such Summons. (There are many more references to the College in this volume, particularly in the Section 'Craft Activities' and in Appendix 9 'The Livery and the Royal College of Veterinary Surgeons – Present Day Links').

1849

The Minutes disclose the problem of covenants arising out of Indentures of Apprentices as they were affected by a Master dying intestate.

'The Clerk reported that James Allen the late Apprentice of Thomas Cook deceased had applied to him to be turned over to Mr. Charles Thomas Harper of 9 Exmouth Street Clerkenwell in the County of Middlesex Smith Citizen and Farrier of London. And the said Thomas Cook having died intestate and no Administration to his effects having been granted, a summons had been issued from the Lord

Mayors Court against his Grace the Lord Archbishop of Canterbury upon whom the said Apprentice had devolved to show cause why the said Lord Archbishop did not fulfill the Covenants of the said Indenture of Apprenticeship. And his Grace the said Lord Archbishop having suffered Judgment by default the said Apprentice had been duly and lawfully turned over to the said Charles Thomas Harper accordingly'.

When the above minute was read the Author wondered as to the connection of the transfer of an apprentice from a deceased Master with the Lord Mayor's Court and the Lord Archbishop of Canterbury so he sought the advice of Mr. Stanley Heather the Comptroller and City Solicitor of the Corporation of London who gave this explanation:

'The Canon Law took its rise from the toleration afforded by the Emperor Constantine to the Christian religion and the permission he gave to the Christian Church to manage its own affairs. In these early days Canon Law followed closely the model of Roman Law but gradually a voluminous body of Canon Law for dealing with ecclesiastical matters was built up. William I decreed that ecclesiastical matters should be administered in the Courts of the Church itself instead of the old secular courts and thence forward they became important institutions with a large and lucrative business.

In addition to jurisdiction in ecclesiastical matters such as punishment of offences against doctrine and morality and the control of marriage and divorce, the Church acquired jurisdiction in some matters quite secular in nature, notably the administration so far as personal property was concerned of the estates of deceased persons. It is to be noted that real property matters were not included. Fierce and bitter struggles between the Church Courts and the Royal Courts followed on matters of jurisdiction but the grant of Probates and Letters of Administration and decisions as to the validity of Wills, dealing again with personal property only, remained with the Church Courts.

In dealing with purely secular business such as the Probate of Wills and the administration of the estates of deceased persons, the Church Courts relied upon that body of Roman Law known as the Corpus Juris Civilis to distinguish it from the Canon Law which continued to apply to purely ecclesiastical matters.

In 1875 the jurisdiction of the Church Courts in secular matters was transferred to the High Court by the Judicature Acts, the practical effect being that the legal principles upon which the Church Courts decisions had been made were expressly incorporated into the laws of England.'

In the same year the Minutes show the lack of administration or, again, was it poverty of the Company? Probably both for a letter was received from the Office of Woods, Forests and Land

Revenues stating that the annual sum of 13s. 4d. payable by the Company 'that they might be a body corporate' had not been paid since 10th October 1832 and demanding payments. £16. 6s. 8d. was subsequently paid. It will be noted in the Ordinances No.33, (appendix) this is the Fee Farm Rent now payable to the Crown Estate Commissioners under the Charter – if it was unpaid for forty days after demand the Company's rights shall cease. These arrears of seventeen years do not seem to have had much effect.

In 1855 the Clerk reported the seizure of the Company's Chair and other goods and chattels which had been for years left at the George and Vulture for Arrears of Rent alleged to be due to the Landlord, (meetings were held at one period in this historic tavern) and it had been left to the Clerk 'to obtain the same on payment of such sum as he may deem fair and just'. The Clerk however was unable to get any reply from a Mr. Lucena (the Landlord) and it was not until a year later that the matter was reported to the Court when a letter was received from the Landlord demanding 25 guineas for the return of the Robes and Chair, which had been seized with other goods at the George and Vulture, for Rent. The Company declined to pay and decided to order four new Gowns and to offer 5 guineas to procure the Chair. In January 1857 it was reported that the Landlord's Clerk – a Mr. Mills – now possessed the Gowns and Chair and he refused to part with any of the items at the offered price. Finally, the Company decided to buy a new Chair and the robes at a sum not exceeding 20 guineas; but in June, the Master (Mr. Ditchman) reported that at last he had obtained the Gowns and Chair for £16. 6s. 0d. and that they had been delivered to the Landlord of Radleys Hotel in Bridge Street, Blackfriars – the Company's new meeting place. It had taken two years to recover their possession It is interesting to note that Mr. Ditchman, who had been a Warden during the period of this dispute, later became a Master for two years.

In 1864 THE VETERINARIAN (the journal of the Royal College of Veterinary Surgeons) describes the breaking of a farriers' strike in the Midlands.

As had been said, Wining and Dining appeared to be the main subject of the Minutes but obviously the Clerk (Sidney Smith about whom more appears in the section on CLERKS) was worried as to the expenditure on Dinners and some Liverymen when elected refused to accept office.

In 1871 the Court resolved –

'That the Charter Rules and Bye Laws of the Company and all documents showing how such Charter was granted and relating thereto should be printed and one hundred copies thereof be bound in Mauve Cloth with the Seal of the Company stamped on the covers at a cost not to exceed £12. 12s. 0d.'

It transpired that the Printer's Estimate for the printing of the Charter etc. was £24 8s. 0d. and the number of copies was reduced to fifty.

1872

The Minutes report that a fire-proof safe be bought to contain the Books and Papers of the Company at a price not exceeding Thirty guineas.

In January 1873 the Court became interested in the education regarding its trade for this Minute appears:

'Resolved That this Court cordially supports the furtherance of Technical education as evidenced by the resolution passed at a Meeting held at the Mansion House on the 10th day of January 1872 And that the opinion of the Members of this Court on the best means of the Company advancing the question of technical education be requested at the next Court'.

Nothing did appear in the Minutes of the next Court or any other Court Minutes until three years later when it was –

'Resolved that a sum not exceeding £50 be granted by this Court out of the funds of the Company for one year for the purpose of furthering by way of prizes or otherwise as may be deemed desirable the art trade and mystery of Farriers and that the same amount be granted in after years if the Court should so direct',

and a Committee was appointed for this purpose and advertising was authorised and the Minutes disclose that the Technical Education Committee reported:

1877

'That no Competitors came forward for the 2nd and 3rd Prizes. That only two of the four persons who paid their entrance fees for the first prize sent in Essays. That the judges . . . decided that neither of them evinced sufficient merit to entitle either writer to the 1st Prize'

In the meantime, the Committee on Technical Education referred to above, being Members of Livery Companies, the Chamberlain acting as Secretary, had been convened by the Lord Mayor to consider a letter from the Chairman of Crystal Palace Company on the subject of technical education, in particular by an Exhibition of Works of Art and Manufacture owned by Livery Companies. Many meetings of a Committee representing the Corporation and Livery Companies were held throughout 1872 and a Conference of the City Companies and International Exhibitors took place at Marlborough House in July 1873 in the presence of HRH The Prince of Wales to discuss Technical Education. In 1877 the Corporation, through the City side of the Gresham Committee, conferred with the Mercers Company to consider a scheme for a National System of Technical Education and the Corporation contributed in 1880 the sum of £10,000 over a period of five years. which was paid out of City's Cash.

In December 1876 the Farriers Company offered prizes for an essay on the treatment of horses in health and disease (open to Members of the Royal College of Veterinary Surgeons and students at the Royal Veterinary College) and for sets of horse-shoes (open to Army and civilian farriers), the competition to be judged by a panel from the Company and the Royal College of Veterinary Surgeons Council. In the event, very few entries were received and no prize was awarded.

From the above it can be concluded that from the earliest days of the veterinary profession, the desirability of a good working relationship between farriers and veterinary surgeons was recognised. There were some differences of opinion over 'territory' but by the 1870's a cooperative spirit was well established between the Farriers Company and the Royal College of Veterinary Surgeons.

At this period, follows a considerable flux of new Members and in 1879 a Committee was appointed to look into and report on the Expenditure of the Company on Dinners etc. The cost of entertainments had risen from £34 in 1869 to £170 in 1877 and £162 in 1878. This was partly accounted for by the rapid increase in membership and the Livery having been invited to the November Dinners.

The Committee made various recommendations in a long Report fully entered on the Minutes, including the raising of fees.

On joining the Court from £20 to £50. On any member of the Court (other than the present members) taking Office as Warden £10 and as Master £25.

The fee for Freedom remained at £1 4s 0d. and for Livery £10.

In 1882 the Bye Laws were reprinted including all the amendments made between 1871 and 1882 and were summarised in the Minutes, dealing with fines which had been increased; Insurance of possessions; wearing of Badges; Robes and Mace; Clerks and Beadles wearing their Gowns; notice of Motions to be given to the Clerk 14 days before the Court; Clerk to keep a Cash Book and balance it with the Bank Book; all moneys to go through the Bank; Clerk deputed to admit to Freedom and Livery; Regulations as to expenditure on Dinners; Sums paid for Apprentices to be invested as Capital; Quarterage in arrear – if unpaid for two years, after a written demand, the member and his widow and children to be ineligible for relief, Such members also shall not be invited to dinners of the Company; Beadles to be paid for each attendance and not on annual Salary; Beadle to collect the Quarterage. (The last two references are mentioned in the section on Beadles).

This was indeed a sweep of up to ten years alterations in the

Ordinances. Included in the recommendations a Finance Committee was to be appointed.

26th January 1883

In 1883, a Committee was appointed to consider the holding of an Exhibition relating to the past and present trade of Farriery. A Guarantee Fund received support from Members of the Court to the extent of £375.

The Committee's report was as follows:

1. The whole of the Members of the Company have been invited to add their names to a fund for guaranteeing the expenses and up to the present time the sum of £985 has been promised.
2. The Committee have determined to prefix the word 'International' to the title of the Exhibition.
3. The attention of the Committee has been directed to obtaining Noblemen and gentlemen to become Vice-Presidents or to serve as members of a General Committee. Alderman Hadley (the Alderman next in rotation for Lord Mayor) has consented to become Chairman of the Committee.
4. To form both a Competition Branch and a Loan Branch. Several Noblemen and gentlemen have already promised articles toward the Loan Collection.
5. Several of the City Companies have officially taken notice of the scheme and appointed Representatives to serve on the General Committee

The Exhibition Committee further reported an interview with the Clerk of the Loriners Company; the following proposal was agreed subject to confirmation –

'The Loriners' Company to give £100 towards expenses and six prizes, amounting to £80. The £100 to be returned if the receipts exceed the expenses. The prize classes to be embodied in the programme and to be stated as given by the Loriners' Company. Judges for these classes to be nominated by the Loriners' Company. Master and Wardens of Loriners' Company to be included on the General Committee'.

Later on suggestions had been made by the promoters of the International Health Exhibition that the Farriers' Exhibition should form a part of the larger event, but in the event of no satisfactory arrangement being made with the Committee of the proposed National Health Exhibition, the Farriers' Exhibition be (with the consent of the Loriners' Company) postponed until 1885.

At the meeting in May 1884 the Clerk laid before the Court a statement of the disbursements and liabilities in connection with the late intended Farriers' Exhibition amounting in all to £70 12s 0d.

It was Resolved that the £70 12s 0d. to be paid . . . and that the Clerk be requested to accept a present of £29 8s 0d. as a slight recognition of his valuable and esteemed services. Correspondence with the promoters of the Health Exhibition was discussed.

Resolved that the Clerk write to the Executive Committee of the International Health Exhibition repudiating any obligation to subscribe and pointing out the loss sustained by the Company in having to withdraw their intended Exhibition of Farriery.

The Company had done its best to deal with Farriery but to no avail. However, the Livery as a whole was also taking an interest in the activities of the Livery Companies, for in the same year, a circular letter was read from the Town Clerk enclosing copy of the following Resolution; passed at the Common Hall on 29th September last:

'That in view of the importance of encouraging the manufactures of the Kingdom the Guilds be hereby Exhorted to assist the spread of scientific and artistic knowledge among the workmen of their respective Guilds'

In 1885 it was Resolved –

'That henceforth all Members of the Company being elected Assistants shall previously to being admitted Members of the Court sign an agreement in the following words, viz:
"We the undersigned do severally and each for himself promise on his respective word of honour that if he shall have the misfortune to become Bankrupt or take advantage of any Act of Parliament for the relief of Insolvent Debtors or make any Assignment for the benefit of or compound with his Creditors he will within 21 days of any such event happening unconditionally resign his office of Assistant of the Company" '

11th January 1887
The Company, two years later, in 1887 –

'Resolved That a Committee be now appointed to consider and report to the Court whether it is desirable that the Company should open a Registry for the entry therein of the names, addresses and ages of any Master and Journeyman Farriers who shall pass a practical examination in the art of making shoes for and shoeing horses as the Company (in connection with the Royal College of Veterinary Surgeons of England or some other Body or person having suitable forges) may direct or how otherwise to celebrate the Jubilee year' (Queen Victoria's Golden Jubilee)

1887
The Court decided to celebrate the Jubilee by inviting the Livery to Dinner at the Albion Hotel on 12th May. £140 was subscribed by the Court.

1888

Now, at last, we find the Company being interested in the Registration of Farriers, for the following Minute appears:

> 'The Committee considering the proposed Farriers' Registration Scheme reported that they had been in touch with the Royal Agricultural Society asking for their assistance; the Society were considering the matter'.

The Registration Committee reported that the Royal Agricultural Society had suggested that the Company should present its Freedom free of cost to the two first prize takers at their Horse Shoeing competition to take place at Nottingham on 10th July.

It was reported that the Freedom of the Company conferred upon the prize winners at the Royal Agricultural Society's Competition would be handed to them by the Master at the Court Dinner, in a polished mahogany box.

It was Resolved –

> 'That the Freedom of the Company be offered to the first prize takers at the Horse Shoeing Competition to be held by the Royal Agricultural Society at Windsor Great Park next year. That in addition the Court present prizes not exceeding in all £60 to the best competitors'.

1889

Members of the Court subscribed the whole of the above £60, but naturally all the enthusiasm of the Court regarding 'registration' was costing money and it is not surprising to find that the Company's Auditor (a member of the Court) drew special attention to the fact that the expenditure for the year had again exceeded the Income. A Committee was appointed to consider the matter, and economies were suggested. In the meantime, a Member of the Court Mr. George Burt (Immediate Past Master) had donated £100, Mr. Nathaniel Louis Cohen (who had recently been elected an Assistant) £5, and Mr. Warden Wimbush £30. All these amounts were to be paid into a Special Account at the Bank to be termed 'Registration Account', and in 1889 a draft scheme for the National Registration of Farriers as prepared by Mr. Arnold Herbert from instructions furnished by Mr. Nathaniel L. Cohen in July last together with an outline scheme by Professor John Wortley Axe for the establishment of an Institute of Horse Shoeing had been sent to the Members of the Court. (Professor Axe of the Royal Veterinary College was the Author of several volumes on 'The Horse').

And it was Resolved –

> 'That it is desirable to establish an organization under the auspices of the Company for the promotion of skilled Farriery and the registration of duly qualified Farriers in London and throughout the country'.

So after sixteen years, for it had been resolved in 1873, the Company was to carry out its purpose of the Registering of Shoesmiths.

We now come to the Meeting at the Mansion House in 1890, referred to at the commencement of this History.

To enable readers to follow the history of the company during the Twentieth Century, it has been felt advisable to change the rhythm of the book. Firstly because the Registration Scheme had become the principal objective and whilst naturally the Court Minutes contained many other items of interest they have been dealt with in the various chapters. Secondly, it has been easier to cover this twentieth century period when dealing with the chapters on Masters and Clerks. It can be said that this is not a consequential or logical reason but, as has been said, the book has been written with the object of informing the members of the Company and others interested in Farriery, of the story of the Farriers Company, over the past six hundred years has been revealed in other chapters.

Before leaving the History of the Company the Author hopes that the following account of a ceremony known as the 'Quit Rent Services' is so connected with the Farriers as to be of interest to readers.

Ceremony of the Quit Rent Services
Each year a ceremony takes place which is the oldest in this country next to that of the Coronation, closely allied to the history of the Worshipful Company of Farriers. It is in respect of a tenement called the Forge in the parish of St. Clement Danes in the Strand and horse shoes and nails form part of the ceremony. The Author has accordingly included extracts from the Address by the Queen's Remembrancer, Master Grundy, given in October 1965. The author was present and copies were sent to all Liverymen. It was in 1965 that the Lord Mayor, Sir James Miller GBE and the Sheriff, attended for the first time since 1859. The author had the privilege of attending the 1978 ceremony when Master Jacob QC explained the unique position of his office:

'In 1859, by the Queen's Remembrancer's Act of that year, the then Senior Master of the Court of Exchequer was appointed to be the Queens Remembrancer and since the Judicature Acts of 1873 – 1875, the Senior Master of the Supreme Court takes on the mantle of the Queen's Remembrancer. I am myself the 20th Master since 1859 who has had the privilege and distinction of holding the office of the Queen's Remembrancer, which remains today the last surviving office of the ancient Court of Exchequer.'

Master Grundy described this Ceremony in these terms:
'Let me now tell you about the Forge. It is a simple story. In the

year 1235, Henry III, there was an itinerant farrier, by name Walter le Brun. He came up the Strand travelling towards the walls of the City, the Western gateway of which was where Fetter Lane now joins Fleet Street. It was not the Strand, the thoroughfare as we know it; there were no buildings on either side, and to the north was all open country. It was "De Stranda" – the river bank – and the ground to the south sloped gently and uninterruptedly down to the Thames. On reaching St. Clement's Church – not the St. Clement Danes which replaced it in 1630 – but a church dating from Saxon times – Walter put up a forge. It is recorded in the Great Roll of the Exchequer, 1235, Henry III, that "Walter le Brun, Farrier in the Strand", was to have a piece of ground in the parish of St. Clement to place a forge there, he rendering yearly six horse-shoes for it. The origin of this quaint grant is not known but tradition has it that it was connected with some incident in the Knights Templars' Tilting Yard. Many of you may know that on the other side of the Strand opposite these Courts, which were not built until 1881, is The Temple, which has long been the seat of lawyers but in the time of Henry III was the abode of the Knights Templars, the Crusaders. Matthew Parris, in his "History of England" written in that reign, referring to the Temple, said: "These Templars at this time were in so great glory that they entertained the Nobility, Foreign Ambassadors, and the Prince himself very often". It may therefore easily be imagined, may it not, that in the year 1235 the Knights Templars gave a special entertainment to the young King to celebrate his forthcoming marriage to Eleanor of Provence in the following january, that one of the features of the entertainment was a tilting match, and that during the tournament some of the large Flemish horses on which the Knights were mounted, and which were trained to stand fast on their forefeet in battle, may in the melee have cast a shoe and required to be re-shod, or that some of the Knights' armour needed repair. This called for the immediate assistance of the local farrier; and so promptly and so deftly did Walter le Brun carry out the necessary work, that the King there and then rewarded him by granting him the site of the land on which his forge stood. And this may very well be true because it was so like Henry III; he was prodigal with his favours, especially when it came to giving one of his subjects the property he had taken from another.

'The location of the site can be fixed with reasonable certainty. In the Memoranda Rolls 1272–73, Edward I, it is recorded that Walter the Farrier at the Stone Cross rendered "sex ferra equorum cum clavibus", six horse-shoes with nails, for the site of a forge, which he held from the King, "ex opposito Crucis lapindeaeP, opposite the stone Cross. It was customary in early times to erect a symbolical cross outside a church, and from an old print showing the open nature of the country at that time there appears a stone cross a few feet to the north of St. Clement's Church. It has been said that this cross was erected by William Rufus in memory of his mother, Matilda, whose body had rested there on its way to Westminster Abbey for burial. This then would place the exact site of the Forge very close to where Australia House stands today. "There are other entries in the Great Roll of the Exchequer showing that in the reigns of Edward I, II, III and Richard II, descendants and successors of Walter le Brun rendered these services, but towards the end of Richard's reign the Knights Templars fell into disrepute and were evicted from the Temple, and in the ensuing riots the Forge was demolished. There is no evidence that the Corporation ever came into possession of the site of this Forge, but from the time it disappeared the Corporation has every year tendered to the Crown six large horse-shodes to fit the forefeet of three large Flemish horses and sixty-one nails; ten nails for each shoe, and one over. But let me now surprise you! The horse-shoes and the nails that will be rendered today are the same shoes and nails that have been rendered every year for over 560 years, and after today's ceremony they will be kept in safe custody in the Queen's Remembrancer's Office until next year's ceremony takes place, when they will be handed to the Corporation to be rendered once again to the Crown. Is not this clear proof that these horse shoes and these nails were forged in the smithy in the Strand? So ends my account of the ceremony you are going to see. In book form it might, in simple words, be called – "The Smith and The Crown".'

Master Grundy commented:

'You will readily understand, will you not, that since 1859 it has not been necessary for the Lord Mayor of London and his Sheriffs to attend the ceremony officially; nor, indeed, have they attended it officially or personally until today. But the ceremony of 1965 is an historic occasion. For the first time for 105 years we are honoured by the presence of a Lord Mayor of London in the person of Sir James Miller who, by coming with his Sheriffs to witness this ceremony, has restored to it not a little of the glory which surrounded it in the years when it was performed before a distinguished assembly in the Court of Exchequer at Westminster Hall. By coming here Sir James Miller has also added greatly to the public interest in an ancient ceremony which has long been an example of the happy rela-tionship existing between the City of London and the Crown. I said "long", not "always", because, as you may know, there were occasions in our history – in the reigns of King John and King Charles the First – when relations were beligerent rather than cordial.'

Meeting and Dining Places

The Company, through lack of finance and not owning a Hall for any considerable time, was not able to hold large banquets, nor to entertain the Lord Mayor and Sheriffs until fairly recently. Certainly there were no references between 1719 and 1809. Even in 1876 Alderman Sir Thomas White, a Past Master of the Company, when Lord Mayor does not appear to have been specially entertained by the Company. It can only be imagined that 'Charity Begins at Home' operated in those days because members of the company certainly did not stint themselves. The extracts of the Minutes contain numerous references to the details of their own Dinners, particularly on the 9th November in each year following the Lord Mayor's Procession. Details of the Banquet in 1739 show the bills of the Pastrycook amounted to £3. 0s. 0d., the Poulterers £3. 0s. 0d., the Butcher for beef £1. 7s. 5d., for Hams £1. 5s. 5d. and for Bacon and Chines 16/–. A total of £9. 8s. 10d. And for this large sum they had '24 ffowles boiled and roasted, 4 Hams abt sixteen pounds each, 2 Turkeys, 2 Chines abt 12 pounds each, 2 Leggs of Lamb, 3 Marrow puddings and three Apple Pies.'

In the eighteenth century meetings had for some considerable while been held at the Half Moon Tavern, Cheapside, but there had been some dissatisfaction and in October 1768 –

'it was taken into Consideration what House the Company should remove to on Lord Mayor's Day . . . Afterwards several Houses were proposed to the Court particularly the Sun Tavern in Honey Lane Market and ffeathers Tavern in Cheapside, and the George and Vulture Tavern in Cornhill, which Houses being severally put up It was Agreed to Remove to the George and Vulture Tavern'.

Other Meeting places and dining rooms mentioned in the Minutes contained a colourful number of hostelries, presumably in a private room and it included the following:

The Guildhall Coffee House, near Guildhall
The Crown Tavern at Cripplegate
The Red Cross, Red Cross Street
Blackwell's Coffee House, Queen Street
The Pope's Head Tavern in Cornhill
The White Horse, Cripplegate
The New Castle Coffee House on St. Mary Hill, Billingsgate
The George and Vulture, Cornhill (of Dickensian fame)
Artichoke Tavern, Blackwall
Radleys Hotel, Bridge Street
Albion Tavern, Aldersgate Street

Ship and Turtle, Leadenhall Street
De Keyser Royal Hotel, Victoria (sic)
Monico Restaurant (Installation of H. Roper Barratt 1921)
Cannon Street Hotel

The Clerk's Office was sometimes used as a venue of the meetings, and presumably the Court proceeded to the nearest or most convenient hostelry.

From 1942 to 1977 the Court of the Company was greatly privileged to meet regularly at Tallow Chandlers Hall in Dowgate Hill, one of the very few Halls in the City which were not destroyed or seriously damaged by enemy action in World War II. After the destruction wrought by the Great Fire of 1666, the building of the present Hall was commenced in 1670 and, including its decoration, took several years to complete. The principal public rooms are the Parlour and Banquet Hall on the first floor and the Court Room above. The Hall was badly damaged in 1944. Today we are facing a position that may have influenced our predecessors, the question of cost of the meals, with the present inflation it may be that our successors will repair to the 'nearest and most convenient hostelry, public house, or even cafe'. What is certain that the menu will not contain the provisions similar to that selected in 1739 as quoted supra.

On pages 46/7 will be found a list of Court and Livery Dinners and Masters' Receptions held between 1940 and 1979. The Court decided that, whilst the Company had received every courtesy and kindness from the Company of Tallow Chandlers for 35 years, they should move the Court Meetings to the Hall of the Company of Inn Holders where it held its first meeting and luncheon on 24th June 1977 and the Company is now happily settled in this delightful Hall.

Returning to the Dinners held by the Company during the last century, Queen Victoria's Jubilee in 1887 was celebrated by the Court inviting the Livery to Dinner at the Albion Hotel on May 12th and subscribing £140. This seems to be the first reference to the Livery being entertained by the Court. There are no details of the numbers attending or whether any Dinner Fee was paid by the members of the Livery. Following the Golden Jubilee Dinner, the Minutes were examined to find out how the Diamond Jubilee in 1897 was celebrated. There was no mention made, not surprisingly, for the following Resolution of the 4th August 1897 read as follows:

'That this Court be indebted to Messrs Ring and Brymer and the Albion Tavern Company for banquets held by this Company in November 1896 and July 1897 and that it is contrary to the dignity and good repute of the Company not to pay its debts. That a sufficient sum of Consols be forthwith sold out to pay and discharge all indebtedness of the Company to the present time. That no further banquet be held by the Company until it has sufficient funds in hand to pay all expenses consequent upon such banquets out of its receipts and without any further infraction upon it capital.'

'The Motion being put to the vote, there were
For   2
Against   3

and same was lost. Notwithstanding, and in manner unknown, the Account of Ring & Brymer, a leading firm of City Caterers, was paid. Incidentally, the present Chairman of this firm is Colonel Sir Lindsay Roberts Ring, GBE, who was Lord Mayor in 1975.

No Dinner was held in 1898 and the Master in commenting on this fact wrote to the Clerk as follows:

'I have avoided some expense owing to there having been no Dinner and I enclose a cheque.'

No sum was mentioned in the Minutes.

In 1902 a Dinner was arranged to be held on the 3rd July to celebrate the Coronation of King Edward VII (postponed to 7th July due to the severe illness of the King). At the Dinner the Veterinary Officer of the Colonial and Indian Troops was invited. Due, as usual, to the finance of the Company and to avoid depleting the funds, it was limited to 20, and members of the Court agreed to subscribe a sum not exceeding two guineas to a Guarantee Fund to be drawn on to the amount by which the cost of the Dinner exceeded the average cost of the dinners of the last three years. (Inflation was less heard of in those days!) However, the Dinner was postponed indefinitely and in fact there is no mention in the Minutes that it was ever held. The Minutes remain silent on the question of any more Dinners until 1911 when it was arranged that the Inaugural Dinner of the new Master, James Coote Garnham be held on 25th July 1911, and ladies to be invited. It is curious that whenever the name Garnham appears, it is always followed by the mention of 'ladies'! This Dinner and the finances of Dinners in general is not again mentioned until the 1925 resolution that the Master's responsibility for any deficit be limited to £75 (other than his personal guests and the balance of deficit be charged to the Court pro rata.) In November 1928 the Clerk reminded the Court that the Annual Dinner was generally held in January and that in order to be assured of the Lord Mayor's attendance, he had fixed the 18th January 1929 for the Dinner. The Court expressed its assent and that the matter in connection therewith be left in the hands of the Master and Clerk.

The above Minute has been recorded for it appears in every year until 1933 that there are no details of any of the Dinners, where they were held or who attended them.

After 1933 there are not even the usual references to an Annual Dinner, but in October 1937 the following appears:
'That in view of the financial position of the Company the Annual Dinner should not be held.' The Master was then Sir Frederick Senier JP.

In 1938 the usual Minute mentions that a Dinner be held. The Author was admitted to the Company in January 1936 and his recollection and his own financial records show that a Dinner was held in 1938 and the Dining fee was £2. 10s. 0d, (The members did not pay a dining fee). On the 16th January 1940 the Minutes record that 'owing to the present War and International situation the Master (R. Barlow Tyler) has decided to abandon the holding of his Installation Dinner. It had been arranged to be held at the Mercers Hall and it was a great regret to have to cancel the Dinner and he expressed the hope that under happier conditions, the Farriers Company might have another opportunity of accepting the hospitality of the Worshipful Company of Mercers.

The next reference to a Livery function appears in April 1942 when arrangements were made to hold a Livery luncheon on 18th May at which the Lord Mayor (Sir Samuel Joseph) was to be invited – but in June the Minutes show that the Lord Mayor preferred that the luncheon be cancelled in view of the recent demands by the Government for economy and restrictions on entertaining. It will be seen from the list of Luncheons, Dinners and Receptions from 1940–1979 that the Court Dinner in 1974, when Brigadier Clabby was Master, was not held at the request of the Lord Mayor, Sir Hugh Wontner, due to the labour difficulties known as 'the three day working week.' (See further reference page 85.)

It will have been noted that arrangements for Livery Dinners have been 'left in the hands of the Masters and Clerks.' Nowadays all the arrangements are made by a Financial and Social Committee consisting of the Master, Wardens and a number of Past Masters, who report to the Court for their approval – a sign of democracy and efficiency. It is hoped that the Annual Court Dinner, Livery Dinner and Master's Reception will continue and none of the difficulties described above, financial, Wars, labour troubles etc will interfere with the Company's opportunities of entertaining the Lord Mayor and other guests of the Livery Companies and Members' personal guests, for hospitality in the Livery and especially in the City of London is the root and branch of all the Livery Companies.

Court and Livery Dinners from 1940 to 1979

*Ladies invited

Year	Master	Court Dinner	Livery Dinner	Master's Reception
1940	Barlow Tyler	Cancelled due to Outbreak of War		
1941-42		Livery Luncheon Cancelled due to Resolution by Government		
1943-44	R W Buckingham	WAR	Tallow Chandlers	
1944-45	G B Garnham	WAR	Tallow Chandlers	Victory Luncheon
1945-46	Walter Rose		Grocers*	
1946-47	Cyprian Whiteley		Mansion Hse & Grocers*	Apothecaries Conference of Master Farrier & Blacksmith
1947-48	W. Newcome Wright	Tallow Chandlers	Vintners	
1948-49	E P Paxman	Tallow Chandlers	Drapers	Tallow Chandlers
1949	F M Garnham		Grocers*	
1949-50	H A Brown	Tallow Chandlers	Grocers Vintners*	
1950-51	G H Fenton	Mansion Hse	Mansion Hse	Tallow Chandlers
1951-52	G A Warley	Goldsmiths	Grocers	
1952-53	Oswald Lewis	Cutlers	Drapers	
1953-54	J B Buxton	Tallow Chandlers	Grocers	
1954-55	S R Walker	Armourers	Mansion Hse*	
1955-56	L B Prince	Apothecaries	Drapers	
1956-57	His Grace the Duke of Devonshire	Armourers	Guildhall* (600th Anniversary)	
1957-58	J Stroud	Vintners	Grocers	
1958-59	G Bowman	Apothecaries	Grocers	
1959-60	G Allison-Beer	Innholders	Mansion Hse*	
1960-61	Sir L Hollinghurst	Armourers	Grocers	HQS Wellington
1961-62	Rt Hon Sir John Smyth	Cutlers	Manion Hse*	House of Commons
1962-63	Sir F Lord	Armourers	Mansion Hse*	
1963-64	J E Lines	Bakers	Mansion Hse*	Livery Hall Guildhall

Year	Master	Court Dinner	Livery Dinner	Master's Reception
1964-65	Dr W R Wooldridge	Cutlers	Mansion Hse*	London University
1965-66	R A Brown	Armourers	Mansion Hse*	Cutlers
1966-67	Alec Hobson	Innholders	Mansion Hse*	Rural Industries Bureau (now Cosira) at Wimbledon
1967-68	George Smith	Pewterers	Mansion Hse*	Armourers
1968-69	A J Barsham	Apothecaries	Mansion Hse*	Armoury house
1969-70	R W V Neathercoat	Cutlers	Clothworkers*	Pavilion Rd London
1970-71	E H Newcome Wright	Armourers	Mansion Hse*	
1971-72	Sir Hugh Linstead	Innholders	Drapers*	Pharmaceutical Society of GB
1972-73	K J Lines	Pewterers	Drapers	HQS Wellington
1973-74	John Clabby	Cancelled (due to 3 day week)	Mansion Hse*	Royal College of Veterinary Surgeons
1974-75	M A P Simons	Innholders*	Mansion Hse*	Buckingham Palace Royal Mews
1975-76	A G Smith	Innholders*	Mansion Hse*	Fellows Restaurant Regents Park Zoo
1976-77	F Bell	Innholders	Mansion Hse*	St John's Wood Barracks (The home of RHA)
1977-78	Dorian Williams	Innholders	Mansion Hse*	Pendry Manor, Tring
1978-79	David Gibson	Innholders	Mansion Hse*	Equine Research station and Jockey Club Rooms Newmarket

Some Eighteenth Century dwelling places and descriptions of Freemen of the Company

Lives with the Serjant ffarrier.
"   on Broadstreet Hill
"   in Dogg Lane Bethnall Green
"   in Ludgate Street
"   in Menoris
"   at Cow Cross a Butcher
"   in Austin fryers
"   at Ring & Pearl ffenchurch street
"   at a Haberdasher of Hatts in Cornhill
"   by Hoxton Square but Officer at Poultry Compter
"   on Mount Hill, a Backon Man
"   at a Cellar under Furnival's Inn Holborne a Victualler
"   in old Fullers Gardens
"   on London Bridge a Haberdasher
"   in a passage facing Mercers Chappell
"   atte the Leather Breeches against St. Sepulchres Church
"   at the Thatched House Petty France
"   at Stratford near Bow in Essex
A Hogg Butcher at Mr. Talbutts
An Oyle Man near Pump at Aldgate
A Blacksmith in Wormwood Street
A Linnendraper Aldersgate Street
Lives in Welclose square Bricklayer

St. Eloi, The Patron Saint of Farriers

The Patron Saint of Farriers is St. Eloi, Treasurer to Dagobert, King of the Franks, and afterwards Bishop of Noyon. He is known in Latin as St. Eligius, and in English sometimes as St. Loo.

The legend is that there was a horse that was possessed of the devil, and would not stand still to be reshod. The owner took him to the Saint, who cut off a leg, nailed the shoe on, and then put the leg back on the stump. On his making the sign of the Cross it was miraculously reunited, to the admiration of all beholders.

St. Eligius is generally represented with an anvil, having a horse's leg in his hand. He appears thus on the rood screen of the Parish Church of Hempstead in Norfolk. He is not included in the English calendar, but his date in the Roman calendar is December 1st, the anniversary of his death in 660 A.D.

CHAPTER 2
Masters

To cover the history of the Chair and its influence on the Company is not unlike a speaker proposing the Toast of the Guests at a Banquet. He has two alternatives; firstly to mention a number of well-known personalities, described sometimes as reading from a telephone directory, giving a brief description of their attributes; or secondly to mention no-one, but remark that all guests are welcome and to end with the one who will reply for all the others. In a list of 248 persons who have acted as Master during a period of six centuries, appears to be an almost insuperable task.

In reading through the Minutes of the Court – each and every one of the masters carried out his duties to the best of his abilities – almost every one received a Resolution of thanks at the end of his year of office and it is of interest to see in the list that on some occasions Masters have occupied the Chair more than once for various reasons, principally due to death of the Master in office or due to lack of candidates especially in the 18th and 19th centuries, or due to the outbreak of Wars when Wardens on Service were unable to succeed to that office. It will be noticed that family tradition has been very strong in the Company and fathers and sons serving the Company over the years.

The Author began this Chapter in the sense that the Company's history was in fact the History of People who had for various reasons joined the Farriers' Company, and whilst all Livery Companies pay tribute to their long list of Masters and Wardens, by publishing a list of those persons who had reached the Chair with the date, it seemed to the Author that more should be attributed to the holders of this office, thus this Chapter became Biographical, particularly over the last sixty years.

When an interesting event has happened, the Master in the year has been mentioned. Eventually, as is explained later in the Chapter, it became easier to write a Biography for each Master. The Chapter on Masters necessarily covers much of the History of the Company and it is hoped that readers will find it more personal than other Livery Company histories – for these latter years must necessarily be also *autobiographical* when an author of such a history has the unique privilege of watching and participating, as a Liveryman since 1936, an Assistant since 1946 and a Past Master since 1955 – denied obviously to any outside author.

On page 90 there is a list of Masters beginning in 1673 to 1979 (excluding those untraced between 1675 and 1718).

As has been mentioned in Chapter 1, the Company was first established by the Court of Mayor and Aldermen as a Fellowship in 1356. The Mayor was Henry Pycard and it is of interest that over the door in the Vintners Hall there is an inscription that Henry Pycard entertained FIVE KINGS to Dinner in 1363 – Edward III, David of Scotland, John of France, Waldemer III of Denmark and Amadeus of Cyprus (and thus originated the Vintners' custom of Five Cheers instead of the usual Three!)

Henry Pycard and the Aldermen of the City chose from the Master Farriers of the City two Masters; 'the most sufficient men, and the best knowing; that is to say Richard de Hertele and John de Oxenford; whom the said Mayor caused to be sworn, and gave them full power to oversee and govern the said trade, and to espy into the defaults thereof, if any such they should find, at all times that they might think proper.'

In the Ordinances of Farriers there is an addition of later date where it is stated that 'because that in the said Articles all the grievances of their trade were not fully set forth, the good folks the said farriers presented a plaint unto John Notte, Mayor, and the Aldermen of the said city . . . and prayed that the same might be added, in form as follows, to the Articles aforesaid:

'To the honourable Lords, the Mayor and Aldermen of the City of London, pray the good folks of the same city, farriers, that whereas many persons, as well denizens as foreigners, are served by the same farriers, some by tally, and others on credit without tally; the same persons, for malice, not caring to pay them for their labour, do go away to others of the same trade, in deceit of those who have served them beforehand, so as to delay them of payment of their debt; may it please your high Lordships, as a work of charity . . .'

These are the earliest references to the Masters and due to the destruction of the Records of the Company in the fire of 1666, we can only deal with the Masters from 1673–1674 (the date of the Company's Charter). Gregory Costen was to hold office until the

Feast of the Nativity of St. John the Baptist (ie Midsummer Day) 1674 and thereafter Andrew Snape (who was Sergeant-Farrier to King Charles II and had a forge roughly where today stands Nurse Edith Cavell's statue opposite St. Martin in the Fields.) The election of Masters, Wardens and Assistants takes place on the Feast of Nativity, yearly, for ever unless on a Sunday in which case the Monday following. This date remained the only fixed date in the Calendar of Court meetings.

Following the Various Power Acts of the Common Council 1958 Saturdays are excluded from the holding of Common Hall and the Farriers Company have also excluded Saturdays – so departing from the word 'for ever' in the Charter. The Master should be someone who has been a Warden. In practice it is normally the Upper Warden. In the Charter there is the power of the Court to fill for themselves a vacancy caused by the death of the Master in office and there are seven references to 'died in office'. Frederick Malcolm Garnham, the father of the present Senior Past Master George Garnham (1944–45) was Master in 1920–21 and when Edward Paxman (1948–49), George Warley (1951–52) and James Buxton (1953–54), died in office, Frederick, being the Senior Past Master was elected Master for the remainder of each year, and thus became entitled to wear his Past Master's badge with four red ribbons. It is of interest to note that James Coote Garnham the elder brother of Frederick Malcolm Garnham, had been Master in 1911.

From the many references to the Masters' 'Hands', for example, in 1723 '(Out of money remaining in the Master's hands at the time of the Audit) it is agreed and ordered that about one hundred pounds of the said Ballance be forthwith laid out in South Sea Stock . . .'. It appears Masters controlled the finances of the Company. There is nothing of great interest outside the usual references to the Master's accounts for moneys and his approval of Dinner menus following the Lord Mayor's Procession, until January 1749 when 'A Motion was also made and the Question put whether a Great Chair be provided at the Company's expense for the Use of the Master for the time being provided the Expense doth not exceed ffive Guineas. It was carried in the Affirmative'.

However, in July, it was reported 'Paid for a Chair for the Master for the time being, as per Order of Court £15.15. 0d.'

It appears that the chair was destroyed by Enemy Action in 1941. Thus for nearly two hundred years the Master, for the time being, had his own Chair.

Reference to the balancing of the Master's Accounts is made in the Minutes of 22nd July 1756 – 'The Master's Accounts for 1755–56 exactly balanced and there was no balance to hand over to the new Master. The last payment reads: 'Paid for Sundry Extraordinary Expenses on account of the Charter and other Business £17.12.6d'. A nice piece of accountancy! As has been stated the Master of the Company held the Balance of the Company in his hands and accounted for moneys at the end of his year. In 1795 'Mr. Merrick, the late Master, informed the Court that he was not at present prepared to pay the Balance of his Account but offered to assign over to the Company his Interest in a Building Society to which he belonged and which interest he stated to be of nearly the value of such Balance (£103.3s.0d) (including the Poor Fund). (It should be noted that the term building society had a different meaning then than today. In 1781 a society was formed in Birmingham to build properties, each member with one share being entitled to a house of £70 value. These societies were *terminating*. There are similar mutual housing associations in England and America today, including those where all the members use their own skills for the group as a whole to accumulate a credit of house towards their own house. In 1846 came an experiment in *permanent* management on the modern model, four years later there were 2,000 societies and later legislation included an Act in 1874 which laid the foundations of the modern form. In Mr. Merrick's case he was in fact offering to give to the Company his interest in his house.) 'Whereupon it was referred to Mr. Salmon the Master and Mr. Edward Clark to examine into the value of such Interest and act on the Occasion as they shall judge best, and most for the Advantage of the Company.' In the following January 'The Clerk acquainted the Court that since the last Court Mr. Wm Merrick the late Master had become Bankrupt. And that in consequence of directions from the Master for that purpose he, (the Clerk) had written to Messrs. Lambert and Doe, Mr. Merrick's sureties, desiring their attendance at this Court to pay over the Balance due from the said Mr. Merrick, but that the said Messrs. Lambert and Doe had not attended. Whereupon ordered that the Clerk write again to them and require immediate payment of such Balance.'

In February – 'The Clerk reported that . . . he had written to Mr. Merrick's sureties for payment of the balance . . .. That in consequence thereof Application had been made by Mr. Heslop, Mr. Doe's Attorney, desiring to be furnished with a copy of Mr. Merrick's Bond and which with the Master's consent had been sent him accordingly.' The Court then agreed to take proceedings against Messrs. Lambert and Doe. 17th February – "The Clerk informed the Committee that since the last Court application had been made to him by Mr. Lambert who offered to pay his Moiety of the balance of £64.3.0d due on 'Mr. Merrick's Account, on having a discharge from the Company from any further Claim respecting such Balance.' (The Balance was not £64.3.0d but £106.3.0d) 'Resolved that it is the opinion of this Committee that it will not be advisable for the Company to accept the said Mr. Lambert's proposal.'

In April – 'The Master and Wardens were requested to wait on Mr. Merrick and his Assignees to enquire whether the said Assignees intend to make any claim in respect of Mr. Merrick's Interest in the Building Society, which he assigned over in December last in part of the Balance due from him to the Company." and two weeks later:

'The Clerk reported that in the Action commenced against Messrs. Lambert Defendants had obtained a Judge's Order to stay all further proceedings on payment of the Debt and Costs.'

The said Messrs. Lambert and Doe now attended and expressed their willingness to pay the Debt and Costs, but requested a little time for that purpose. Whereupon resolved that the Sum of Forty pounds thereof be paid on Saturday next and the remainder of the 20th day of May next. And thereupon Ordered that the Clerk deliver up Mr. Merrick's Bond to the said Messrs. Lambert and Doe.'

There are no further references to Mr. Merrick, so it is presumed that any balance still owing was written off!

There are some instances where poverty has affected a Past Master or prevented a Warden from taking the Chair. In 1790 'Mr. Henry Thorowgood desired leave to resign his seat at the Court of Assistants, which was granted. Ordered that the sume of ffive pounds paid by Mr. Thorowgood on his Admission into the Court of Assistants be returned to him again out of the Company's Stock. Ordered that the sum of Three Guineas advanced by Mr. Bevarn to Mr. Thorowgood some time ago be repaid him out of the Poors Box.'

Henry Thorowgood had been Master in 1785/86, and as early as 1766 he had shown great generosity when he presented the Company with an engraved plate of their Arms to be used for summons to the Company. Throughout the period he had been an active member of the Court. It appears that he was the musician who provided music for the Lord Mayor's Show, for in 1772 a Minute shows 'Paid the Porters carrying back Mr. Thorowgood's Harpsichord 3s 0d' and he was a member of the Committee set up to consider the Warrant of Sir Fletcher Norton Knight Speaker of the House of Commons regarding the petition of John Roberts who had complained of an undue Election and Return for the City of London and requiring the Clerk to attend the House of Commons with such books or papers as were required. In 1779 he was one of the donors of the Hammer presented to the Court. Again in 1782, he presented the Company with a desk for the Clerk's use in the Court Room. Obviously Mr. Thorowgood had fallen on bad times for he resigned from the Court in 1790. In 1791 'Ordered that Mr. Henry Thorowgood be excused paying the Quarterage due from him at Lady Day last'.

Again in 1813 'Mr. John Veal in Rotation for Master of the Company for the year ensuing have now represented to the Court his inability to serve the said Office on account of his pecuniary circumstances and having requested that he might be allowed to withdraw himself from the situation of this Court and that the fine paid on his Admission may be returned to him.'

'Resolved Unanimously that the said Mr. Veal be excused from being any longer a Member of this Court and that the Fine paid on his Admission be returned to him and the same (being £5) was now returned to him accordingly.'

In 1848 the Minutes of the Court went into very great detail regarding the accounts of Mr. Jonathan Lucas, the late Master, when it appeared that moneys were due from him. 'The Accounts showed that there would be a balance due thereon to him of £8.1s.7d provided a sum of £6.18s.0d due to the Beadle in respect of his Salary was paid – and that exclusive of such £6.18s.0d there was still a balance of £1.3s.7d provided the Tavern Bill was paid. It however appeared that although the customary allowance had been made to the late Master the Tavern Bills for the last two Dinners amounting to £24.6s.0d still remained unpaid.'

'After some discussion Mr. Lucas stated that his expenditure had exceeded the allowance made to him. That £3.6s.1d was all that he had in hand and he required that the Court should increase his allowance to the full amount he had expended. The Court declined to entertain such proposition – and Mr. Lucas thereupon placed the sum of £3.6s.1d on the Table and stated that he should leave the Company to settle the matter as they might think proper.'

'The Clerk was desired to take possession of the £3.6s.1d and to apply the same together with the £1.3s.7d before named towards payment of the late Master's Tavern Bills.

'It was moved and seconded.'

'That Mr. Lucas the late Master having refused to pay certain Tavern Bills in accordance with the rule and custom of former Masters the Court feeling that it is due to themselves as a matter of honour that the same should be forthwith settled resolved that each member with the exception of Mr. Lucas be requested to pay the sum of £1.1.0d – which question put was carried unanimously.'

In the following November the following Minutes appear:
'It was moved and seconded and resolved that the Clerk write to Mr. Lucas pointing out the part of the Charter of the Com-

pany applicable to the removal of Members of the Court for just and reasonable Cause and requesting him to amend his Accounts conformable to the customary forms of the Company the part of the Charter referred to will be taken into consideration with reference to his case at the next Meeting – And the Clerk was also directed to suggest that the Court supposed it might be his intention to tender his resignation as a Member of the Court.'

June 1849:

It was moved and seconded that the Court taking into consideration the circumstances of the late Master Mr. Jonathan Lucas not having passed his accounts do hereby remove the said Jonathan Lucas from the Office of one of the Assistants and of the Common Council of this Company.'
This appears to be the only reference to a Past Master being removed from the Court.

In 1860 Mr. Edward Lawrence, who was elected Master, declined to serve the office for the year ensuing. The Court instructed the Clerk to write to him reminding him of the Fine to be imposed by the Charter if he refused to serve the Office. Mr. Lawrence duly paid £10 in lieu of serving the Office of Master.

In October 1883 the current Master, James Waddell and his brother William Waddell, who was Upper Warden, were removed from their respective offices and from the Court as Bankruptcy petitions had been served against both gentlemen. The Minutes state that 'Messrs. Waddell had been absent from their business for some time.'

The above paragraphs may seem of no consequence to the reader in a book covering six centuries – but they have been inserted for the reason that the Court meetings had very little of interest to discuss. It must be remembered that any matters dealing with the trade of farriery was the concern of the Registration Committee of which full Minutes were kept and which form other parts of this book.

In July 1890 Mr. Barnes Wimbush was elected Master and at the following meeting Sir William Hardiman's death was reported. He had been taken ill shortly after his election. Lady Hardiman's letter read as follows:

'You will recollect I daresay that this time last year how very grieved Sir William was that the serious illness prevented him being able to attend your meeting and one of the most grievious disappointments he endured . . . I was most grateful at the attention shown by the presence shown by a deputation of the Farriers at his funeral.'
(It was in 1890 that the meeting was held at the Mansion House,

but Mr. Sidney Smith was Master.)

In 1891 Mr. Hyman Montague FSA was elected Master. His name is especially mentioned for two reasons. Firstly, his grandson, Mr. Ronald Simon was a distinguished member of the Court of Common council (1961–1971), not a member of this Company but a member of the Company of Solicitors. He was the Chairman of the Music Committee of the Corporation and was a most enthusiastic supporter of the Barbican Arts Centre.

In February 1971 whilst the author was Chief Commoner, a stormy debate took place in Common Council as to whether the Barbican Arts Centre should be continued in view of the inflationary costs. The debate continued for a record time within living memory and eventually it was decided by 19 votes to proceed with the construction. Sadly, Mr. Ronald Simon died in the following April.

Secondly, the author and Mr. Ronald Simon were in residence at Cambridge in 1919 and were closely connected in business and in Corporation affairs. In 1969 Ronald Simon offered his grandfather's Farriers Past Master's Badge, presented in 1892 to Past Master Montague, to the author. Mr. Hyman Montague presented the Company with a Silver Salver of the year 1736 and he died in 1892.

1892–3

He was succeeded by Mr. Francis Campbell Bayard LLM and the Minutes contain a list of the following ceremonies at which he had attended as Master of the Company:

6th February 1893	A meeting of the Guilds Defence Institution at Goldsmiths Hall.
15th February 1893	A meeting of the Minor Companies called by Mr. Alderman Davies at Guildhall Tavern
1st March 1893	The Mansion House Dinner given by the Right Honourable the Lord Mayor to the Masters of the City Livery Companies.
13th May 1893	The opening ceremony of the Gardening and Forestry Exhibition at Earls Court.
7th June 1893	The Annual Dinner of the Royal College of Veterinary Surgeons at the Holborn Restaurant.
9th June 1893	The Election Dinner of the Tin Plate Workers Company at the Ironmongers Hall.

The Author has not come across such a list of a Master's Civic Meetings and Functions. It may have been something to put in the Minutes book for, apart from a note postponing the date of the next meeting, in consequence of the marriage of HRH The Duke of York and The Princess Mary following on the day of the meeting, (the Royal pair became King George V and Queen Mary), there was little of interest to report during Mr. Bayard's year of office.

On 4th January 1900 the Master (Thomas Dollar MRCVS) received a letter from the Lord Mayor asking him to bring to the notice of the Court the Patriotic Movement in progress in the City, for the equipment and dispatch to the Seat of War in South Africa a Volunteer contingent and requested the Company to subscribe to the CITY OF LONDON IMPERIAL VOLUNTEER FUND.

The Master headed the Appeal with a donation of £25 and 15 members of the Court donated £5 each, making a total of £100 which was forwarded to the Lord Mayor and included in the list of contributions by the City Companies. In August 1901 the Company received a letter from the War Office on the recommendation of Field Marshal Earl Roberts, Commander in Chief. His Majesty the King Edward VII had approved of the presentation of the South African War Medal to the Company in commemoration of the spontaneous and patriotic liberality shown by the Company in helping to raise the City of London Imperial Volunteers – the medal bearing the clasps earned by the regiment in War.

It may be of interest that in October 1900 the Court gave the Honorary Freedom of the Company to four officers: Captain Orr, Hon. Lieutenant Ridler, Veterinary Lieutenant Morgan and Veterinary Lieutenant Mulvey in recognition of the eminent service to the Country which attached to the Farriery and Veterinary Department of the City of London Volunteers whilst on active service in South Africa.

A further connection of the Company with the Services can be mentioned for during 1956 an association was entered into with the 51st Signal Regiment of the Royal Corps of Signals. This association enabled the Company and the Regiment to begin an interchange of visits. An exchange of gifts in the form of the Company's and Regiment's Crests were made. The Master (Leslie Prince) and George Garnham (Master 1944–45) paid a visit to the Regiment's Summer Camp in Chester at the invitation of Colonel Lovegrove.

It is of interest to note that in the middle of the nineteenth century there were Telegraph Companies in the City of London Volunteers – part of the Royal Engineers. In 1919 the Corps of Signals was formed, to be renamed in 1920, the Royal Corps of Signals.

In 1939 at the outbreak of War the Regiment joined the British Expeditionary Force in France and took part in the evacuation of Dunkirk. It was re-formed as 51 L of C Signal Regiment TA and existed until 1950 when it turned into the Supplementary Reserve. In 1935 King George V gave the Unit the honorary title of 'City of London Signals'. In the 1930's they lost all their horses and were completely equipped with mechanical vehicles. The regiment still wear their pre-war undressed uniform with spurs. When the Corps was adopted by the Farriers Company in 1956, General Sir Hubert Rance was Honorary Colonel. General Rance in 1945 was appointed Chief Civil Affairs Officer in Burma, and later in 1946 the last British Governor of Burma, for in January 1948 Burma became a Sovereign Republic without following the example of India of remaining a member of the Commonwealth.

We now come to a name which has played a very important part in the Company's history: SYDNEY SMITH was Clerk of the Company 1850–1869, about whom there is a full description in the 'Clerks' section. SIDNEY his son and Arthur Gerald his grandson both became Masters. SIDNEY who joined the Company in 1864, became Master 1869–70 and until 1903 almost controlled the affairs of the Company. In July 1903 the following letter was received from Past Master Sidney Smith:

'I joined this Livery in 1864 and was elected Assistant in 1866. I find that my eyesight is so impaired that I cannot hope to be again permitted to attend meetings and must ask the Court to permit me to retire from office the duties which I can no longer perform.

With all cordial and good wishes for the Company's future. Believe me to remain,
Ever yours faithfully,
Sidney Smith'

The Court asked the Clerk to write to Sidney Smith asking him to reconsider his decision to resign and to leave his name on the list of members of the Court and hope that his eyesight would improve so that he could attend future meetings.

His death was reported in January 1912 – he had not attended the Court since 1900 – but nevertheless his Obituary recorded in the Minutes was rather terse:

'That a letter be sent to the family of the deceased expressing sincere sympathy and condolences of the Court in the loss they have sustained.'

Having regard to his great services one would have expected a little more detailed description, but it must be remembered that the members of the Court in 1912 were probably unaware of the extent of his service prior to 1900 – in fact he had resigned from the Court in 1909 – he had been Master in 1869–70 and 1870–71 and yet again in 1890 he was acting Master, for Sir William Hardiman's long illness again had prevented him from being in the

Chair for the whole of his year in office. Again, it was Sidney Smith who was in the Chair when the Mansion House Meeting took place on the 2nd January 1890, of which a full description appears in the Craft Activities section.

In 1884 Sidney Smith presented the Company with a Chairman's Hammer inscribed with the Arms of the Company on retiring from his office as Master, which he had served for the third time – he was unaware that he would again be serving as Master in 1889–90. In 1895 a painting of Sidney Smith was officially presented – then it mysteriously disappeared until 1973 when the present editor bought it from a Blackheath antique dealer who had found in in a nearby stable!

Sydney's son, Arthur Gerald, and grandson of SIDNEY became Master in 1900–01 and 1901–02 and again in 1908–09. The Minutes do not say why he remained in office but it is assumed that the Upper Warden CLAUDE BEDDINGTON in 1900 was away at War in South Africa, for in January 1900 the following Minutes appeared:

'A letter was read from Mr. Warden Beddington stating his inability to attend the Court to make his declaration as Middle Warden owing to an important engagement with regard to the Imperial Yeomanry.'

and again in 1900:

'Owing to the continued absence of Claude Beddington in Africa he was unable to attend to make his declaration as Upper Warden of the City.'

So it appears that Claude Beddington following his War Service never became Master. In October 1900 the Minutes recorded that the Court sent its congratulations to Beddington on his second marriage to Miss Francis Murlock and further its pleasure upon his safe return (though severely wounded near Johannesburg) from his service with the Imperial Yeomanry in South Africa.

Arthur Gerald Smith, having served two years as Master, as described above, again became Upper Warden in 1907 and Master for the third time in 1909. His grandfather was Clerk for 19 years, and his father Master four times.

In November 1899 a meeting was called at the Clerk's Office and the following was the sole business transacted:

'Arthur Sidney Smith son of Charles James Smith of Shenley Albermarle Road, Beckenham in the County of Kent, solicitor, was this day bound apprentice to the said Charles James Smith for the term of 5 years.'
Consideration, Natural Love and Affection
Signed, William W. Dollar.'

Obviously with father and son, consideration would be natural love and affection. In normal apprenticeships consideration was substantial, for in 1897 the Minutes show that Abraham Solomon

Wilkes was bound apprentice to John Robert Cooper (about whom much follows) for the term of 5 years – Consideration £262.10s.0d and again in 1901 two more cases of apprenticeships for £315 and £350. (The author, who keeps writing of himself, was for three years Articled as an Accountant in 1922, his father paying a premium of £525).

To return to the Smith family – Charles James Smith became Master in 1919–20 and so ends the Sidney Smith's family connections with the Company, apart from the generous gifts, detailed later, of Miss Sarah Smith.

On 24th June 1895 John Robert Cooper was elected Master of the Company. This followed a curious incident. At a special meeting of the Court held on 3rd May the Upper Warden, Mr. Nathaniel Louis Cohen, intimated that he did not intend to serve the office of Master of the Company, should he be elected, and at that meeting a long discussion took place as to the selection of a Master. Mr. Cohen must have been a busy man for when in 1894 he was elected Upper Warden, these words were added to the normal Resolution – 'but without undertaking by him to serve on the Registration Committee'. The question of the validity of this meeting and the powers of the Court to select a Master until the 24th June were debated. A vote was taken and it was resolved that under the special circumstances the Court had full powers to elect a Master and John Robert Cooper was elected Master on 24th June and took the Chair on 4th July 1895. This was to become a busy year for John Cooper for he became Sheriff on 28th September 1895. At his first meeting on the 4th July the following Resolution was approved:

'That in consequence of the Master as one of the Sheriffs having to attend the Lord Mayor's Banquet at the Guildhall on the 9th November next the Livery Dinner be held on Wednesday 13th November.'

The words 'having to attend' were possibly unfortunately chosen in view of the Sheriff being one of the hosts of the Banquet! In October Mr. Sherriff Cooper was in the Chair at a special Court and it was arranged that as the Master would appear in the Lord Mayor's Procession in the capacity of Sheriff, Mr. Past Master Jackson should act as Master on that day. The meeting was held at 10.30 am on Saturday 9th November and promptly adjourned. At the previous meeting the sum of £65 was voted by the Court and a committee appointed to make all the necessary arrangements in supporting the Master as one of the Sheriffs in the Lord Mayor's Show. Incidentally, Mr. Sheriff Cooper took the Chair at seven out of nine meetings during his year of office.

Mr. J.R. Cooper was a generous benefactor to the Company. In 1881 he presented a Rose Water dish which is fully described elsewhere, and in 1882 he presented the Master's Gold Chain of Office, and in 1895 the Banner of the Donor's Arms, and in the following year a photograph album in red Morocco. Unfortunately the Banner and Album no longer exist. At this point in the history of the Company the author cannot resist recording that he was elected Sheriff on the 24th June 1954, took office on the 28th September and was at the time Upper Warden. On the 24th June 1955 he was elected Master of the Company and duly made his declaration on the 13th September. Thus whilst in no way emulating Mr. Cooper's year, he was both Sheriff and Master for 15 days.

In January 1929 Past Master Cooper was presented with a Silver Tray subscribed for by his fellow members of the Court whose signatures were engraved thereon to record his long and efficient service as a member of the Company. The Master (Archibald Brown) in making the presentation emphasized that the occasion was one that should hold a very important place in the History of the Company. He had been Master three times during the period of his fifty-four years membership. In thanking his colleagues, Mr. Cooper expressed his sincere appreciation of the honour that had been bestowed upon him, one that would keep alive in his memory his cherished and long-standing association with the Company.

Mr. Cooper died in January 1931.

On the 24th June 1899 Mr. Thomas Aitken Dollar MRCVS was elected Master. The Dollar family were well represented in the Company – John Archibald Watt Dollar MRCVS was made a member of the Court; in the following year Mr. William Watt Dollar was Middle Warden and John Archibald Watt Dollar became Renter Warden. Mr. William Watt Dollar became Master in 1902 but Archibald never reached the Chair. He was, however, elected Middle and Upper Warden but in June 1903 the Minutes record the following:

'Mr. Warden Bayard withdrew his proposed motion of censure on Mr. Warden J.A.W. Dollar of which he had given notice 'That this Court having considered the observations by Mr. Warden J.A.W. Dollar at a Meeting of the Royal College of Veterinary Surgeons held on the 16th May and having read a letter by him addressed to the Editor of the 'Veterinary Record' and published in the issue of the 23rd May with reference to the Registration Scheme, is of the opinion that Mr. Warden J.A.W. Dollar is deserving of the censure of this Court and resolves that he be not elected to any office in connection with the Company.'

Then followed two Resolutions:

'That Mr. Past Master J.R. Cooper be elected Master:

'That Mr. J.A.W. Dollar be elected Master.'
The voting was as follows:

    For Past Master J.R. Cooper   5
    For J.A.W. Dollar   4

and accordingly Mr. Cooper was elected for a second term of office. A very close decision.

The background of this censure is fully discussed in the section dealing with the Craft Activities, including the Arbitration with Mr. Past Master Lambert who was appointed Arbiter, requesting a report be made to the Court. On 23rd February 1978 Mr. Past Master Garnham telephoned the author to say that a Mr. Ivor William Dollar, having recently discovered that his father Mr. J.A.W. Dollar and other relatives had been members of the Company, desired to join the Company by patrimony, and Mr. I.W. Dollar was admitted to the Company on 6th September 1978. An echo of the past!

It was in July 1902 that, owing to the King's illness, it was decided that the proposed Coronation Dinner (being the Master's, Mr. W.W. Dollar's Inauguration) be not held, and a letter was received from the Home Office in August thanking the Company for its loyal and sympathetic resolution received by His Majesty on the occasion of his severe illness.

In December 1903 Charles Clifton Tollit of 79 Gresham Street joined the Company. He never became a member of the Court so why should his name be mentioned? The reason was that Mr. Tollit owned the well-known stationery shop in Cheapside, Tollit and Harvey, and the author distinctly remembers Mr. Tollit supplying him with a Cash Book in 1922.

In 1949 Mr. Tollit was nominated to fill a vacancy on the Court but was not successful in a ballot which took place – the successful candidate being Major Brennan de Vine, who felt unable to accept the nomination, so the second name in the ballot, Mr. George Allison-Beer was elected. More about Mr. Allison-Beer will follow, but to return to Mr. Tollit – he died in 1965 without standing again for election to the Court.

1905 seems to have passed without any undue comment, save that at the November meeting Mr. James Coote Garnham was made Free of the Company and he eventually became Master in 1911. This is the beginning of yet another Farrier Dynasty in the Company's history. His brother Malcolm was Master four times, uncle of George of whom much will be heard of later, and great-uncle of Mrs. Diana Pagan, the first lady to join the Livery.

In the early part of the twentieth century the Court were having great difficulties. The Registration Committee were struggling to keep its scheme alive, there were no moneys available, the Court subsidising it to the maximum of £100 per annum out of its very meagre funds. One can repeat that Finance, or its absence, has been the chief influence on the activities of the Company. The total of the General Fund, for example, in 1907 amounted to £133. It certainly had a few properties which brought in about £50 per annum, and £891 of 2½% Consolidated Stock. The fee paid to the Clerk was £50 per annum. Nevertheless the Company bravely carried on – it had its dignity and much can be deduced from the Minutes that, despite its financial difficulties, it held its head high in Farriery. Charles Sheather surprisingly was Master for 3 years (1905–08), no reasons being given for his re-elections, so one must assume that there was no-one available to take his place in the absence of Assistants at that time.

James Coote Garnham who was admitted to the Livery in 1905 was Master in 1911, followed by Ernest John Marsh, William Barry Gregar, John D. Best and Robert McConnell (3 years, 1915–1918), the latter carrying on during World War 1 when very few meetings were held. However, there were some significant happenings. A letter was received from the Board of Agriculture asking to know if the Company would be willing to nominate a witness to attend and give evidence before the Departmental Committee on Agricultural Education. The Master (Mr. C. Sheather) was nominated. However the Minutes make no further reference to the matter.

In 1910 it was suggested that a Church service be held, and arrangements made to hold it at St. Paul's – following a notice to all members of the Livery, who numbered approximately 60, very few members notified their intention to be present – so, sadly, the arrangements were cancelled. From a perusal of the Minutes it would appear that over forty years elapsed before the question of holding a Church service arose and it was not until 1953 that during the Mastership of Mr. Oswald Lewis that the service eventually took place on the 6th January 1953 at St. Mary Wool-noth, followed by a lunch at Tallow Chandlers Hall and fully described in the Minute Book, attended by over 50 including ladies. This annual service continued to be held although the Minutes do not contain any details. The author has happy memories of the service at St. Sepulchres during his Mastership in 1955, and leading the Company and their ladies across Newgate Street (with the help of the City Police) to Cutlers' Hall. The Record tells us that in 1970 when the present Chaplain Rev. Preb. F.A.F. Poulden A.K.C. was elected it was hoped that all annual services would be held on the election of the new Master and happily these services have continued.

This account of Masters has wandered – we left off during the War. In August 1914 the Company received a letter from Buckingham Palace from Edward Prince of Wales (later King

Edward VIII) asking the Company to subscribe to a National Relief Fund to alleviate the acute distress which inevitably arose in consequence of the War – a donation of one hundred guineas was made by the Company. Also in 1914 a letter had been received from a Guilds Hall Provisional Committee founded for the purpose of establishing a Common Hall for the use of hall-less and other Livery Companies. The Master, Mr. Herbert Oldfield was nominated a representative and a fee of £2.10.0d was paid towards the expenses of the Committee. The subject of Halls keeps coming up over the years – nothing appears in the Minutes as to what happened to the 1914 Committee. The next reference was in 1943 when the Master of the Glaziers informed the Company that a scheme was afoot of building after the War a large Hall for use of companies needing accommodation. The Court decided to follow up the matter with great interest. Again no further references – but in 1945 the Court itself became very interested when Mr. W. Newcome Wright, the Middle Warden, raised the question whether it might not be possible in conjunction with some other Livery Companies for this Company to acquire a Hall of its own. After consideration he had come to the conclusion that the acquisition of a hall was beyond the Company's means and it was unsatisfactory to do it in conjunction with other Companies. However, nothing daunted Newcome Wright for in 1949 the matter was again raised and a committee consisting of the Master, the Wardens, Past Master Newcome Wright, Past Master Whiteley and L.B. Prince was appointed to examine the possibility of acquiring a site for a Hall either alone or with other companies. This committee sat many times, in the memory of the author. The Company of Coachmakers and other Companies had suggested a site in Noble Street, but Past Masters Newcome Wright and Whiteley considered the site unsuitable for joint use and it was decided to take no further action. So ended the matter and no further efforts have been made to acquire a hall, although the matter was raised in 1975 by an approach from the Glaziers and Paint Stainers Companies but it was considered to be beyond the resources of the Company. In 1977 the Glaziers with the Scientific Instrument Makers had indeed acquired a splendid new Hall in a converted warehouse at the south side of the Thames, opposite the Fishmongers Hall.

But back to the Masters. The War had ended on 11th November, 1918 and the Court met on Thursday the 21st and the Minutes read as follows:

AT A QUARTERLY COURT of the Worshipful Company of Farriers held at the Cannon Street Hotel in the City of London on Thursday the 21st day of November 1918
Present: The Master (H.R. Oldfield Esq.)

2 Wardens
4 Past Masters

It was proposed by the Master and seconded by Mr. Past Master Cooper

THAT this Court desires to express its gratitude to the Most High for being permitted to witness the termination of the greatest War between Good and Evil that the World has ever seen, for the ultimate victory of Right over Wrong and for the re-birth of those principles of Justice Honor Equality and Brotherly Love that have been the foundation of our National existence, of our Progress and our Prosperity.

Carried unanimously.

Apart from the reading of the Minutes of the last Court and two Meetings and the presentation of a Statement of Funds, viz:

General Fund	£190	4	3
Poor & Orphan Fund	19	12	11
	£209	17	2

no other business was transacted at the Court.

Four years of War and the hope that it had been the War to end all Wars!

The Company remembers with pride the assistance which during the period of the War 1914–18, through the Registration Scheme, it was able to afford to the military authorities by providing them with the names of upwards of 4,500 qualified farriers when they were in desperate need of shoeing smiths in the various theatres of war. Amongst the Past Masters who were present at that meeting was H. Roper Barrett who was free of the Company by Patrimony in 1916 and elected to the Court in the same year. The Minutes of the 9th September 1943 containing the detailed Obituary will give readers some idea of what a remarkable life Past Master Roper Barrett lived.

'The late Mr. Herbert Roper Barrett joined the Farriers Company in 1916 and was elected as an Assistant in the same year. He served as a Warden in 1918–21 and again in 1935–36. He ably served the office of Master on two occasions, in 1921–22 and 1933–34. By profession he was a solicitor. He was elected to the Common Council in 1910 and became Chief Commoner in 1924 and a Deputy in 1941. In 1907 he was appointed Vestry Clerk of St. Peter upon Cornhill and in 1942 was Chairman of the Board of Income Tax Commissioners (Schedule E) for the City of London. In the world of sport he was well known as a Lawn Tennis player having played in the first Davis Cup team in 1900. In 1909, 1912 and 1913 he won the Wimbledon Doubles Championship with various partners and was a member of the Davis Cup team for years, including being non-playing Captain.

In 1933 he was a non-playing Captain of the team which won the Cup for Britain. In 1934 he was Chairman of the Lawn Tennis Association. He also played football for the Casuals, the Corinthians and Surrey.'

From a book published in 1977 '100 years of Wimbledon' written by Lance Tingay, the Daily Telegraph Correspondent, one further detail emerges. Roper Barrett played often at Wimbledon under different pseudonyms; in 1898 as A.L. Gydear, in 1900 as J. Verne and in 1901 as D'Agger. One wonders why. It may of course be to hide his identity – he had been born in 1873 and so as a young man in his twenties he may not have wished his office to know of his absence – who knows? In any event, the Corporation of London and the Farriers Company must have been very proud of their Chief Commoner and Past Master. The Minutes from the year 1916–43 show what an active man he was in the Company – scarcely a meeting took place without Roper Barrett making his contribution.

Reference has been made to Roper Barrett being 'Chief Commoner'. To many of our readers this title or appointment will not be known so the author has thought fit to interrupt this chapter with an explanation of this office, which was aptly summed up at the Dinner given by the City Lands and Bridge House Estates Committee at Clothworkers Hall on 24th July 1978 where on the Menu Card it read:

'In rural England a Commoner is a person who has joint rights with others in the common lands of a manor, and for centuries the Commanalty of London has enjoyed similar rights in the land in and around the City.'

A Charter of Henry VI (1444) confirmed to the citizens, that is to the Commoners, all Common soils and water courses, thus recognising the City's Estate, and the management of this common estate was entrusted by the citizens to their elected representatives in Common Council who subsequently delegated much of their authority to the City Lands Committee.

The Chairman of the City Lands Committee presides as a trustee for the Citizens and should ensure that the common Estate of Citizens is not wasted but preserved for the enjoyment of generations of Commoners to come. There is thus a certain aptness in attaching the title of Chief Commoner to the Chairman of the City Lands Committee, who is Chief Commoner in deed as well as in name.

The growth of the expression is easily understood. It is based upon the responsibility for the City's estate and reinforced later by the prominence of the Chairman of the City Lands Committee which by reason of its antiquity and the importance of its work has always been considered the premier Committee of the Corporation. The Committee has charge of the Corporation's main assets and through this control of the source of revenue it has always exercised a great influence on the policy and activities of the Corporation.

Of latter years the Committee took over the control of the building and maintenance of the City's four bridges, together with the source of income derived from these estates. In 1967 an official badge was purchased in order that the incumbent of the Chair of the City Lands and Bridge House Estates Committee could be recognised on all official and semi-official occasions as the 'Chief Commoner'.

The following members of the Company have been appointed to the office of Chief Commoner –

1924 Deputy H. Roper Barrett (Master 1921–22 and 1933–34)
1952 (Coronation year) Deputy S.R. Walker (Master 1954–55)
1971 Deputy L.B. Prince (Master 1955–56)

The title 'Deputy' will have been noticed and is possibly one not understood by persons not with the City of London.

The office of Deputy has an historical background and Miss Masters, Deputy Keeper of Records, recently reported in great depth its history and possible definition and the duties of the holder of that office.

In brief, the first mention of Deputy appears in 1495 in the Great Chronicle when 'in the absence of Alderman Sir Henry Colet he charged Robert Fabyn to hold the Wardmote and to have the rule as a depute'. Over the years the Deputy is appointed at each Annual Wardmote by the Alderman of the Ward. Under the Act of Common Council of 1952 he may preside in the absence of his Alderman at a by-election of a Common Councilman but not at the Annual Election because the Deputy is himself not a member of Common Council (the members of Common Council are elected annually).

In general, however, the duties and responsibilities of a Deputy are not laid down and may vary from Ward to Ward but generally he deputises for and assists the Alderman of the Ward in Common Council matters and acts as the leader and spokesman of the Members of his Ward. The Deputy has to ensure that the Ward is represented on Committees and, after consulting members, informs the Town Clerk which particular member is to sit on a particular Committee.

It is the Deputy who introduces a new member in Common Council and instructs the new member in the etiquette of Committees and the Court of Common Council.

In perusing the Minutes it is difficult to omit references to 'items of interest' for, back in 1914 HRH Prince of Wales (the late Edward VIII) made an appeal to the National Relief Fund to which the Company donated £105 (bearing in mind that the state of its finance which has been described, it was indeed a generous gesture).

In 1916 a Minute reports a letter from the City Livery Club, which had been founded in 1914, stating that this Club regrets the abolition of Parliament and Livery vote and asking the Company to appoint a representative to attend a conference in the Common Hall. The Clerk was instructed to attend. Curious that the City Livery Club should take such a lead. It proved a momentous decision, for the City of London is today not truly represented by its working public. and despite much discussion it has proved a delicate subject in the Corporation of London's defence against many attacks on the City.

1925

It would not be out of place to make a reference to the Company's connection with the City of London. Whilst in its earlier years the Company attended Lord Mayor's Shows, entertained Lord Mayors at annual dinners, it has tended to look after its trade, and quite rightly so, perhaps to the detriment of its remembering it is one of the Livery Companies of the City. The author, in reading the Minutes, feels that this is due to two reasons; firstly that it is so closely connected with the Veterinary profession and farriery, and secondly, the lack of finance to be able to contribute to City charities. It will be seen on page 17 that since 1757 nine Past Masters have been members of the Court of Common Council.

After the Second World War it was found that the Court needed strengthening. A Resolution was passed that the Court be increased and it stated that it should include at least one member of the Court of Common Council. On the passing of that Resolution, William Newcome Wright, Cyprian Whiteley and Samuel Walker were elected members of the Court. It will be seen that the three members of the Court of Common Council became Masters. It is hoped that the 1943 Resolution be borne in mind. In March 1979 Arthur Bryan Wilson, Deputy of the Aldersgate Ward, was elected to the Court.

For the next fourteen years, until the outbreak of the Second World War, the Minutes disclose many interesting matters regarding the affairs of the Company and the author has picked out a few items of possibly exceptional interest. Other items fall into the various sections of this book – in particular, the financial situation of the Company which was still a source of anxiety. The Registration Committee was in existence but making very little progress.

In 1924 Henry Cyril Else was unable to act as Master so in January 1925 Past Master Francis Robinson was Acting Master, and in March 1925 the Clerk Benjamin Popham died and his

The Company's Float in the Lord Mayor's Show 1925. Frank Piper, the donor of this photograph, is on the Float.

Miss Pat Smythe, OBE, receiving the Freedom of the Farriers Company from the Master, Leslie B. Prince, in 1955

HRH The Princess Anne, Mrs. Mark Phill
on receiving the Freedom of the City

g to the Chamberlain of London's Address
on the 27th February 1976 in Guildhall.

HRH The Princess Anne, Mrs. Mark Phillips, signing the Declaration on her Admission to the Company on 8th February 1977.

HRH The Princess Anne, Mrs. Mark Phillips, at a Court Dinner with the Author and guests.

partner William Starkie was elected Acting Clerk. So for six months the Company had an Acting Master and an Acting Clerk. Starkie was elected Clerk in June 1925.

Else died in 1955 at the age of 89. He had been Chairman of a large Iron & Steel Works and was President of the British Wire & Rollers Association and many other Trade Associations. All his life he had taken a very active interest in St. John's Ambulance Brigade and was made a Knight of the Venerable Order of St. John.

In November 1925 the Master (J.T. Sanders) informed the Court that he had arranged with Mr. A.C. Stanley Stone, a member of the Court of Common Council, to prepare a Historical Record of the Company and requested the Court's permission for Mr. Stone to have access to such books and records as he required. Permission was given. However, there is no further mention of this matter in the Minutes, so it would appear that Mr. Stone was unequal to the task!

At the same meeting a request was received from the Victoria and Albert Museum that the Company might be willing to allow its Plate to be exhibited. The request was agreed to, subject to proper safeguards regarding insurance.

1926

Sir George Rowland Blades, Bart., MP, Lord Mayor Elect, a Liveryman of the Company, was made an Honorary Liveryman of the Company.

The Glaziers Company was preparing to bring a case before the High Court on the taxation of fees received by Livery Companies and had requested the Farriers Company to make a contribution towards expenses. It was decided to take no action.

1927

In order to have closer co-operation between the Company and working farriers, it was agreed that the National Master Farriers and Blacksmiths Association and the Amalgamated Society of Farriers and Blacksmiths be invited to nominate Master Farriers and Shoeing Smiths holding the Certificate of Associate of the Company for election to the Livery on payment of the usual fees but without fine for steward.

Mr. Ernest Beaumont FWCF, in consideration of the able and efficient manner in which he had prepared the 'Emblematic Car' descriptive of the trade of the Company for representation in the Lord Mayor's Procession for the years 1926 and 1927, was made free of the Company by redemption. He paid the fine and fees.

An appeal was made to the Livery for a gift towards the London University New Building Fund, which resulted in a donation of £45; a gracious letter of thanks was received from the Vice-

Chancellor for the Company's generous gift which they made towards the erection of a University Hall on the Bloomsbury site.

1934
A letter was received from the Ulster Society for Prevention of Cruelty to Animals inviting one of the members of the Company to attend a meeting to be held in Belfast. Past Master Sanders was asked to represent the Company.

1939
In December it was agreed that Members of the Court engaged on Active Service shall be exempt from Fine for non-attendance at Court.
Returning to our Masters:

Sir Edward Manville MP 1922–23
Edward Manville MP was knighted in the New Year's Honours List of 1923. Later references show that two more Masters were also Members of Parliament, Sir John Smyth Bt. VC, MC (1961–66) and Sir Hugh Linstead OBE, LLD, FPS (1971–73). It was during Manville's year as Master that a Resolution was passed 'That whenever the numbers of the Livery exceed 120, all persons desirous of joining the Company should be fined for Stewards in addition to paying the usual fee of £11.10s.0d.'. This quarterage collected in June 1923 showed 73 names, but this cannot be taken as an accurate number for there were possibly members who had not paid their quarterage by that date.

F.J. Robinson 1923–24
Francis John Robinson, elected Master 1923, played a very active part in Company affairs. He was acting Master in Henry Else's absence in 1925. It was he, as Chairman of the Subcommittee in 1942, who investigated the affairs of the Company when the Clerk, Mr. Starkie, found himself in difficulties. This has been fully discussed in the Section on 'Clerks'.

Robson, who later became Clerk, and Walter Rose were the two gentlemen who unravelled the affairs of the Company described later. Both Robson and Rose were invited to be Clerks of the Company – Rose for a short period in 1941–42 was acting Clerk but due to his many other activities he declined, and thus it was that Robson was elected Clerk, but Rose was later elected to the Court and became Master in 1945–46.

Ernest T. Neathercoat CBE 1935–36 1938–39
As we proceed through the list of Masters in the 'Thirties', one would like to deal with each, and if Ernest Tom Neathercoat CBE is mentioned it is partly for sentimental reasons, for the author was admitted in his year of Master of the Company in 1936. He was again Master in 1938–39 and his son Russell William became

Master 34 years later. Another example of family tradition.

At the meeting when Ernest Neathercoat was proposed as Master elect, there were only eight members present, seven of whom were Past Masters. Mr. R. Barlow-Tyler was elected Middle Warden (later to be Master 1939–40).

R. Barlow-Tyler 1939–40

It was during this period that many Resolutions were passed regarding the necessary Quorum that was needed to be present at a Court meeting. It was eventually decided to be five (including Master and three Wardens). The War very much interfered with the attendance of the Court. On the 7th September 1940 the following members of the Court were present:

PM F.M. Garnham, PM A.G.J. Brown, H.A. Brown, G.B. Garnham

The Meeting was adjourned to the 15th October 1940.

15th October – those present:

PM F.J. Robinson, PM A.J. Brown, H.A. Brown

The Meeting was again adjourned and no further meetings were called 'till Master (Barlow-Tyler) recovered in health and the existing state of emergency less acute.'

R.W. Buckingham 1937–38; 1940–41; 1941–42; 1942–43; 1943–44

On 26th November 1940 a meeting was held with Warden Mr. H. Oswald Lewis in the Chair when Mr. Barlow-Tyler's death was reported and R.W. Buckingham was elected Master. Mr. Buckingham remained in office for four years until he was succeeded by George Garnham in 1944–45. To those who remember Robert William Buckingham, nothing need be said, however, as there are but a few living who knew him, let it be said that he was the Rock upon which the Company relied during the War. It was he who held the Company together – a stickler for the carrying out of the Ordinances and Regulations – one such instance:

The 24th June 1950 was on a Saturday, and accordingly the Court met on Monday, 26th June. Buckingham raised the point that the Court should have met on Midsummer Day 24th June notwithstanding that day fell on a Saturday. It was explained that Tallow Chandlers' Hall (where the Court then met) would not allow the use of the Hall on a Saturday. Buckingham held that the meeting was illegal in accordance with the dates laid down in the Charter and called for a report from the Clerk. At the next meeting the Clerk reported in the following terms:

'The alteration in date did not conflict with the Spirit of the Charter and Ancient Bye-Laws';

the matter received no further comment.

'Bob' Buckingham left the residue of his estate to the Company amounting to £13,000. In his Dedication to the second Supplementary History (1962–72) the author wrote these words:

> 'My dedication to the late Past Master Robert Buckingham is due to his years of devotion to the Company and his great generosity in bequeathing the residue of his estate to the Company, which enabled the Company to make a substantial grant to the Appeal Fund now open to members of the Livery and to the general public in respect to the Registration and Apprenticeship and Training Scheme.'

1944–79

The Masters so far come into the Historical category. The following are those Masters referred at the beginning of the chapter as having been known at first hand and by the author and the reminiscences became autobiographical rather than biographical.

G. Garnham 1944–45

George Garnham followed the four years of the Mastership of Robert Buckingham and much has been written of George and his family. Let it be said that George still fathers the Company. Every new Master relies on his knowledge and wise counsel. But his own year of office was a difficult one – the last year of the War. On the day he was elected Master in the Tallowchandlers Hall it was reported that on account of the anticipated lack of accommodation due to enemy action, only three out of the ten men whose applications for the Freedom and Livery had been approved at the last Court, had been summoned for admission. The Court consisted of 19 members, of which 14 were present. The number on the Livery was 121 (including the 7 not then admitted). During the year 23 new members were admitted.

The Registration Committee was to be reformed but it was decided that nothing could be done until after the War. On 10th July 1945 the Victory Luncheon was held at Tallowchandlers Hall with a total attendance of 83 of which 12 were visitors. It was during George's year that notice of a Motion was given by Past Master Buckingham that a Masonic Lodge should be formed in connection with the Company (see page 201). It was in July 1945 that a discussion took place as to a permanent home for the Company by acquiring a site for a Hall – one of many future discussions.

The Company was in dire straits – its Registration Committee still functioning – but due to lack of finance not able to do more than present medals at Horse Shows.

W. Rose 1945–46

Walter Rose, joined the Company in 1942 following his work with Robson in putting the administration of the Company in order. The Author was personally acquainted with Walter Rose, the Secretary to his Sheriffs Committee in 1953 when he fought an election on Saturday, 26th June, coinciding with the Test Match

versus Australia at Lords and Wimbledon not the most conve-
nient time to attract City voters to Guildhall! (The Author was
defeated by Alderman Edmund Stockdale and the late Mr.
Norman Tremellen but happily was unopposed in 1954). Walter
Rose was in fact a City man, being a member of the Needlemakers
Company and later to be its Master.

C.C.O. Whiteley 1946–47

Then followed Cyprian Whiteley in 1946–47 – again a great personal friend who did much to help the Author in his Civic
activities and it was in his year of office that the Author was
elected to the Court of the Company. Whiteley was a Deputy of
the Ward of Cordwainers, a very well-known personality in the
City as a Surveyor in the firm of Chesterton and Sons, and he did
much to reconstruct the Company.

W. Newcome Wright 1947–48

Then followed Newcome Wright, who later became Deputy of
the Ward of Bishopsgate Without and is referred to whenever the
possible building or acquisition of a Livery Hall is raised.

Thus for three years the Masters were members of the Court of
Common Council, followed by Edward Philip Paxman who was
the first of three Masters in the next six years to die during their
year of office.

E.P. Paxman MA JP 1948–49

E.P. Paxman, MA, JP, introduced by Buckingham, became
Master in 1948, died at the early age of 47, serving only six months
as Master. He had been Managing Director of Ruston and Horn-
sby, Chairman of British International Combustion Engine
Research Association. During his six years association with the
Company he had shown very great interest in the Company (as
with other Guilds, the Farriers welcome the modern equipments
of the craft, as heavy engineering is of both farriery and smithing).

H.A. Brown 1949–50

Then followed H.A. Brown, the son of Past Master Archibald
Brown (1928–29) who had joined the Company in 1933. He had
been elected to the three Wardens' Chairs and was one of the very
few able to attend Court meetings during the War and, but for his
War duties, he would have been Master 1944–45 instead of
George Garnham and would ipso facto have been contemporary
Senior Past Master. He gave great service to the Company and
devoted much of his time to Social and Church matters and was
responsible for the election of the Rev. Preb. F.A. Poulden AKC,
the present Chaplain.

The Robson History was published in 1949. It had been produced by Mr. Duffield of Leeds, a member of the Livery.

It was during his year that the Company made two presentations: A Silver Challenge Cup to the Royal Agricultural Society for competition at the Royal Show to be held in trust for the National Master Farriers Association and An Oaken Stand to hold table plans and the like to the Tallow Chandlers Company.

G.H. Fenton 1950–51

George Herbert Fenton joined the Company in September 1943 and proved a very remarkable man who 'woke up' the Company which, as has been seen, had been very dormant during the War years. Between the years 1943 until his death in 1959, he introduced no less than 49 members to the Company of whom three became Masters, viz; His Grace the Duke of Devonshire 1956–57; Sir Leslie Hollinghurst GBE, KCB, DFC, 1960–61 and Sir John Smyth VC, MC, MP 1961–62. Among those introduced were Professor Hindle SCD, FRS and the Rev. Charles Cocup CBE who was the Administrator of the Diocese of Gibraltar and Chaplain to his Majesty the King. Fenton was the donor of the Silver Loving Cup presented to commemorate his marriage in 1948, and also the gift of Fifty Guineas as a Thanksgiving for the Victory in Europe in 1945.

G.A. Warley 1951–52

G.A. Warley, a Chartered Accountant (a close colleague of Fenton) became Master in 1951–52 but sadly he died in office. He had performed a great service and it was during his year that the approach came from the Coachmakers Company for a Hall to be built for the convenience of Livery Companies connected with Transport, reference to which has been made elsewhere.

Oswald Lewis 1952–53

A Member of Parliament for Colchester (1929–34), a son of the Founder of John Lewis and Company of Oxford Street, was admitted to the Livery on the 20th September, 1938 and on the same day invited to join the Court. At the same meeting, a resolution was passed that the quorum of the Court to enable it to carry out its business shall consist of not less than five members including the Master and Wardens. There now being three vacancies, steps were taken to fill the remaining two. In fact, with the outbreak of War, it was not until March 1940 that there were additions to the Court, viz: Harry Archibald Brown (Master 1949–50) and George Garnham (Master 1944–45). Lewis was made Renter Warden in 1939–40, Middle in 1940–41 and Upper in 1941–42, but due to War Duties was prevented from taking the Mastership. He eventually became Master in 1952. It was in his year that His Grace the Duke of Beaufort KG, PC, GCVO, Master of the Horse, was granted the Honorary Freedom of the Company. This was the first time that a holder of the ancient office of Master of the Horse had been associated with the Company. A Guild Service was held for the first time at St. Mary Woolnoth – the beginning of the Company's annual Services.

J.B. Buxton 1953–54

In 1953–54 Professor James Basil Buxton was yet another to die in office. He had been Chairman of the Registration Committee in 1946–53. The Registration Committee inaugurated in 1890, had been carrying out its work under great difficulties due to lack of financial assistance, since the Company ran three Examinations at different levels for the efficiency of Farriers, awarding medals at Agricultural Shows. In the early part of this century candidates averaged 80–100 but when Professor Buxton was Chairman the average number was 44. His sudden death was a great shock both to the Company and to the Veterinary College for he had been Principal and Dean since 1936 succeeding his distinguished predecessor, Sir Frederick Hobday CMG who had launched the appeal known as the NOSE-BAG FUND. It was the pivot of an appeal for two hundred and fifty million farthings (£250,000) in order to rebuild the Royal Veterinary College's tumbledown premises in Camden Town. Buxton had an outstanding career. Himself an alumnus of the Royal Veterinary College, Veterinary Superintendent at the Wellcome Laboratories, Professor of Animal Pathology at Cambridge. He was President of the Royal College of Veterinary Surgeons in 1932. In 1953 he was elected Chairman of a Scientific advisory committee to assist the Animal Health Trust in the development of its research programmes. The Royal Veterinary College had become a School of the University of London in 1949. The new curriculum for the degree of Bachelor of Veterinary Medicine was being considered and the preparations were being made to petition for a new Charter and negotiations were being conducted for the purchase of a field station. In all these affairs he was one of the principal architects. His life was dedicated to the College and he died, as he wished, in its service.

S.R. Walker CBE 1954–55

Then came Samuel Richard Walker, known throughout the City, not unnaturally, as 'Johnny'. He had a farriery connection in the 1914–18 War and received his Cold Shoeing certificate in 1914. He joined the Territorials in 1909, Queen Victoria Rifles, and 1st King Edward's Horse in 1913, was commissioned in 1916 in the Royal Field Artillery and became Brigade Signalling Officer.

He had joined the Corporation in 1943, elected Chief Commoner in 1952, received the CBE in 1955 and only retired from the Corporation in 1977. It was he in 1955 who had inaugurated the appeal to the Livery for funds, later to become part of the Charity

Trust. 'Johnny' conceived the idea of inviting Miss Pat Smythe to accept the Honorary Freedom of the Company and sponsored an invitation to HRH The Princess Anne to accept the Honorary Freedom of the Company. He was one of the three donors of the stained glass window in the Crypt of Guildhall.

L.B. Prince CBE 1955–56

The Author followed as Master. He subscribed to the traditions of the Company and not unnaturally supported the formation of the Golfing Society and was in the team that was second in the Connaught Cup Match in 1958. He was elected Sheriff in 1954, Chief Commoner in 1971; he received the CBE ln 1973 and was elected President of the City Livery Club in the same year. Only five gentleman have held these three appointments, viz: Sir George Cullum Welch Bt, OBE, MC (who was Lord Mayor in the Company's 600th anniversary year) Sir Lionel Denny GBE (Lord Mayor 1965), Stanley Wells MBE and S.R. Walker CBE. The Author formed what is known as the 'Past Five Club' who entertain each another annually. Sadly, Stanley Wells died in 1975 but the annual luncheon still continues. In 1971 Prince was appointed by the Corporation of the City of London as a Member of the Council of the Royal Veterinary College. He has been the Company's representative on the Board of Governors of the St. Martin in the Fields High School for Girls since 1959. He also was one of the three donors of the window in the Guildhall Crypt.

Both Deputy Walker and Deputy Prince were elected Sheriffs in 1957 and 1955 respectively and on *both* occasions they were presented with an Illuminated Address and the Master and Wardens rode in the Lord Mayor's Procession in an open landau drawn by a pair of greys. *Both* were Presidents of the City Livery Club in 1955 and 1973 respectively, although the former's Mother Company was the Founders, the latter's only Company was the Farriers. L.B. Prince was thus the first Farrier to be elected as President of the City Livery Club.

He was the Author of the Supplementary Histories in 1962 and 1972.

His son Michael (1951) and two sons-in-law Ivor Lewisohn (1951) and Norman Mann (1968) are members of the Livery.

His Grace the Duke of Devonshire MC 1956–57

It was in 1956 that the Clerk Leonard Robson conceived the idea of celebrating the 600th Anniversary of the Company's Fellowship in 1356 – (see Appendix) His Grace the Duke of Devonshire was elected to the Court in 1951 following the sudden death of his father the 10th Duke, and having been permitted by the Court to assume the seniority of his father elected thereto in 1947. He had shown great interest in the Registration Committee. At this time, the Racecourse Totalisation Charity Trust had been established and was giving the Company financial support for its work in farriery, their grant in 1956 amounted to £250, until a doubt arose as to whether the Company was using the grant as well as it might. In 1958, realising the implication of the situation, it was decided to re-stimulate this important activity. Full details of this work appears in the Chapter on Craft Activities.

J. Stroud 1957–58

John Stroud was elected Master in 1957. He had joined the Company in 1935. He later became Mayor of Basingstoke in 1952 and re-elected 1953 for the Coronation Year 1953–54. He still continues to show great interest and gives much time to the Company's affairs, being a member of the the the Finance and Social Committee. He was made Honorary Freeman of the Borough of Basingstoke on 14th March 1974.

During his year of office he presented on behalf of the Company an Illuminated Address at Guildhall to Mr. Past Master S.R. Walker CBE on his election as Sheriff. In 1958 he presented His Grace the Duke of Beaufort to the Chamberlain of London for Admission to the Freedom of the City of London.

He also presented Lord Harding of Petherton to receive the Freedom of the City. (see Appendix)

G. Bowman 1958–59

George Bowman FWCF followed in 1958. He was the first Master in modern times who was a practising farrier. On his election to the Court in 1946 he was President of the National Master Farriers and Blacksmiths Association and as he held the Associate's Diploma by Examination, he was appointed a Fellow of the Worshipful Company of Farriers Honoris Causa. It was to be thirty years before a practising farrier was to join the Court, viz: Howard John Cooper FWCF in 1977. In 1954 Bowman succeeded the late Professor Buxton as Chairman of the Registration Committee. Until his death in 1962 Bowman had given great service to the Company and to the farriery trade. In 1960 he had given the Company £100 to provide for the 'Farrier Prize' to be presented annually to the pupils of St. Martin in the Fields High School for Girls.

G. Allison-Beer 1959–60

In 1959 Deputy George Allison-Beer, at the date of his election as Master, was the Senior Member of the Livery, having been admitted in 1920. The highlight of his year was the Royal Show at Cambridge; The Master and his wife had the honour of being invited to the luncheon and being presented to HM The Queen Mother, who showed her interest in the Company in the questions she asked the Master regarding the forge which she visited accompanied by Mr.H.C. Ablett the President of the

National Master Farriers Association. Allison-Beer was the third of the three donors of the stained glass window in the Crypt, Guildhall.

Three Knights followed as Masters:
1960–61   Sir Leslie Norman Hollinghurst GBE, KCB, DFC
1961–62   Sir John Smyth, Bart. VC, MC, MP
1062–63   Sir Frank Lord OBE, MA, JP
Each in his own field gave much lustre to the Company.

Sir Leslie Hollinghurst 1960–61
Air Chief Marshal Sir Leslie Hollinghurst GBE, KCB, DFC introduced by Fenton in 1951, had a very distinguished career in the Royal Air Force, served in the Royal Flying Corps in the 1914–18 War and was Director General RAF in 1940. Member of the Air Council 1945–48.

In 1960 it was agreed that Ordinance 63 should be amended to include the words 'and in exceptional circumstances may admit to such Honorary Fellowship persons who in the opinion of the Court have rendered exceptional Service to the Company.' Accordingly, Mr. Herbert Cyril Ablett was presented with an Illuminated Certificate recording the award to him of the Honorary Fellowship of the Company in recognition of his outstanding services to farriery, and also Mr. R. Armstrong RSS, Farrier to the British Olympic Team for many years, was accorded the similar award of Honorary Fellowship.

In 1961 a member of the Livery had found difficulty in finding an experienced farrier to shoe the horses used in his cartage business in East London and he was considering having his horses put down; the Company had referred him to Messrs. Whitbread Ltd. who readily agreed to the horses being taken to their forge.

Sir John Smyth 1961–62
Brigadier the Rt. Hon. Sir John Smyth, Bt VC, MC, MP also introduced by Fenton in 1951, became Master in 1961. He had entered the Army in 1912 and was awarded the VC in the 1914–18 War. He retired in 1942 and became Military Correspondent for the Daily Sketch and Sunday Times, also Lawn Tennis Correspondent for the Sunday Times 1946–51, News of the World 1956–57. A Member of Parliament for Norwood 1959–66; Parliamentary Secretary of Ministry of Pensions 1951–56. He was the first Chairman of Victoria Cross Association 1956 (Centenary of the VC) and President 1966. In July 1972 the Company was represented at a Remembrance Service for the Victoria Cross and George Cross Association in St. Martin-in-the Fields. It was while he was Parliamentary Secretary of the Ministry of Pensions that he approached the Company as to whether it would consider

taking up one of the eight Foundation Governorships of St. Martin-in-the-Fields High School for Girls under the provisions of the Education Act of 1944. Smyth had been Governor himself 1950–52. The Company accepted and a reference to the school will be found (appendix). Smyth has continued his Journalistic career and has written many books, his latest publication being Milestones. He is still an Honorary Assistant of the Court. Each year he arranges for girls from St. Martins to visit the Wimbledon Tennis Championships.

Sir Frank Lord 1962–63

The last of the Company's three Knights, Sir Frank Lord KBE, Master in 1962, was Mayor of Oldham, High Sheriff of Lancaster. He died in 1974. He was a most respected and popular person who did much for the Company during the twenty years he served on the Court. His son, Peter, was elected to the Court of Assistants in 1972, but due to his many other activities was not able to take his place as a Warden. In 1979 he was elected Master of the Barbers Company and was also elected to the Court of the Royal College of Surgeons. In June 1979 he regretfully submitted his resignation as a Member of the Farriers Court.

J.E. Lines 1963–64

J.E. Lines, the next Master, joined the Company in 1938, the Court in 1954, and became Master in 1963. Father of Kenneth Lines (Master 1965) and grand-father of Peter and Stuart, members of the Livery.

In 1963 Mr. Robert Armstrong, an Honorary Fellow of the Company, acted as farrier to the British Equestrian team at the Olympic Games in Tokyo and this was the fifth occasion on which he had acted in such a capacity.

Dr. W.R. Wooldridge CBE 1964–65

In 1964 Dr. W.R. Wooldridge CBE who had joined the Company in 1947, was the Author of the History of the Registration Committee (1951–61) which was included in the Supplementary History 1949–61 and included in the Chapter 'Craft Activities'. Sadly Dr. Wooldridge died shortly before the conclusion of his year of office. Dr. Wooldridge CBE, PhD, MSc, DVSc, FRCVS, FRICS, had been the Chairman of the Registration Committee since its reconstitution in June 1959 up to the time of his death. He brought a fund of knowledge and immense enthusiasm and energy to the Committee and was largely concerned with the groundwork of the Company's Apprenticeship Scheme. Already successful in developing the Animal Health Trust of which he was Director, he it was who collaborated in bringing together representatives of the various organisations concerned with the horse with the object of discussing in the broadest way the future of farriery.

From that meeting stemmed the Animal Health Trust Farriery Committee under Dr. Wooldridge's Chairmanship.

R.A. Brown 1965–66

R.A. Brown OBE was admitted to the Livery in 1947. He was Secretary of the National Horse Association of Great Britain for 24 years and of the British Horse Society for 16 years. He joined the Company in 1958 and became Master in 1965. He was the donor of Badges presented to each new member of the Livery.

Alec Hobson 1966–67

Alec Hobson CBE, MVO was the subject of a Resolution of the Court on 10th December 1957:

'That in view of his great services to Agriculture as Secretary of the Royal Agricultural Society of England, he be invited to become a Freeman and Liveryman of the Company'

and on the 11th March 1958 he was admitted to the Freedom by the Master of the Company. He was admitted to the Court in 1961 and elected Master in 1966. Alec Hobson continued the History of the Registration Committee (begun by Dr. Wooldridge) from 1962–72 in the Supplementary History, and which is included in the chapter on 'Craft Activities'.

He was one of the three Past Masters to whom the Supplementary History was dedicated: 'To Alec Hobson for his untiring energy in acting as Chairman to the Registration Committee (1966–72) and for editing the History of the Registration Committee 1962–72').

G.H. Smith 1967–68

George Hamilton Smith was elected Master in 1967–68 and his son Arthur George Smith in 1975–76. They played a very inportant part in the Company's activities. In the Author's second Supplement, George Hamilton Smith was the third of the three Past Masters to whom the Volume was dedicated. The dedication in 1972 read as follows: 'To George Hamilton Smith for his many generosities in every way to the Company for his energy and enthusiasm in establishing a Fund to ensure the future of the Company's vital and important schemes on behalf of the horse'.

In 1956 – three years before George Smith became a member of the Court – he was invited to make an appeal to the Livery in order to purchase a Loving Cup to celebrate the 600th anniversary of the formation of the Company. So magnanimous was the response that a George III Silver Gilt Loving Cup and a book containing the names of the subscribers was presented to the Company. He was a generous benefactor to his Appeal.

A.J. Barsham 1968–69
Then followed Alfred John Barsham B.Com.FCA. He had been admitted to the Livery in 1945, to the Court in 1962, and Master in 1968. He became Honorary Treasurer of the Charitable Trust in 1967 and later became Honorary Accountant to the Livery. The words the author wrote in his Supplementary History in 1972: 'The Company is very indebted to him for all the work he has put into this onerous task' is an understatement, for at the date of this publication in 1980 he is still looking after the affairs of the Charitable Trust and also the full accounts of the Livery. Included in this volume is an account of the Charitable Trust edited by him. His three children are members of the Livery – John Gordon (1976), Margaret Anne (1978) and Michael Keith (1978).

R.W.V. Neathercoat DFC 1969–70
The son of Ernest Tom Neathercoat, Master in 1935–36 and 1938–39, he launched the General Appeal under the title 'No, Foot, No Horse' and the Duke of Beaufort presided at a Reception on the 30th October 1969, receiving the support of H.M. The Queen and H.M. The Queen Mother.

It was in 1969 that the Company's Honorary Freeman Major Derek Allhusen (in 1975 he became a Liveryman) had captained the Equestrian Team that had won the European Championship. On the 17th March 1970 the Clerk referred to the request by the City Police showing the Company's Coat of Arms which might be displayed in their new Saddle room, and approval for the purchase of such plaque and its donation to the Mounted Branch was approved and presented to the Acting Commissioner of the City of London Police.

In March 1970 the Master reported the Brochure that he had received from the Worshipful Company of Carmen concerning their Tercentenary Appeal and it was agreed that the Company would give a donation of ten guineas towards such appeal.

Mr. Past Master R.A. Brown observed that in 1879 Veterinary Surgeons were originally all Farriers and a separate fine had been originated when the Veterinary Surgeons received their Charter and he though that this distinction should be continued. There was some support for this view and a general discussion took place on how many rates of fines there should be. After hearing from the Veterinary Surgeons on the Court that their professions did not wish to be singled out for such kind of preferential treatment but were pleased with the honour that had been accorded to them and the recommendations were unanimously approved.

The Master pointed out that Past Master Smyth had virtually retired and he therefore suggested creating Honorary Assistants. Any member of the Court who so desired could become an

Honorary Assistant who would receive all papers and be entitled to attend and, with leave of the Court, speak at Court meetings but could not vote. The Court agreed that the Master should investigate this matter further.

At this point in the Company's history a great enthusiasm had been introduced into the Company, with the Registration Committee submitting various schemes to the Court which, whilst carrying out the objective of the Company, nevertheless required financing. As has been seen from time to time the enthusiasm had always been damped through lack of moneys. Appeals had been launched but sadly moneys were never sufficient. It will thus be seen that the Masters from 1970 onwards were preoccupied in boosting the New Appeal.

E.H. Newcome Wright 1970–71

Edward Howard Newcome Wright, the son of William Newcome Wright, Master 1947–48, had been appointed Clerk to the Company in 1958 until his retirement in 1963. In 1962 he had been elected to the Court in recognition of the Services he had rendered to the Company. A Solicitor by profession, he was instrumental in advising the Court on the formation of the Charitable Trust. During his year of office his experience of having been a former Clerk and having been associated in the revival of the Company's work for the Craft, helped him to recognise there was much more to be done if the future of the farriery trade was to be made secure, and it was to the Company that all interested parties should look to achieve what was necessary to overcome the unsatisfactory position then obtaining. He had in mind that the Company was a Livery Company of the City of London and one of the Oldest Guilds recorded, so it was largely in this connection that the Liverymen could enhance the growing reputation of the Farriers. Newcome Wright was to play an important part in the work of the Company through its Registration Committee, and in particular with that which culminated in the passing by Parliament of the Farriers' (Registration) Act 1975.

24th June 1971

The Clerk reported that only some 17 copies remained of the History of the Company compiled by the late Mr. Robson. He asked the Court if they wished further copies to be produced by facsimile printing or whether there should be a complete new addition to the history comprising both the original and supplementary history and also bringing it up to date. Mr. Past Master Hobson suggested that a 'young' Librarian might be invited to re-write the whole of the history and be given access to such documents as the Company had.
(N.B. Mr. Prince not present).

However, at the next meeting the Clerk reported that there were 92 copies of the History of the Company and there was therefore no necessity to make a decision at the present time as to facsimile reprinting or engaging the services of someone completely to rewrite the history in a modern fashion. Mr. Past Master Deputy Prince said that he was starting work on a further supplement to take the history of the Company up to the end of the sixties. He hoped to complete this work by the end of 1972 – events having prevented him from completing it by the end of 1971. He had been Chief Commoner. (The Supplement was completed in 1973 at a cost of approximately £520, a specially bound copy had been sent to HRH The Princess Anne).

Sir Hugh Linstead 1971–72

Sir Hugh Linstead had joined the Company in 1936 and was admitted to the Court in 1965. He has had a very distinguished career in the pharmaceutical world, having been Secretary of the Pharmaceutical Society of Great Britain 1926–64, served on many Government Committees and been Member of Parliament for Putney in 1942–64. Sir Hugh received the Pharmaceutical Society's Gold Medal in 1971. During his year of office, HRH The Princess Anne was admitted to the Freedom of the Company, and on 23rd June 1972 the following were admitted to the Freedom without Fine by virtue of their eminence in the fields in which the Company was interested –

The Hon. John Jacob Astor, MBE, Legion of Honour, French Croix de Guerre
Walter Oswald Case – Editor of 'Horse and Hound'
Jack Raymond Reynolds, CB, OBE – Director General, British Horse Society

and on 19th September 1972 –

David Anthony Thomas Fane, KCVO, 15th Earl of Westmorland
All of these were later admitted to the Livery.

In 1978 The Earl of Westmorland succeeded the Duke of Beaufort, KG, PC, GCVO, and Honorary Freeman, as Master of the Horse.

During his year the Registration Committee was making great strides. Much has been written in the chapter on Craft Activities of the great interest shown by Sir Hugh; suffice it to say that his year of office was the beginning of great service to the Company and Craft.

K.J. Lines 1972–73

Kenneth Lines, son of Jack Lines, Master 1963–64, had joined the Company in 1948 and was a member of the Court in 1965 – no-one could have shown more keenness as a Liveryman during the quarter of a century of his connection with the Company. His year as Master coincided with the tremendous growth of the Company. The Apprentice Scheme was progressing, 28 new entrants, bringing the total to 118 (in 1978 the total was 169), the draft Farriers (Registration) Bill had been finalised and approved in principle by the trade, horse owners and others concerned. Its process through Parliament was of necessity slow. He, among other Masters of Livery Companies, was a guest at the Royal Albert Hall when HM Queen Elizabeth the Queen Mother, Chancellor of the University of London, made the presentation of Degrees to Graduates. It was during his year that the Company attended the International Horse Show at Wembley Stadium. As the seats were given to the Company, the proceeds of the sales, approximately £800, benefitted the Company's Charitable Trust. This has now become an annual event.

In 1973 Lord Hill of Luton was admitted to the Freedom and Livery without payment of Fine in consideration of his eminence in public life.

On 20th March 1973 James Richard Attfield, AFCL, was awarded Honorary Fellowship in recognition of his services to the Company and in acknowledgement of his outstanding service to the farriery trade for many years past.

In September 1973 the Clerk reported that a new Livery List of Members was being prepared and he produced a list of 15 Liverymen for whom he had no addresses. The Court decided that their names should be included marked 'No Address'.

Brigadier John Clabby, CBE, MRCVS 1973–74
Brigadier John Clabby was admitted to the Livery in 1964 and appointed to the Court in 1967. He had been much associated with the late Dr. Wooldridge at the Animal Health Trust. In 1974 he had been appointed President of the British Equine Veterinary Association. Clabby was Chief Executive Officer for eleven years and retired in 1977. He had given outstanding service to the Trust and has now established the Coxland Stud at Ewhurst, Surrey.

During his year of office the marriage of HRH The Princess Anne and Captain Mark Phillips took place and Clabby was a guest at the Wedding in Westminster Abbey. Captain Phillips was granted the Freedom of the Company and both Princess Anne and Captain Phillips attended the Master's Reception at the Royal College of Veterinary Surgeons in Belgrave Square. Immediately prior to this Reception, for the first time, a joint meeting was held with the Veterinary History Society and three excellent papers were read –
The History of the Horse by Col. J. Hickman, MA, FRCVS
(Author of 'Farriery')

The History of the Worshipful Company of Farriers by Mr. M.A.P. Simons (later to be Master 1974–75)

The Development of Veterinary Science from the Art and Craft of Farriers by Emeritus Professor L.P. Pugh, CBE, MA, BSc, FRCVS (a member of the Livery) Author of 'From Farriery to Veterinary Medicines 1785–1795', Past President Royal College of Veterinary Surgeons.

Clabby naturally played a very large part in the Company's farriery activities and in 1979 succeeded Sir Hugh Linstead as Chairman of the Registration Committee.

At the December Court Lunch Earl Ferrers, whose ancestors had a close connection with the Company in its early days, was the Guest of the Master; there were also present the Masters of the Carmen, Loriners, Saddlers and Wheelwrights and the Prime Warden of the Blacksmiths.

It was unfortunate that the Master's Court Dinner arranged for February 1974 was cancelled owing to the stringencies imposed by the 'three day week'. However, he had the compensation of presiding over a large gathering at the Mansion House when the Company celebrated the Three Hundredth Anniversary of the granting of the Royal Charter by King Charles II. Alderman Sir Charles Trinder (Lord Mayor 1968–69) presided in place of Sir Hugh Wontner, Lord Mayor, who was attending a State Banquet in honour of HM The Queen of Denmark. The Author had the privilege of proposing the Civic Toast, thus achieving the unusual 'double' for he had proposed the Guests in 1956 at the Sixth Hundredth Anniversary Dinner in Guildhall of the Fellowship of Marshalls. The Response by Sir Charles, noted in the City for his sense of Parody, is worth quoting in part, as an example of his ready wit, by adapting a well known Nursery Rhyme thus:

'This is the House that Dance built,
This is the Mayor, the great Sir Hugh, who lives in the
House that Dance built
This is the Man who carries the Sword
In a far finer hat than I can afford
In front of the Mayor, that fine Sir Hugh,
To whom all Civic honour is due,
And who lives in the House that Dance built.

This is the man who carries the Mace
And Commonly cries all over the place;
He envies the man who bears the Sword,
For it weighs far less, as the scales record,
In front of the Mayor who's named Sir Hugh
Who is sorry he can't be here with you
And who lives in the House that Dance built.

Then there's that Marshall chap besides
Who never falls off the horse he rides,
And therefore sets an impossible pace
For the panting fellow who carries the Mace
Who envies the Man who bears the Sword
With a bearing that even the Guards applaud
In front of the Mayor, the great Sir Hugh,
Whose visitors come in a constant queue
Who is Clerk of the Royal Kitchens too
Who is seized of the worth of a horse's shoe,
Especially if it's nailed on by you
To whom all Civic honour is due
Who is sorry he can't be here with you
In this wonderful House that Dance built.'

M.A.P. Simons 1974–75

The Company was reaching a very high point in its history. It had some very distinguished veterinary personnel on its Court; Michael Simons MRCVS followed Clabby. Parliament was being involved to legislate for farriery in the 20th century to protect the horse from injury and to re-affirm the responsibilities of the Company. Simons, whose paper on the History of the Company has been referred to supra had a very busy year. It was Simons who had drawn up the pamphlet with the theme 'No Foot – No Horse' which was used for the National Appeal referred to in the Section on 'Charitable Trust'. In those four words was summarised 'The complete dependance of the horse on the farrier. In the skilful hands of the man who trims and shoes the horse's feet rests the health, comfort and usefulness of every horse in the British Isles'.

The year's Record shows that he represented the Company on eight official occasions, twenty-four Court and Committee meetings, visited the Royal Show and both Schools of Farriery. How different from the proceedings of the lean years in the early part of the century already described. The Author has quoted the figures of 1974–75 only because they were summarised in the 'Record', they were really not very different from other years in the seventies.

The number of members in the Livery was increasing, eighteen new members, but sadly nine deaths reported, including His Honour Judge Montague Berryman who had been admitted in 1930, a member of the Court for ten years and who had reluctantly resigned in 1961 due to his important judicial work; and Ernest Charles Winn, Renter Warden 1972–73, Middle Warden 1973–74. Winn was to be installed as Upper Warden in September 1974 but his illness prevented him from attending and he died on 20th December 1974; Harry Brown, Master 1949–50 and H.C. Ablett FWCF who was awarded a Fellowship honoris causa in 1960 and had served on the Registration Committee for many years; also two other Fellows – James Ibbotson and William Kemp. Ibbotson was a long standing member of the Registration Committee and did great work in promoting the Company's Farriery Apprentice Scheme, including training several apprentices himself. Kemp was an examiner for the Company's farriery examinations for many years.

Again, the Company attended the Royal International Horse Show. Colonel Sir Michael Ansell, Director of the Show, and an Honorary Freeman of the Company, procured free tickets and the proceeds contributed £530 for the benefit of the Charitable Trust.

Several Livery Companies and City Institutions donated trees to enhance the beauty of our City of London. Due to the generosity of the Court, every member of which subscribed individually, a tree was bought by the Company and was ceremoniously planted by the Upper Warden, Mr. Arthur Smith, assisted by the Clerk, on the 26th February 1975. The tree is a red-twigged lime and is situated at the corner of Cheapside and Foster Lane. This is expected to thrive better in the urban situation than the traditional 'spreading chestnut tree'.

A.G. Smith 1975–76
Arthur Smith followed as Master. Arthur split the rhythm of Veterinary Masters, although his value to the Company was in no way diminished by his lack of such qualifications. He showed a similar enthusiasm as his father George. His devotion to detail, his attention to duty and to the furtherance of the Company and its Liverymen have been paramount and he would say his reward was the moment, when as Master, he led the deputation into Guildhall for HRH The Princess Anne Mrs. Mark Phillips to be given the Freedom of the City of London.

On 17th December 1975 Lord Newall was admitted into the Livery without Fine in recognition of his services in respect of the Farriers (Registration) Act 1975.

Professor F.R. Bell, BSc, PhD, FRCVS 1976–77
Professor Fred Bell with all his experience in the Veterinary world, a member of the Council of the Royal Veterinary College, as Chairman of the Division of Clinical Studies and Professor of Experimental Veterinary Medicine, and Head, Department of Medicine, entered his year as Master in the Silver Jubilee year of HM The Queen. It was also the year that HRH The Princess Anne was admitted into the Livery. His Reception took place at the St. John's Wood Barracks the home of the King's Troop of the Royal Horse Artillery who performed the 'Ceremony of Sunset' in the presence of a large company, including Her Royal Highness and Captain Mark Phillips.

It was also the year when the Farriers (Registration) Bill had finally become Law in all its aspects. The Farriers Registration Council was formed under the Chairmanship of Sir Hugh Linstead. In the Record for 1977 the following Past Masters were specially mentioned as having contributed so much to the culmination of the work – Clabby, Simons, Arthur Smith, Linstead, and whilst the Author has paid tribute to their contributions in dealing with their year's work, it is worth repetition.

Professor Bell's Paper entitled 'The Days of the Farriers', written in 1977 is included in the Appendices. In congratulating Professor Bell on his year as Master, particular mention was made of his help in the educational side of the Company and his encouragement to the Examination Board.

The Author has quoted the 'Record' on several occasions and he cannot refrain from the quote in the 1976–77 edition:

'The History of the Company compiled by a former Clerk, Mr. L.R. Robson, in 1949 is now out of print and the Court is indebted to Past Master Mr. Deputy Leslie Prince for undertaking to compile a complete new History from the Company's beginning to the present day. This is no easy task and the Court is well aware of the work involved and the time consumed in such a monumental work.'

Dorian Williams, OBE, MFH, 1977–78
Dorian Williams is a name as well known as any in the Horse World, inter alia as Chairman of the British Horse Society. He was admitted to the Livery in 1962, a member of the Court in 1972. His television voice known to millions describing Show-Jumping was now familiar to members of the Company and particularly to the Court. He is himself a celebrated author of so many books that he will not, it is hoped, take exception to a quote from his own book, 'Master of One' on his reactions to becoming Master of the Farriers Company:

'In 1977 I was elected Master of the Worshipful Company of Farriers, one of the great City Livery Companies, an honour which as a simple country bumpkin I greatly appreciated. To be a part of something that goes back six hundred years is fascinating and challenging . . .'

Having been a spectator at so many great ceremonial occasions, either watching on television, in the crowd outside the Palace, as a special mounted police officer in the Mall, and greatly honoured as a guest at Princess Anne's wedding, it was a unique privilege for me to be part of such ceremonial when Princess Anne was made a Freeman of the City. I am not so naive as to think that the world would come to an end if the City of London's famous Livery Companies were disbanded; nevertheless, convinced that they have a vital role to play, I believe passionately in their retention as something traditional, deep-rooted and of absorbing historical interest. The survival of so much that is worthwhile is frequently based on the illogical and anachronistic, but is nevertheless entirely justified. I cannot pretend that hidden away in one of my early photographic albums there is a picture of little Dorian standing on the steps of the Mansion House dreaming of the day when he would be Lord Mayor of London. But I cannot deny that to preside at the Great Livery Banquet in the famous Egyptian Hall in the Mansion House, entertaining as my guest the Lord Mayor himself, made me feel very proud.'

Possibly the first Master of Fox Hounds who has been Master of the Company – no other member has been found in the Minute books – the Author was astounded, as many others have been, in reading his Autobiography, at his prowess, not only as a horseman, but also his acting abilities, his skill as a Director of Drama and his care of Pendley Manor, Tring, as demonstrated at his Masters reception where many members of the Company were entertained in the presence of HRH The Princess Ann Mrs. Mark Phillips – who arrived below lowering skies in a helicopter – to a programme described by one Liveryman as a unique amalgam of 'Champion Ponies, Shakespeare, a Princess and Strawberries and Cream'! The Author particularly appreciated Dorian's many references in his speeches at Court and Livery meetings to the necessity for the Company to remember as a Livery Company its close association with the City of London.

Jubilee 1952–1977

To mark the occasion of the Silver Jubilee of HM The Queen all Livery Companies were approached by the Corporation of London to have erected in Cheapside their Armorial Bearings. The Company readily acceded to this request and the Arms of the Company were seen in Cheapside, on each side, erected on a pole and they remained there until the end of the Jubilee celebrations.

In addition an exhibition was held in July 1977 in the Courtyard of Guildhall. Mr. E.P. Stern FWCF, a member of the Company, set up a forge which was of great interest to the general public. Horse Shoes had been for sale and the proceeds were given to the Queen's Jubilee Trust.

The Guildhall Library held the City and Crown Exhibition and the Company lent some of their treasures which were much appreciated.

W. David Gibson 1978–79

Gibson was admitted to the Livery in 1966, became a member of the Court in 1972. He had retired as a Major in the Welsh Guards in 1957. A great horseman, he had won the Grand Military four times, and in 1957 he rode in the Grand National – a feat unparalleled for a member of the Company – unfortunately his horse fell at the last fence and Gibson broke his collar bone.

In the mid sixties he was appointed Senior Steward of the National Hunt Committee and in 1970 Deputy Senior Steward of the Jockey Club. His experience with horses was of much value to the Court, for it will have been seen how the Company was progressing towards its goal – that of getting the Parliamentary powers in Farriery achieved in 1975 when the Farriers Act became law.

When he was elected Master in 1978 David Gibson, notwithstanding that his residence was in Perthshire, recognised the responsibilities of the Company laid down by the Act and with his equine background was much in the saddle. One of his first duties was to welcome HRH The Princess Anne Mrs. Mark Phillips to the Court. His 'Master's Reception' was held at Newmarket. In the true sense of the words he and his wife were very much 'At Home' to the Livery during a tour of the Equine Research Station and the Jockey Club Rooms. The former is now the Headquarters of the Animal Health Trust whilst the latter houses the original coffee room where the club was established in 1771.

So ends this History written through the Biographies of the Masters and it is hoped that many Liverymen will have been reminded of the events of each year. Obviously some happenings have not been mentioned – it would have been impossible to deal with every item that is recorded in great detail in the Minute Books and in the Record. Suffice it to say that this Chapter has only ended as the History of the Company has been brought up to date.

The Masters of the Company

1673–74 Gregory Costen	1726–27 William Browning
1674–75 Andrew Snape	1727–28 Phillip Dewerth
1675–1718 Unknown	1728–29 John Rogers
1718–19 John Wood	1729–30 John Lewis
1719–20 George Collingwood	1730–31 William Wells
1720–21 Nathaniel Preston	1731–32 Thomas Cotton
1721–22 John Edwards	1732–33 William Wackett
1722–23 Seth Adams	1733–34 William May
1723–24 James Martin (died in office)	1734–35 John Siddall
	1735–36 Thomas Deane
April 1724 Thomas Potter	1736–37 Nicholas Cooke
1724–25 William Every (died in office)	1737– Matthew Woodyard
	July 1737 William May (Deputy Master)
Feb 1725 Henry Sheldon	
1725–26 John Wackett	1738–39 John Sewell

1739–40 Richard Strutton	1787–88 William Box
1740–41 John Bromley	1788–89 Robert Bovarn
1741–42 Francis Cockayne	1789–90 William Pryor
1742–43 James Townsend	1790–91 Ebenezer Clark
1743–44 Thomas Winsmore	1791–92 Edmund Kershaw
1744–45 Andrew Ward	1792–93 John Edwards
1745–46 Samuel Wilson	1793–94 Robert Pickwoad
1746 Thomas Ingrave (died in office)	1794–95 William Merrick
	1795–96 John Peecock
1746–47 John Lewis	1797–98 Thomas Wilson
1747–48 George Cranston	1798–99 Thomas Pointer
1748–49 Thomas Wackett	1799–1800 Joseph Wood
1749–50 Peter Vandercombe	1800–01 Henry Tadwell
1750–51 Harry Thrupp	1801–02 John Hall
1751–52 Thomas Clarke	1802–03 William Lowdan
1752–53 William Hopkins	1803–04 Thomas White
1753–54 Matthew Allen	1804–05 Joseph Wood
1754–55 David Rice	1805–06 Francis Blackbeard
1755–56 Francis Butler	1806–07 Robert Scratton
1756–57 William Wackett	1807–08 James Robertson
1757–58 Francis Gawthorn	1808–09 Christopher Chryssel Hall
1758–59 William Ash	
1759–60 William Holliday	1809–10 George William Wood
1760–61 Robert Cranston	1810–11 William Layton
1761–62 William Chater	1811–12 Ebenezer Clark
1762–63 George Street	1812–13 Robert Jones
1763–64 John Heath	1813–14 Thomas Watkins
1764–65 Luke Alder	1814–15 George Turner
1765–66 Robert Garrard	1815–16 Joseph Turton
1766–67 Thomas Whitehorne	1816–17 Thomas Dudderidge
1767–68 Matthew Butterworth	1817–18 John Moore Adams
1768–69 Henry Potter	1818–19 Charles Alexander Craig
1769–70 George Townsend	1819–20 John Hassall Gardner
1770–71 Godfrey Wilson	1820–21 Vaun Edwards
1771–72 John Kennett	1821–22 William Watkins
1772–73 John Bunnell	1822–23 William Neall
1773–74 George Shaw	1823–24 Henry Wood
1774–75 John Robinson	1824–25 Henry Surmon
1775–76 Charles Bartrum	1825–26 Thomas Hennington
1776–77 Henry Brooks	1826–27 James Sheppard
1777–78 William Wilson	1827–28 Thomas Hubbock
1778–79 David Rice	1828–29 Thomas Moulden
1779–80 William Odber	1829–30 John George Lacy
1780–81 Thomas Richardson	1820–31 Joseph Henley
1781–82 Richard Green	1831–32 George Cooke
1782–83 John Scott	1832–33 George Mills
1783–84 John Spicer	1833–34 Thomas White
1784–85 Thomas Dickens	1834–35 John Blanch
1785–86 Henry Thorowgood	1835–36 Thomas Hubbock, Junior
1786–87 Edward Clark	1836–37 David William Witton

1837–38 John Burges Watson
1838–39 William Weedon
1839–40 William Coates
1840–41 Charles Marshall
1841–42 Robert Willis Hall
1842–43 James Beeson
1843–44 Josiah Nice
1844–45 Richard Hillier
1845–46 James Covington
1846–47 James Hinde Fyffe
1847–48 Jonathan Lucas
1848–49 John Gardner
1849–50 Penry Lewis
1850–51 Alfred Higgs
1851–52 John Gillingham
1852–53 William Field
1853–54 John Jones
1854–55 George Hill
1855–56 Richard Smith
1856–57 William Patey
1857–58 John Allambridge Howe
1858–59 Thomas Simmons
1859–60 John Ditchman
1860–61 John Ditchman
1861–62 Frederick White
1862–63 William Williams
1863–64 Joseph Hudson
1864–65 Jabez Samuel Gower
1865–66 Jabez Samuel Gower
1866–67 John Burges Watson
1867–68 Wiliam Clark
1868–69 William Field
1869–70 Sidney Smith, Junior
1870–71 Sidney Smith, Junior
1871–72 John Burges Watson
1872–73 Henry Richard Brett
1873–74 Thomas Lawrence
1874–75 Frederick White
1875–76 William Field
1876–77 William Henry Wagstaff
1877–78 Horatio Stewart
1878–79 James Shaw
1879–80 Thomas Henry Watson
1880–81 William Carter
1881–82 John Robert Cooper
1882–83 George Mills
1883–84 James Waddell
    Sidney Smith, Junior
1884–85 John Henry Kays
1885–86 William Hawkins Herbert

1886–87 Cornelius Marshall
    Warmington, MP, QC
1887–88 William Thomas Loveday
1888–89 George Burt, JP
1889–90 Sir William Hardman,
    MA, JP (Acting
    Master during the
    Master's long illness:
    Sidney Smith)
1890–91 Barnes Wimbush, MA
1891–92 Hyman Montague, FSA
1892–93 Francis Campbell Bayard,
    LLM
1893–94 William Joseph Daves
    Andrew
1894–95 William Charles Jackson
1895–96 John Robert Cooper
1896–97 Joseph Pyke
1897–98 Percival Beavor Lambert
1898–99 Walter Daniel Cronin
1899–1900 Thomas Aitken Dollar,
    MRCVS
1900–01 Arthur Gerald Smith
1901–02 Arthur Gerald Smith
1902–03 William Watt Dollar
1903–04 John Robert Cooper
1904–05 Thomas Henry Watson
1905–06 Charles Sheather
1906–07 Charles Sheather
1907–08 Charles Sheather
1908–09 Arthur Gerald Smith
1909–10 Thomas Ashworth
    Richardson
1910–11 William Ballin Hinde
1911–12 James Coote Garnham
1912–13 Ernest John Marsh
1913–14 William Barry Gregar
1914–15 John Duncan Best
1915–16 Robert McConnell
1916–17 Robert McConnell
1917–18 Robert McConnell
1918–19 Herbert Rooke Oldfield
1919–20 Charles James Smith
1920–21 Frederick Malcolm
    Garnham
1921–22 Herbert Roper Barrett
1922–23 Edward Manville, MP
1923–24 Francis John Robinson,
    MA
1924–25 Henry Cyril Else

Jan 1 1925 Acting Master during the Master's absence: Francis John Robinson, MA

1925–26 John Thomas Sanders

1926–27 Sir John Byford

1927–28 Lt Col George Westhead Parkinson

1928–29 Archibald George James Brown

1929–30 Stanley Cyril Else

1930–31 Col Sir Frederick Daniel Green

1931–32 Cecil John Marsh, MA

1932–33 Robert McConnell

1933–34 Herbert Roper Barrett, CC

1934–35 James Godfrey Martin

1935–36 Ernest Tom Neathercoat, CBE, JP

1936–37 Sir Frederick Senior, JP

1937–38 Robert William Buckingham

1938–39 Ernest Tom Neathercoat, CBE, JP

1939–40 Robert Barlow Tyler

1940–41 Robert Barlow Tyler (died in office) Robert William Buckingham

1941–42 Robert William Buckingham

1942–43 Robert William Buckingham

1943–44 Robert William Buckingham

1944–45 George Bird Garnham

1945–46 Walter Rose, CC

1946–47 Col Cyprian Charles Oswald Whiteley, OBE, JP, CC

1947–48 William Newcome Wright, JP, CC

1948–49 Edward Philip Paxman, MA, JP (died in office) Frederick Malcolm Garnham

1949–50 Harry Archibald Brown

1950–51 George Herbert Fenton, FZS, FRGS

1951–52 George Appleton Warley, FCA (died in office) Frederick Malcolm Garnham

1952–53 Oswald Lewis, MA, FZS, FRGS

1953–54 James Basil Buxton, MA, FRCS, DVH (died in office) Frederick Malcolm Garnham

1954–55 Samuel Richard Walker, CBE (Deputy)

1955–56 Leslie Barnett Prince, MA, FCA, CC

1956–57 His Grace the Duke of Devonshire, MC

1957–58 John Stroud

1958–59 George Bowman, JP, FWCF

1959–60 George Allison-Beer (Deputy)

1960–61 Sir Leslie Norman Hollinghurst, GBE, KCB, DFC

1961–62 Sir John Smyth, Bart, VC, MC, MP

1962–63 Sir Frank Lord, OBE, MA, JP

1963–64 John Edward Lines

1964–65 Dr Walter Richard Wooldridge, MSc, DVSc, FRCVS, FRICS

1965–66 Reginald Alfred Brown, OBE

1966–67 Alec Hobson, CBE, MVO

1967–68 George Hamilton Smith

1968–69 Alfred John Barsham, BCom, FCA

1969–70 Russell William Vernon Neathercoat, DFC

1970–71 Edward Howard Newcome Wright

1971–72 Sir Hugh Nicholas Linstead, OBE, LLD, FPS

1972–73 Kenneth John Lines
1973–74 Brigadier John Clabby,
CBE, MRCVS
1974–75 Michael Anthony Peter
Simons, MRCVS
1975–76 Arthur George Smith

1976–77 Professor Frederick
Rowland Bell,
FRCVS
1977–78 Dorian Williams, OBE,
MFH
1978–79 W. David Gibson

The Court 30th June, 1979

	Date of Election to court
Master:	
Major William David Gibson	1972

Wardens:	
Robert William Bulfield, Esq.	1974
Denis Frank Oliver, Esq., B.Sc., MRCVS	1974
George Kendrick Findlay, Esq., LRIBA	1975

Past Masters:	
George Bird Garnham, Esq. (1944–45)	1940
Samuel Richard Walker, Esq., CBE (1954–55)	1943
Mr. Deputy Leslie Barnett Prince, CBE, MA, FCA (1955–56)	1946
John Stroud, Esq. (1957–58)	1946
Reginald Alfred Brown, Esq., OBE (1965–66)	1958
George Hamilton Smith, Esq. (1967–68)	1959
Alfred John Barsham, Esq., BCom, FCA (1968–69)	1962
Russell William Vernon Neathercoat, Esq., DFC (1969–70)	1962
Sir Hugh Nicholas Linstead, OBE, LLD, FPS (1971–72)	1965
Kenneth John Lines, Esq. (1972–73)	1965
Brigadier John Clabby CBE, MRCVS (1973–74)	1967
Michael Anthony Peter Simons, Esq., MRCVS (1974–75)	1967
Arthur George Smith, Esq. (1975–76)	1970
Professor Frederick Rowland Bell, FRCVS (1976–77)	1972
Dorian Joseph George Williams, Esq., OBE, MFH (1977–78)	1972

Assistants in Order of Seniority:	
Eric Arthur Styles, Esq., OBE, FIB	1975
Charles Edward Docwra, Esq.	1976
Howard John Cooper, Esq., FWCF	1977
HRH The Princess Anne. Mrs. Mark Phillips	1978
Mr. Deputy Arthur Brian Wilson FCA	1979

Honorary Assistants:	
His Grace, The Duke of Devonshire, MC (Master 1956–57)	1951
Brigadier the Rt. Hon. Sir John George Smyth, Bt., VC, MC, (Master 1961–62)	1953

John Edward Lines, Esq. (Master 1963–64)   1954
Alec Hobson, Esq., CBE, MVO (Master 1966–67)   1960
Edward Howard Newcome Wright, Esq. (Master 1970–71) 1963

Chaplain:
The Rev. Preb. F.A.F. Poulden, AKC

Clerk:
Franklin Edwin Birch, Esq.

Beadle:
Charles Ellwood

CHAPTER 3
Possessions

Gifts To The Company, etc., 1732–1979

1732   *The Company's Colours*
Presented by William May
Extract from Minutes of the Court 30th October, 1732, raises the question whether this, the first Gift to the Company, was really a gift or a purchase of the highest office in the Company:

'This Court taking into consideration the bad condition of the Company's Colours whereby they are not able to attend on any Lord Mayor's Day as heretofore And Mr. William May a Member of this Company proposing to the Court to make a present to the Company of Colours and Streamers to cost at least fforty pounds Provided the said Court would choose him Master next Midsomer Day ensuing being the day for Election of Master and also that the said Company would attend upon him the Lord Mayors Day then next ensuing

'Upon the Question put whether the Court do agree to the said Proposall it was carried in the affirmative which was signed by the following persons.' (Here follow the names of the Master and sixteen Assistants.)

Not now in existence.

1766   *An engraved Plate of the Company's Arms*
Presented by Henry Thorowgood, Junior
'to be used for Summons's to the Members of the Company.'
Minutes of Court 10th November, 1766.)
Not now in existence.

1779 *A Hammer* (presumably a Gavel)
Presented by William Odber (Master), John Spicer (a Warden), Henry Brooks (Assistant), Henry Thorowgood (Assistant), Edward Clark (Assistant), George Brooks (Assistant).
Not now in existence.

1782 *A Desk* 'for the Clerk's use in the Court Room'.
Presented by Henry Thorowgood.
Not now in existence.

1871 *A Mahogany Table and Footstool* 'for use in connection with the Large Chair of the Company'.
Presented by Mr. Joseph Hudson (Master 1866–67)
Destroyed by Enemy Action at the Depository of Thomas Wallis & Co. Ltd., in May, 1941, when the Master's Chair (the large chair' mentioned above), purchased by the Company in 1749, was also destroyed.

1874 *The Master's Gold and Enamel Badge*
Presented by Mr. Horatio Stewart (Master 1877–78)
The Jewels in the Badge and the Gold Chain were added later.

1875 *A Banner of the Company's Arms*
Presented by Mr. James Shaw, J.P. (Master 1878–79 and Sheriff 1874–75)
Destroyed by fire 1887, together with all the other Banners. They were replaced out of the Insurance Money in the same year.

1876 *Snuff Box*, Horse's Hoof mounted in silver
Presented by Mr. Horatio Stewart (Master 1877–78)
On the lid is engraved the Company's Arms and the inscription 'Presented to the Worshipful Company of Farriers of London by H. Stewart, Esq., Upper Warden, 1876.'

1878 *Jewels added to the Master's Badge*
Presented by Mr. Horatio Stewart.

1878 *Loving Cup and Cover*
Presented by Mr. Horatio Stewart (Master 1877–78)
The cup is supported on three rustic pillars between which is the figure of a smith with implements and anvil, on which is the wording: 'By hammer and hand our art doth stand.' The cover is surmounted by the figure of Concordia and has medallions of the City Arms and those of the Company, also the inscription: 'Presented to the Worshipful Company of Farriers of London by Horatio Stewart, Esq., Master 1877–78', and the motto, 'Concordia res parvae crescunt discordia maximae ditabunter'. (Small things flourish with concord but the greatest things shall be cast down by discord.)
Height 20 inches. Weight 77 oz.

1878 *Five Bannerets of Arms*
Presented by Horatio Stewart (Master 1877–78), John Burgess Watson (Master 1866–67 and 1871–72), William Clark (Master 1867–68), H.R. Brett (Master 1872–73), W.H. Wagstaff (Master 1876–77)

1878 *Six Banners of Arms*
Presented by Samuel Chatwood, Sidney Smith (Master 1869–70, 1870–71 and 1883–84), Horatio Stewart (Master 1877–78), E.M. Hubbock, M.D. Collins, Wynne E. Baxter (Clerk 1877–1906)

1878 *Poor Box, in polished oak*
Presented by Mr. George Burt (Sheriff 1878–79, Master 1888–89)
The inscription reads: 'Worshipful Company of Farriers – Poor Box – Presented by George Burt, Sheriff Elect – on his admission to the Court of Assistants, July, 1878.'

1879 *Banneret* of the Company's Arms
Presented by Mr. George Burt, J.P. (Sheriff 1878–79, Master 1888–89)

1879 *Freeman's Declaration Book*
Presented by Mr. Horatio Stewart (Master 1877–78)

1879 *Liverymen's Declaration Book*
Presented by Mr. James Shaw (Sheriff 1874–75, Master 1878–79)

1881 *Banner of Arms*
Presented by Mr. T.H. Watson (Master 1879–80)

1881 *Rose Water Dish* in parcel Gilt Silver
Presented by Mr. J.R. Cooper (Master 1881–82, 1895–96, 1903–04, Sheriff 1895–96)
With eight medallions embossed: Marshalls appearing before the Mayor, 1356. Granting the Charter, 25th Charles II. 1674. Petitioning the Judges, 1675. Petitioning the Court of Aldermen, 1692. The City Arms. The Company's Arms. The Donor's Arms. Horse Shoeing. The panels are divided by horses' heads mounted to the Dish.
The Inscription: 'Presented to the Worshipful Company of Farriers by John Robert Cooper, Master, 9th November, 1881.'
Diameter 20 inches. Weight 64 oz.

1882 *The Master's Gold Chain of Office*
Presented by Mr. J.R. Cooper, J.P. (Master 1881–82, 1895–96, 1903–04, Sheriff 1895–96)

1882 *Cover for the old Two-handled Cup of 1778*

Presented by Mr. W.H. Wagstaff (Master 1876–77)

The domed cover is surmounted by a figure of Concordia: The inscription reads: 'This cover with figure of Concordia (Mother of Companies) presented to the Worshipful Company of Farriers of London, by W.H. Wagstaff, Esq., Master 1876–7)

1882 *Banner of Arms*
Presented by Mr. William Field (Master 1852–53, 1868–69, 1875–76)

1883 *Facsimile of the Arms of the Company, with Genealogical Tree*
'showing that the Company had been in existence at least as far back as 1312'
Presented by Mr. W.H. Wagstaff (Master 1876–77)

1883 *Loving Cup and Cover*
Presented by Mr. George Mills (Master 1882–83)

A two-handled Loving Cup – the relievo work represents one of the numerous battles fought by the Crusaders against the Infidels; a knight on horseback surmounts the cover.

The total height of Cup and Cover is 24 inches.

Inscription: 'Presented to the Worshipful Company of Farriers of London by George Mills (Master 1882–3) as a memento of the long and pleasant connection of himself and family with the Company, and especially of his father, the late George Mills, Esq., a liveryman for 61 years and who 50 years ago filled the office now held by his son.'

1884 *Silver and Ivory Gavel,* or Chairman's Hammer
Presented by Mr. Sidney Smith (Master 1869–70, 1870–71, 1883–84)

The inscription reads: 'The Gift of Sidney Smith, Esq., to the Farriers' Company of London on retiring from the office of Master, which he had served for the third time. July 1884'.

1884 *Masters, Wardens and Assistants Declaration Book*
Presented by Mr. Barnes Wimbush, MA (Master 1890–91)

1885 *Cigar Box in Coromandel Wood*
Presented by Mr. J.H. Kays (Master 1884–85)

The Inscription on a silver plate on the lid is as follows: 'Presented to the Worshipful Company of Farriers by John Henry Kays, Esq., on his retiring from the office of Master, July, 1885.'

1888 *Claret Jug* in silver
Presented by Mr. W.T. Loveday (Master 1887–88)

Engraved with an elaborate pattern and the Company's Arms.

The Inscription reads: 'The gift of William Thomas Loveday, Esq., to the Worshipful Company of Farriers of London on retiring from the office of Master, July 1888.'

1890 *The Seal of the Company's Arms and Press*
Presented by Mr. Barnes Wimbush, MA (Master, 1890–91)

1892 *Salver, Silver, of the year 1736*
Presented by Mr. Hyman Montague, FSA (Master, 1891–92)
'Piecrust' edge, standing on four feet. The Arms of the Company are engraved on the face, and on the back are the words: 'Presented to the Worshipful Company of Farriers of London by H. Montague, FSA, Master 1891–92.'

1894 *Four Robes for use of the Master and Wardens*
Presented by Mr. W.J.D. Andrew (Master 1893) and Mr. W.C. Jackson (Master 1894–95)

1895 *Banner of the Donor's Arms*
Presented by Mr. J.R. Cooper, JP (Master, 1881–82, 1895–96, 1903–04, Sheriff, 1895–96)

1895 *Portrait of Sidney Smith*, three times Master of the Company (framed and glazed)
Presented by Mr. N.L. Cohen

1896 *Photographic Album* in Red Morocco with Lock
Presented by Mr. Sheriff Cooper (Master, 1881–82, 1895–96, 1903–04)

1896 *Silver Tankard with Lid*
Presented by Mr. Joseph Pyke (Master 1896–97)
Bands of Grape Vine decoration are embossed around the top and bottom of the body; the Arms of the Company are engraved on the lid.
Height 11½ inches. Weight 90 oz.
The Inscription reads: 'Presented to the Worshipful Company of Farriers by Joseph Pyke, Esq., Master 1896–97'.

1900 *Salver, Silver of the year 1773*
Presented by Mrs Harris, widow of the late Hon. Chaplain of the Company.
Standing on four feet, gadrooned edges, made by John Carter.
The Inscription reads: 'Presented to the Rev. Joseph Harris, MA, Honorary Chaplain of the Worshipful Company of Farriers of London, as a token of much esteem from his friends on the Court of Assistants, with whom he has been associated for many years. July 1891.'
The Salver was presented to the Company by his widow in November 1900.

1902 *South African War Medal*
Presented by Horatio Stewart and Francis Campbell Bayard
The seven clasps being those carried by the City of London

Imperial Volunteers during the war. (The Company had contributed £100 to the CIV Funds).

1902 *Silver Frame for the above Medal*
Presented by Mr. Horatio Stewart and Mr. Francis Campbell Bayard

1904 *Paper Weight* – a horse's hoof shod by the donors and mounted in silver
Presented by Mr. J. Thirtle, RSS and Mr. F.B. Mills, RSS

1911 *Banner of Arms*
Presented by Mr. W. Ballin Hinde (Master 1910–11)

1915 *The Clerk's Badge*
Presented by Mr. J. Duncan Best, JP (Master 1914–15)

1928 *The Principles and Practice of Horse Shoeing*
Presented by C.M. Holmes, FWCF

1929 *Portrait of Andrew Snape*, Sergeant Farrier to King Charles II, and second Master of the Company under the King's Charter
Presented by Miss Moore Brabazon

1942 *The Record Book and its compilation*
Presented by Leonard C.F. Robson (Clerk to the Company)

1944 *Bound Photographs of Specimen Pages* from the Earlier Records of the Company
Presented by Mr. E.P. Paxman, MA (Master 1948–49)

1944 *A Copy of a Paper on the Early History of the Veterinary Surgeon in England*, by Dr. Fred Bullock, Assistant
Presented by Leonard C.F. Robson

1945 *A Book entitled 'The Gentleman's Farriery'* by J. Bartlett, Surgeon, 1753
Presented by Mr. G.E. Marden (A Member of the Livery)

1947 *A Black and White Livery Gown*
Presented by Mr. Oswald Lewis, MA (Warden)
(Black and white are the proper colours for the Farriers' Company.)

1948 *Loving Cup and Cover*
Presented by Mr. Herbert Fenton (Master 1950–51)

1950 *Silver Punch Bowl,* in memory of her husband Archibald George James Brown (Master 1928–29) and to commemorate her son's year of office Harry Archibald Brown (Master 1949–50)
Presented by Mrs. Archibald Brown

1950 *Shield bearing Three Horse Shoes of Company's Arms*, as a

compliment of his recent election to the Court of Assistants.
Presented by Leonard Charles Robson

1951 *Freeman's Declaration Book*, to mark admission of his son
Michael Prince and of his son-in-law Ivor Lewisohn as Livery-
men.
Presented by Leslie Barnett Prince, MA, FCA, CC

1951 *Beadle's Gown*
Presented by Mr. Deputy S.R. Walker

1951 *Chaplain's Badge*
Presented by the Chaplain, The Rev. E.G. Turner

1951 *Pair Sheffield Plate Candlesticks*
Presented by Mr. H.C. Else (Master 1924–25) and Family and so
inscribed (received after death of Mr. Past Master Else)

1955 *Silver Gilt Master's Cup* (designed by Omar Ramsden)
Presented by Leslie Barnett Prince, MA, FCA, CC, in commemoration of his year of office as a Sheriff and as Master

1956 *Silver Loving Cup* (designed by Stanley Phillips), engraved
with the names of the Members of the Court to mark 600th
Anniversary of the Foundation
Presented by the Master, Wardens and Court of Assistants

1956 *George III Silver Gilt Loving Cup*, to celebrate the 600th
Anniversary and a Book containing the names of the Subscribers,
organised by Mr. George H. Smith, FZS
Presented by the Members of the Livery

1956 *Wooden Shield of Arms of 51st L of C Signal Regiment*
Presented by the Officers of the Regiment

1957 *Silver Salver* (from the Devonshire Family Plate)
Presented by the 11th Duke of Devonshire (Master 1956–57)

1959 *The Sum of One Hundred Pounds*
Presented by George Bowman, JP, FWCF
To provide an Annual Prize from the Company to the Pupils of
the St. Martin in the Fields High School for Girls.

1961 *An Illuminated Pedigree of the Arms of the Company*
Presented by Sir Frank Lord, OBE, MA, JP (Master 1962–63)
Purchased and completely restored.

1961 *Silver Challenge Cup*
Presented by George Hamilton Smith, FZS (Master 1967–68)
For the Farriers Livery Golfing Society.

1961 *Clock, 'Farriers in Action — Great Exhibition 1851'*
Presented by Mrs. J. Beven

1962   *Past Masters Badge*
   Presented by Mr. George Garnham (Past Master 1944–45)
   Belonging to his Father, Mr. F.M. Garnham (Master 1920–21,
1949, 1952, 1954). To be worn by the Immediate Past Master.

1964   *A Book, 'Treatise upon the Art of Farriery'* printed in 1756
   Presented by Mr. E.H. Newcome Wright (Master 1970–71), in
memory of his Father, Mr. William Newcome Wright (Master
1947–48).

1964   *Silver Shields*
   Presented by Mr. George Smith
   For the Farriers Golfing Society.

1967   *Silver Sugar Sifter*
   Presented by Mrs. Wooldridge
   In memory of her late husband, Dr. W.R. Wooldridge (Master
1964–65).

1968   *Decoration to the Grant of Arms and its Display Case*
   Presented by Mr. George Smith (Master 1967–68)

1968   *Silver Gilt Ewer and Rosewater Dish*
   Presented by Mr. J.L. Marden
   In memory of his Father, Mr. George Marden (Middle Warden
1965–66, elected but did not take office owing to illness).

1969   *Pair of Silver Gilt Candelabra*
   Presented by Mr. George Garnham (Master 1944–45).
   In memory of his Father Mr. F.M. Garnham (Master 1920–21,
1949, 1952, 1954), a matching pair to those presented by Mr. Past
Master Else in 1951.

1969   *Block and Dye of the Company's Registered Armorial Bearings*
   Presented by the former Clerk, Mr. A.G.W. Scott, FCA.

1970   *Pair Early Victorian Port Decanters in Mahogany Case*
   Presented by Mr. R.W.V. Neathercoat (Master 1969–70).
   In memory of his Father, Mr. E.T. Neathercoat (Master
1938–39).

1971   *Gold Pen*
   Presented by Mr. George Garnham (Master 1944–45).
   With which Her Royal Highness The Princess Anne signed the
Declaration as a Freeman, and *Onyx Stand* inscribed to com-
memorate that occasion, both to be used for the signing of
Freemen's and Liverymen's Declarations at Court Meetings and
on other ceremonial occasions.

1971   *Livery Badges*
   Presented by Mr. Reginald Brown (Master 1965–66).

For present and future Members of the Company, to be worn by Liverymen at all Company functions.

1972 *Jewelled Past Master's Badge*
Worn by the late Mr. Thomas A. Richardson (Master 1909–10), presented by his daughters.

1972 *Silver Rose Bowl*
Presented by Mr. J.B. Hill
For the Farriers Golfing Society.

1972 £2,466 final instalment of a total of £13,000 from the Estate of the late Mr. Robert Buckingham (Master 1937–38 and 1940–44).

1972–79 *Pewter Dinner Mats*
1 presented by John Lines (Master 1963–64); 1 presented by Alec Hobson (Master 1966–67); 1 presented by George Smith (Master 1967–68); 3 presented by Sir Hugh Linstead (Master 1971–72); 3 presented by Mr. Joseph N. Cohen 'as thanks for the hospitality received and enjoyment had from attending the Company's functions over many years – a Liveryman of the Tin Plate Workers Company – a lifelong friend of Mr. Senior Past Master George Garnham'. 2 presented by W. David Gibson (Master 1978–79).

1974 *Stained Glass Window* – erected in the Crypt of the Guildhall donated by Mr. Deputy S.R. Walker CBE, Mr. Deputy Leslie B. Prince, CBE, MA, and Mr. G. Allison-Beer.

1974 *Book Matches* – 5,000 printed with the Company's name. Anonymous Donor.

1975 *Book* – 'The Panorama of London' published in 1830 and signed by the grandfather of the donor, E. Howard Newcome Wright (Clerk 1958–63, Master 1970–71).

1976 *Silver Cup* engraved 'Horse Shoeing Championship of London 5th April 1930, presented by the Mustad Horse Nail Company' – presented by Mr. R.A. Lovell.

1978 *Silver Cup for Wardens* – presented by George Garnham (Master 1944–45) to mark the 100th Anniversary of a member of the Garnham family being admitted a member of the Company on 26th June 1878.

1978 *Lectern* for Master's use at functions, in oak embelished with horse-shoes – presented by Dorian Williams (Master 1977–78).

1979 *Book* – 'Ptolemy Tortoise' written and presented by Sir Edmund Stockdale (Lord Mayor 1959).

Book – 'London and The Guilds of Europe' written and presented by John Kennedy Melling.

Books – 2 copies of 'Practical Farriery' by W.J. Miles and a copy of 'Royal Newmarket' by R.C. Lyle – presented by Fred Newington (son-in-law of the Clerk).

In addition to the above-mentioned gifts the Company owns the following articles:
An Ivory and Silver Seal, purchased in 1767.
An Hour Glass (running about 10 minutes), 18th Century.
Four Wardens' Badges.
The Beadle's Staff, ebony and silver.
A Table Snuff-Box, made from a colt's hoof, with model of a colt on the lid.

1974   **Stained Glass Window** in the new Wren West Crypt possibly the oldest part of Guildhall with a magnificent vaulted ceiling. The 19 windows were donated by the respective Guilds, installed Monday April 8th, 1974 made by Chapel Studios and designed by Brian D.L. Thomas OBE, FMGP, member of the Court of the Glaziers Company, co-editor of Directory of Master Glass-Painters, whose work can also be seen in St. Paul's Cathedral, Westminster Abbey, City Chambers, and who wrote, for the official booklet these notes on the Farriers' Window:

'One of the City of London's most ancient ceremonies is the annual payment to the Queen's Remembrancer of a "quit rent" granted in 1235 for the site of a forge near St. Clement Danes Church (see supra).

'This, as the window shows, consists of sixty-one nails and six horseshoes. The latter are especially big ones, because this forge served the Knights Templars, who trained their heavy mounts to lash out with their forelegs in battle. The first Charter of the Farriers' Company dates from 1356, and the Grant of Arms was made in 1674.

'At one time Farriers not only shoed horses, but served as horse-leeches, so the implements of both trades are illustrated in the window, including various "surgical shoes" of the kind still produced for the Company by apprentices as set pieces. The range of the farriers' clientelle is demonstrated at the head of the window by life-size renderings of the delicate shoes of a racing horse and a pony in striking contrast with the high shoe of a shire horse. (Contrary to popular belief the "lucky" way of hanging a horseshoe is as shown here, because the Devil is loth to go through the hoop.)

'A few of the many breeds of horse still in use are shown below the Company's Coat of Arms. The farrier is kept in ever-extending employment by the fact that horse riding is second only to fishing as the most practised British sport. In the upper corners of the window are indications of the medals and qualifications awarded by the Company, and at the base are the badges of institutions with which the Company works in close liaison, including the Royal Army Veterinary Corps. At the bottom right are the Arms and Monogram of the donors of the window, Mr. Deputy S.R. Walker, CBE, Mr. Deputy L.B. Prince, CBE, MA and Mr. G. Allison-Beer, lately Deputy. At the centre-base is the Patron Saint of Farriers, St. Eligius, known in England as St. Loo.'

Farriers Clock

In December 1961 the Clerk reported that the Reverend Russell Chapman of Chilbolton acting as Executor of an estate had, with the approval of Mrs. J. Beven, the daughter of the deceased, offered to the Company a grand-father clock believed to have been specially made for the Great Exhibition 1851, depicting in a scene above the clock face a farrier working at his anvil. The farrier strikes blows with his hammer in time with the movement of the clock and at each hour a second figure appears in the scene and strikes the hours on a bell. A condition of the offer was that the clock should be housed in the City. The Clerk reported that as time was short, to prevent the clock being included in an auction sale, he had proceeded to make the best arrangements he could to secure the clock for the Company and that it was now standing in Cutlers Hall by kind permission of the Master, Wardens and Court of that Company who had agreed to house the clock without payment subject, however, to the Company making its own insurance arrangements. Insurance in the sum of £100 had accordingly been effected by the Clerk and suitable letters of thanks had been sent to the Reverend Russell Chapman, Mrs. J. Beven and to the Cutlers Company.

In September 1962 the Clerk reported that he had now heard from the Worshipful Company of Clockmakers in regard to the clock recently given to the Company. He had been advised that the clock was of considerable interest and was most unusual being a fine specimen of its type; the maker, James Poole, was not well known though James M. Poole and John Poole (possibly his sons) were famous chronometer makers: no similar clock was known to the Guild.

In September 1975, Mr. Past Master George Garnham drew attention to the Clockmakers Company collection of timepieces in the new library at Guildhall and wondered if this would not be a better place for the Company's clock as it would be more accessible for Liverymen and others to view it. Its present situation at Cutlers Hall was rarely seen by Members of the Farriers Company other than when Dinners were held there. It was agreed that the Clock be offered to Guildhall on permanent loan provided the Cutlers Company had no objection to its being removed.

In December the Clerk reported that it was not possible for the Company's Clock to be placed on permanent loan with the display of timepieces in Guildhall Library due to reasons of space. Accordingly, Past Master Deputy Walker undertook to see whether the Clock could be housed somewhere in Guildhall where it could be on view to members of the Company and public generally. The Clock has now been accepted by the Corporation of London on permanent loan and, completely restored at a cost of £450, it stands in the Ambulatory in Guildhall. (It is fully insured for the sum of £12,000).

Armorial Bearings
On 24th June 1841 'The Clerk read a letter addressed to him from the Clerk of Christ's Hospital Newgate Street stating that the Governors of Christ's Hospital having appropriated a portion of the Window of their Great Hall to such of the Companies as might be desirous of placing therein their Armorial Bearings and desiring to know whether it will be agreeable to the Farriers Company to contribute their Armorial Bearings (as several Companies named in the Letter had done) the same to be executed on Stained Glass at an expense to the Company of £10. 10s. 0d. Resolved that inasmuch as the Measure would be a useless and unnecessary expense to the Company it is not expedient to adopt it.'

In 1974 a Stained Glass Window depicting the Company's Armorial Bearings was placed in the crypt – the gift of Past Masters S.R. Walker, L.B. Prince and G. Allison-Beer. (See supra for the artist's description)

The Author is indebted to Garter King of Arms, Mr. A.C. Cole, CVO, CC for supplying the following History of the Company's Armorial Bearings.

'There could be no more appropriate device for a farrier or shoesmith than the horseshoes which are the distinctive feature of the Shield of Arms which the Farriers Company has used for many generations in its history.

The earliest records of the Arms which the Company assumed for itself is found in a manuscript of 1591 in the British Museum (Harliean M S 2220) that is to say there is therein depicted Arms of:

'Argent three horseshoes Sable'
A Silver shield with horseshoes placed upon in black is a striking combination and served the Company, it would seem, for a good number of years, without more, but in the 17th Century there is evidence of a Crest being taken into use as also Supporters to Shield, Arms, Crest and Supporters thus constituting the Farriers

Achievement of Arms which are found illustrated in the manner of the time in Richard Wallis's London's Armory published in 1677 and as plate 59 this is reproduced in the 1914 edition of this work compiled by Charles Welch FSA sometime Librarian of the Guildhall Library, he giving the blazon or formal discription of the Armorial Bearings and Supporters used by the Farriers Company as follows:

'Argent three horseshoes Sable pierced of the field. Crest: an arm embowed issuing from clouds on the sinister side all proper holding in the hand a hammer Azure handled and ducally crowned Or. Supporters: two horses Argent.

Motto: Vi et Virtute.

Although the obvious symbolism and general suitability of these Armorial Bearings is apparent, or probably because of this, the Company left it until the 20th century before making application for a formal grant of Armorial Bearings by Letters Patent of the Kings of Arms, this being the only way in which authentic Armorial Bearings can be established, since the Kings of Arms began to exercise their granting powers, first exemplified by Garter King of Arms in 1439 when he devised "Insignia in the form of Arms" to and for the Drapers Company.

The irregularity of the use which Farriers had made of Arms, Crest and Supporters, notwithstanding their suitability as significant of the craft, having been remarked, in 1968 the Farriers under their corporate name of the Master, Wardens, Assistants and Commonalty of the Company of Farryers of London petitioned by Memorial that the Kings of Arms might grant and confirm the Arms Crest and Supporters which had been hitherto used so as to enable them to bear and use the same in future with such distinction as might be considered fit and proper, with minor differences, to prevent confusion with any similar Arms Crest and Supporters already on the Register maintained at the College of Arms.

Letters Patents under the hands and seals of the Kings of Arms were duly issued, the description or blazon thereof being in the language of heraldry as follows:

"Argent three horseshoes on a bordure Sable three nails pallwise Argent and for the Crest an arm embowed issuing from clouds from the sinister side all proper holding in the hand a Farrier's hammer Azure hafted and crowned Or, 'and for the Supporters,' on either side a horse Argent gorged with a collar pendant therefrom a sword Gules".

These Armorial Bearings and Supporters were granted and confirmed to be borne and used for ever hereafter by the Master, Wardens, Assistants and Commonalty of the Company of Farryers of London on its Common Seal or otherwise according to the Laws of Arms.

It will be observed that the distinctions which were necessary were carefully conceived so as not to alter the essential nature of the devices which had been used by the Farriers in that as regards the Arms a black border was added with three nails thereon significant in themselves of the Farriers craft, crowned rather than having a ducal coronet ensigning its head, and the horses as Supporters were linked with the City of London by having a City sword, representing that of St. Paul, attached to a collar about each horses neck, red upon white, in allusion to the City's colours of Argent and Gules'.

Incidentally the City sword of St. Paul, contrary to popular belief, *pre-dates* the famous Wat Tyler dagger used by Mayor Sir William Wadworth at Blackheath.

Readers may recognise the similarity to the Arms of the various branches of the Norman family of de Ferres – for example, the present editor's mother's family of Ferres in the West Country bore arms 'Or on a bend sable three horseshoes argent.'

CHAPTER 4

The Craft and the History of the Registration Committee

During 1975 the Farriers Registration Bill finally became Law, under the title Farriers (Registration) Act 1975, through the great effort of Lord Newell and Mr. Michael Mates MP, in steering the Bill through its very tortuous stages. The Act must go a long way to raising and maintaining standards of Farriery in the United Kingdom. The future is mainly in the hands of the Farriers Registration Council set up under the Act, but the National Master Farriers, Blacksmiths' and Agricultural Engineers' Association and the Farriers Company have great responsibility to do all in their power to assist the Council. It is clear that the Act will restore the Company to the premier position it had held in the 14th Century unlike many Guilds whose main purpose had fallen away in the 19th Century following the Industrial Revolution.

It is interesting to note that the Worshipful Company has now gone full circle, if not to 1356 when its jurisdiction was confined to the 'Cities of London and Westminster and seven miles beyond', at least to 1890 when a Registration Committee was set up with the object of registering all existing farriers in the United Kingdom and, presumably, all future entrants to the Trade by examination. As is the case with anything that is not compulsory, the registration scheme was not successful, at least in the long run, and the Act has given that compulsion lacking in the early days of the present Century.

It is worthy to note that under the Interpretation Clause 18 of the Act, the 'Company' means

'The Worshipful Company of Farriers being the Livery Company of the City of London bearing that name and incorporated by Royal Charter dated the seventeenth day of January 1674, granted by the late Majesty King Charles II.'

To quote from the Ordinances of the Farriers:

'The year of Grace 1356
To Henry Pycard, Mayor, and the Aldermen of the City of London, shew the good folks, the Master Farriers of the same city, that whereas many offences and great damages had been committed as against persons of the Court, and the commonalty of the same City and of all the realm, by people not wise therein, who kept forges in the said city, and intermeddles with works of farriery, which they did not understand how to bring to good end; by reason whereof, many horses had been lost, to the great damage of the people:
therefore the said Mayor caused to be summoned before him all the farriers of the said City, and to be chosen among them two Masters, the most sufficient men, and the best knowing; that is to say Richard de Hertele and John de Oxenford; whom the said Mayor caused to be sworn, and gave them full power to oversee and govern the said trade . . .'

Horse shoeing as it is known today probably did not begin until about the ninth century as, before the days of artificial roads, it was not essential for horses to wear shoes – a hippo sandal strapped to the horse's foot, possibly to hobble the horse and not to protect its feet whilst travelling. There is no indication that at that time iron shoes were used. The first Smithies began to appear in about the thirteenth century. In 1235 Walter le Brun, Farrier, put up a forge in the Strand on condition he should pay an annual quit rent. Today this annual payment is celebrated by the Quit Rent Ceremony which is fully described elsewhere in this volume. So perhaps it is not suprising that in 1356 the Mayor summoned the Farriers of the City as many offences and dangers had been committed in the City and the Realm 'by people not wise therein' who kept forges in the City and intermeddles with the works of farriery which they did not understand, with the resultant loss of many horses.

Thus the discipline of the trade began and it is now interesting to note that Section 18 of the 1975 Act interprets 'farriery' to mean any work in connection with the preparation or treatment of the foot of the horse for the immediate reception of a shoe thereon, the fitting by nailing or otherwise of a shoe to the foot or the finish off such work to the foot.

The Minutes of the Company and the Minutes of the Registration Committee (appointed by the Court of the Company) over the many centuries show how the Company has tried to continue to control the trade. Its weakness was the lack of authority to proceed against anyone who created an offence. Over the centuries the Company had done its best to attract all those practising in Farriery to join the Company. This volume has not set out to contain the many references in the Minutes referring to the Farriery trade – what it has tried to do is to show notwithstanding its lack of resources, the attempt to keep its interest in the shoeing of horses and its connection with the City of London. The story of the Registration Committee started in 1890, following the meeting at the Mansion House, described elsewhere. The Court had appointed a Sub-Committee in March 1890 to make arrangements in regard to the Meeting to be held at the Mansion House.

'In May 1890 a report headed "National Examination and Registration of Farriers or Shoeing Smiths" stated that by kind consent of the Rt. Honourable the Lord Mayor (Sir Henry Aaron Isaac) a meeting in furtherance of the objects of the scheme has been fixed for the 2nd June 1890 when his Lordship the Lord Mayor consented to take the Chair. In order to make the meeting a thoroughly representative and successful one, already over 2000 invitations to Noblemen and Gentlemen on the subject asking for this formal approval of the Scheme and their attendance at the meeting.'

Then followed a list of distinguished persons including The Rt. Hon. the Earl of Coventry (Master of Her Majesty's Buckhounds),

'The President of the Royal Agricultural Society, Lord Dorchester etc. etc. and many apologies for non-attendance etc.'

The Report stated that 18 of the leading Livery Companies had been prayed for a grant of moneys towards the object of the Scheme. Then follows a list of donations, including £150 from the Royal Agricultural Society payable in three instalments conditional on the whole Guarantee Fund of £200 per annum being raised;

The Drapers Company	£150
N & M Rothschild and Son	£ 52. 10. 0d;
The Leathersellers	£ 21. 0. 0d,

Making a sum of £668. 9. 0d guaranteed to the present date, and that a separate account to be opened at the Bank of England, to be called the 'Farriers Company Registration Account.'

At the Court meeting on the 24th June 1890 the Minutes give a very detailed account of the proceedings of the Meeting at the Mansion House presided over by the Lord Mayor. It is reported that there was a very good attendance and the meeting was most successful, listing out some of the important people who were present.

Among the Resolutions passed were those to the effect:
'1 that it was highly desirable that arrangements be made to promote the Technical Instruction and Systematic Registration of Farriers

or Shoeing Smiths throughout the country and;

2   that the meeting approve of the Scheme and amended in conference by the Farriers Company, the Royal Agricultural Society and the Royal College of Veterinary Surgeons;

3   that the Farriers Company proceed at once to organise the Registration Committee and that Subscription be invited from the public towards the expenses of working the Scheme.'

The Registration Committee set up at the Mansion House, met at the Albion Tavern, Aldersgate Street in the City of London on the 3rd June 1890. The President of the Royal Agricultural Society of England, the Rt. Hon. Lord Moreton, was elected Chairman for the ensuing year.

'That Mr. Wynne Edwin Baxter (Clerk of the Company) be elected Secretary of the Committee and the Services of Mr. Thomas Hancock be continued as Clerk of the Registration Committee at a salary of £2, he to give his entire time to the duties.'

It is of interest to note that Mr. Fred John Young of the well known firm of Turquands Young and Company had been appointed Auditor.

'That two rooms at 9 Lawrence Pountney Hill (the Clerk's office) at £90 per annum including rates, taxes and attendance. Following instructions given to the Secretary regarding the carrying out of the Scheme, it was agreed that the next meeting be held 28th July 1890 at the Guildhall. It was also agreed that the Master of the Worshipful Company of Farriers be Vice Chairman for the ensuing year.'

The Minutes concluded as follows:

'It was understood that the Master of the Farriers Company retired at the end of the ensuing year become Chairman for the next year and the President of the Veterinary College, Vice Chairman, and so on.'

The first Minute Book of the Registration Committee covering seventeen years (1890–1907) contains 455 pages. Finance again played its main part, for the list of subscriptions promised mentioned in the Minutes of the second meeting showed a total of £1439.5s.0d (received £783.3s.0d) of which £300 was promised by the Farriers Company and of which £100 had been paid. Reference has been made to the appeals to the Senior Livery Companies and Seven Companies, viz: The Drapers, Mercers, Grocers, Clothworkers, Leathersellers, Merchant-Taylors and the Salters, together had contributed a total sum of £315.

It was from this point that the work of the Registration Committee and Farriery began to spread its wings. In 1356 and again in the Charter of 1674 the 'Area' means the Cities of London and Westminster or within seven miles thereof. In 1890 the Registration Committee consisting of representatives of the Royal

Agricultural Society of England, the Royal College of Veterinary Surgeons and the Worshipful Company of Farriers was formed to carry out the Scheme of the Worshipful Company of Farriers for the National Registration of Farriers or Shoeing Smiths to cover the United Kingdom.

In 1891 the first Report gave a list containing the names and addresses of the men registered up to the 15th August 1891 of no less than 3230 of the applications received and passed, and Certificates of Registration signed by the Master and Clerk of the Farriers Company. The list beginning alphabetically with the Army, Anglesea to York – 58 towns and cities. 900 copies of the list had been sold to Registered Shoeing Smiths at one shilling each, and postage. The Cash Statement showed that £1127.17s.0d had been received in subscriptions and donations towards the objects of the Scheme; Registration Fees amounted to £889, Examination Fees £4.0s.0d, Sales of Lists to £13.11s.11d (sic). Total receipts £2035.8s.11d, Expenditure £1093.16s.4½d – a *surplus* of £930.11s.6½d – a strange word in the History of the Company. However, this position did not last for long. Annual deficits ate into the small working capital and by 1895 this sum was reduced to less than £100 and the Annual Report on that year read:

'The Committee realising that their funds were becoming small, and with a view of placing the Scheme upon a footing to secure in continuity, appointed a Sub-Committee to enquire into the matter . . . The Committee then most earnestly and with confidence appeal to the horse-owning public.''

This Appeal brought in very little money, and resulted in a later Minute:

"Your Committee is asked whether they can suggest any better means to approach such persons including Vestries, Railway Companies, Brewers, Carrying Agents etc.'

The Minutes disclosed year by year the activities of the Registration Scheme but it is evident that the Scheme was not really progressing in the sense of the 1890 optimism. In 1902 the Report disclosed that during 1899 only 281 Smiths were examined, 205 passed as RSS and that the balance of Receipts over Expenditure was £3.4s.9d, but by 1901 it had become a deficit of £99.8s.11d and in 1902 a deficit of £115.16s.5d.

The Report for 1902 read as follows:

'The Committee much regret that the Funds placed at their disposal for the purpose of organising and carrying on the Scheme, have now been reduced to £100 and if the deficit for the coming year is a similar amount to that in this year just closed, the whole of the funds will be exhausted and a liability created. It is necessary therefore that

115

immediate steps should be taken for the purpose of obtaining fresh moneys.'

In the meantime the finances of the Company itself were at its lowest – an example of its position is shown as follows:

A Resolution which appeared in December 1903:

'It was proposed by the Master that the following cheques be drawn:

Quarters Clerical Assistance	25.	0.	0d
Geo Smith & Co Advisory	11.	2.	10d
Baxter & Co (standing of type re list)	1.	1.	2d
H.W. Brown (Books supplied)	1.	18.	8d
Petty Cash	5.	0.	0d
	£44.	2.	8d

With a note following that these cheques shall not be paid away till the balance at the Bankers had been materially increased.'

In February 1903 the Registration Committee had decided to obtain a referendum from the County Council's Agricultural and other bodies. It was sent by the Company and read as follows:

'Dear Sir
As you are probably aware, it is now over 10 years since the Scheme for the Registration of Farriers was inaugurated, and, in the opinion of the Committee, ample time has now been given for a second judgement to be formed of the value of the Scheme to those in whose interest it was started.
The Committee are desirous of obtaining the opinion of those competent to judge on the matter, and they would be much obliged if you would kindly fill in the answers to the Questions on the enclosed form and return the same to me at your earliest convenience.
I am, Dear Sir,
Yours faithfully,
Wynne E. Baxter, Clerk.'

And the Questions were:

'1   Is the Scheme in your opinion a benefit to the Farriers generally?
2   Have the Classes which have been formed in various parts of the Country been a means of increasing the interest of the men in the Trade, and of producing better workmen?
3   Do you consider that the Examinations are conducted in such a manner as to thoroughly test the efficiency of those concerned?'

In February 1904 the Clerk reported that the answers had now been received from all the Bodies, Societies and Institutions upon the scope and effect of the whole Registration Scheme and that without exception the replies, although couched in different terms, were in favour of the continuation of the Committee's functions as a benefit to the trade and the Country. The Council of

The Farriers Clock – made for the Great Exhibition 1851, depicting in a scene above the clock face a farrier working at his anvil.

Some of the Company's Silver (from left to right). Back: The J.R. Cooper Rose Water Dish, The Herbert Fenton Loving Cup, The George Mills Loving Cup. Middle: The Horatio Stewart Loving Cup, The Two-handled Cup of 1778, The Joseph Pyke Tankard. Front: The Montague Salver, The Harris Salver.

Master's and Wardens' Chain and Badges. From left: The Clerk's Badge. The Master's Badge and Chain and a Court Medal. A Warden's Badge.

the Royal College of Veterinary Surgeons were especially thanked for their favourable opinion as to the effect of the Scheme. Their opinions, of course, were a great encouragement to the Committee. Accordingly it was decided that the following towns would be selected for holding examinations and arranged when desirable:

Chester, Melton Mowbray, Brighton or Chichester, Cardiff, Carlisle, Stafford, Ross, Cambridge, Northampton and London. Two Past Masters of the Company, Mr. Campbell Bayard (1892–93) and Mr. Barnes Wimbush (1890–91) as representatives of the Company were elected to serve on the Provincial Committee for Yorkshire and other Provincial Committees invited the Company to have discussion with a view to the revival of the Registration Scheme.

(At the next meeting Mr. Thurtle and Mr. Mills, members of the Company and appointed members of the Registration Committee, presented to the Company a splendid piece of workmanship contained in the Mounted Hoof shod by them).

In June 1903 the Dollar family were at issue with the Company and the Chapter on Masters give details which took place at the Court meeting. A Report had been made to the Court regarding Mr. J.A.W. Dollar's letter to the 'Veterinary Record' which caused a controversy at a meeting of the Royal College of Veterinary Surgeons. This very detailed report shows that there had been 'trouble and misunderstanding'. Mr. Dollar had made certain charges against the Registration Committee including the charge that the letters RSS have 'in a vast number of instances been misused by farriers in order to give the public a false impression of the nature of their qualifications.'

'That the Registration Committee had flooded the country with densly ignorant farriers' and that 'for some years there has been no legally elected Registration Committee, the body of which has assumed that name being constituted quite otherwise than provided in the original prospectus.'

The Report continues that Mr. Dollar's charges had not been substantiated although the names of offenders who have been convicted of a breach of the Veterinary Surgeons Act of 1881 had not been removed from the Register. The Report clearly shows that there certainly had been troubles with the Registration Committee and concluded:

'From the letter to the Clerk dated 25th June 1903 it seems that Mr. Dollar was under the impression that I (Past Master Lambert – the Arbiter) had been entrusted with the duty of stating whether in my opinion 'the operations of the Registration Committee should continue.' This is not the view which I take of my position. I understand that I was to look into the question in dispute, and do what I could to state those questions and the facts bearing upon them in such a form as to furnish material which might be of service to the Court in considering what course it will be expedient to take. This I have endeavoured to do.'

Finally, the Court passed the following Resolution:

'that the Registration Committee having performed their most difficult task to the best of their ability, be requested to continue their exertions in connection with the Registration Scheme which in the opinion of the Court, although capable of improvement, is still doing a useful and beneficial work.'

Then appeared in 1904 a Report surveying the work of the Committee from 1890, recommending that all Shoeing Smiths above the age of 23 and having had three years practical experience, should be admitted without examination up to 31st December 1890, later extended to 31st March 1891, subject to two satisfactory testimonials. 3,800 applicants had been received and by 15th August 1,901 had been registered.

So matters continued – year by year the financial position did not improve. It is almost unbelievable that such financial frustration had not weakened the efforts of all those concerned. It is supposed that such reports as shown in the 1906 Report revived their optimism:

The Committee Report of 31st May 1906 read as follows:
1   That in their opinion the Scheme should not be under any circumstances, abandoned especially considering the trouble and expense that have been bestowed upon it for so many years and the large experience which has been gained with regard to the working of the Scheme and the numerous evidences of success and appreciation which have been given by Shoeing Smiths and others throughout the country, and the knowledge that in Victoria, Australia and New Zealand a similar scheme is shortly expected to be formed and the Committee of the Registration Scheme has been asked to advise the Education Department of these Colonies with regard to the matter.
2   That the Committee strongly recommend the Court to grant such a sum of money, not exceeding £100 per annum as may be found necessary for the working of the Scheme.
3   That in order to consolidate the financial basis of the Scheme, and to extend its scope, efforts should be made to obtain grants and subscriptions from suitable sources.'

So the Registration Committee continued when in 1910 an apprenticeship scheme appears to have been started. The Minutes of the 28th April 1910 of the Court of the Company contain the following:

'The Registration Committee beg to report that the decision of the Court to provide a sum of £50 per annum for inaugurating an Apprenticeship Scheme, such Scheme to be left to the Committee to formulate, was accepted by the Committee with much pleasure and at their first meeting on the 16th February last the matter was discussed at considerable length. Having regard to the funds available, the Committee decided to limit the Scheme to the sons of registered shoeing smiths and an advertisement was inserted in the Farriers Journal inviting applications from Apprentices and Masters desirous of taking advantage of the scheme. Only two applications on behalf of Apprentices however have been received, one from a Country Farrier Instructor on behalf of his son and one from a Master who desired to apprentice his son to himself. The latter application was rejected by the Committee as not being within the spirit of the scheme and consequently there remained only one applicant to select from.

Under these circumstances the Committee have not felt justified in proceeding further with the Scheme until the Court had had an opportunity of again considering the matter. The Committee are of the opinion that in view of these facts there appears to be no desire on the part of the Registered Shoeing Smiths to take advantage of the Company's Scheme. They therefore beg to suggest that in lieu thereof the Court should place at their disposal a sum to be expended in Prizes to encourage candidates to be examined for the Company's Certificates which they consider would give a great stimulus to the Registration Scheme and would be the means of inducing a larger number of candidates to enter for the Examination.'

In consequence, the Court passed the following Resolution:

'That in view of the facts disclosed by the Report of the Registration Committee the Court are of the opinion that the Apprenticeship Scheme should not be definitely abandoned but they are agreeable and hereby authorise the Committee to expend at their direction the sum of £25 out of the £50 already voted for presenting medals, prizes or awards to advance the Registration Scheme and that the balance of £25 be for the present retained by the Committee on account of the Apprenticeship Scheme.'

At this point the Author has considered that enough has been written to give readers the story of the 'Struggle of Two Decades' for the survival of the Company's Farriers Scheme – starting at the high point of the Mansion House Meeting in 1890 to its nadir in 1910. The Registration Committee remained in being – reports appearing year after year but only the awarding of medals being subsidised by the Company.

At this point in the history of the Registration Scheme it is regretted that the records between the years 1907–1938 are not available, the Minute book having been lost. Fortunately, the Court Minutes do from time to time show the recommendations of the Registration Committee and it is from this source that the author continues his narrative.

In 1909 there was a recommendation from the Registration

Committee that Associates of the Company be permitted to use the letters AFCL (Associate of the Farriers Company London) and after some discussion the recommendation of the Committee was adopted. This is an interesting Minute for as recently as June 1979 a discussion took place in the Court as to whether these letters be continued. It appears that there is no society or organisation known as the Association of the Farriers Company London but it was a qualification passed by candidates who were examined by County Education Authorities Technical Schools. At this recent Court Meeting it was pointed out that the Trade would object to any alterations in this traditional qualification, although it would seem to be illogical to allow the letters to be used by Farriers of a non-existent body.

In 1918 two Members of the Amalgamated Society of Farriers were added to the Committee.

In 1921 there appears in the Court Minutes a reference to the Alteration of Rules with a view to improving the status of Associates and Registered Shoeing Smiths and the syllabus for the RSS was set out in full with all the necessary questions that candidates be required to answer for the RSS Certificate or AFCL Examination. These questions are so detailed and technical as would take up too much space in this volume but it is interesting to see that the syllabus contains the following: 'That all examiners provide themselves with a set of shoes surgical or otherwise so as to determine the knowledge of the candidates in the application of the various shoes used in horse-shoeing'.

During the period from 1909–1938 the Registration Committee Minutes do not contain many items of interest other than the detailing of prizes and medals presented at Horse Competitions through the Royal Agricultural Society.

The Company was still subsidising the Registration Committee to a maximum of £50 and each year the election of members of the Registration Committee was recorded.

In 1928 the Registration Committee was showing a very considerable decrease in the number of men examined in comparison with the previous four years and it was decided to strengthen the membership of the Committee by inviting the various Societies interested in the horse to nominate members.

In 1928 the Court reconsidered the recommendation of the Registration Committee with reference to the progress made in the proposed scheme for the compulsory registration of Farriers and Shoeing Smiths. After due consideration the Court came to the conclusion that having regard to the general political situation and the consequent pressure of business in the House of Commons, it would be practically impossible for a Private Member's Bill to have a chance of being passed and consequently it was agreed that the matter should stand over.

So it took nearly fifty years for the Farriers Registration Act to be passed in 1975.

In 1930 in a Report the Registration Committee was asked to consider and advise the Court as to the reason of the failure of the workings of the Registration Committee. The Minutes do not disclose any reference to this matter but in 1932 it was obviously finance again, for an appeal was made to all members of the Livery Company for a donation towards the funds of the Registration Scheme.

In 1935 the Annual Report of the Registration Committee for the year ended 31st December 1934 dealt very fully with the position. Again it was pointed out that there was a considerable decrease in the number of men examined and a consequent reduction in the amount of Examination Fees received. The Accounts show a deficiency of £64.6s.4d. A Conference had been held with the representatives of the National Master Farriers and Blacksmiths Association and the Amalgamated Society of Farriers and Blacksmiths and at that Conference it had been recommended that the Court of Assistants be asked to contribute £100 towards the salary of £150 paid to the Clerk of the Registration Committee, that an appeal be made to the two Trade Associations mentioned above for immediate financial assistance, and also that the Court be asked to appeal to the various City Livery Companies and others interested, for donations to enable the work of the Registration Scheme to be continued. It was also proposed that each of the twenty-two Branches of the Trade Associations be asked to inaugurate an organising campaign in each of their centres to bring to the notice of all farriers the benefits they would derive by obtaining certificates of the Farriers Company.

Finally, in view of the pressing need for economy, that all examiners fees be reduced by one-third and only one examiner be required to conduct any AFCL Examination and that the papers relating to the written part of such examination be submitted to an appointed Veterinary Surgeon for adjudication and marking, thus saving the fees and expenses of the personal attendance of a Veterinary Surgeon.

In 1938 the question of Farriery education had been raised by the Ministry of Agriculture and Fisheries.

On the 15th February it was reported that a letter from the Ministry regarding Farriery Education was received in order to arrange a meeting in conjunction with the National Master Farrier and the Blacksmiths Association and the Amalgamated Society of Farriers and Blacksmiths, the National Farmers Union and the Rural District Bureau. The Farriers Company was invited to send representatives.

It was not until January 1940, when the Registration Committee next met, that a report on the above meeting was reported. Mr. Holleyman FWCF, the Vice Chairman of the Registration Committee had represented the Company and he reported that the subject 'Farriery Education' proved to be 'Training of Village Smiths for Tractor Service Works'. He considered that Farriery interests appeared to be lacking and he left the meeting feeling that there was little hope of help for the Craft from Government sources, and it was Resolved:

'THAT the subject of the proposed Compulsory Registration of Farriers through a Parliamentary Bill be deferred until the end of the existing state of War appears to be in sight and the moment seems opportune for further earnest consideration of the matter, and also that the Clerk be directed to inform the Secretary of the Yorkshire Farriers' Education and Demonstration Association of the Committee's interest and views on the subject.'

In the meantime, the Meeting of the Court on 19th December 1939 had considered the whole matter of the Registration Committee. A sub-Committee was set up to examine the whole position. A lengthy report was made and inter alia there appears to have been financial irregularities going back to the year 1931. The word 'irregularities' seems serious but in the Author's opinion only consisted of confused book-keeping. The report quotes:

'I do not know how this happened. I was not the Auditor in those days but it explains clearly the time lag which I could not understand.'

To summarise; the Accounts at 25th June 1939 showed a deficit of £63.15s.0d. The Court decided to clear the deficit by making a grant of £75 which, with the annual subsidy of £100, made the Registration Committee solvent!

The Author, in quoting from Robson's History, published in 1949, which covered the story of the Registration Committee from 1890 to 1948 in rather glowing terms, and omitting any financial worries, can only therefore give a general picture of the farriery trade sponsored by the Company during those years.

'. . . The Company also remembers with pride the assistance which, through this scheme, it was able to afford to the military authorities during the First World War by providing them with the names of upwards of 4,500 qualified farriers when they were in desperate need of shoeing smiths in the various theatres of war.

Since the close of the Second World War the examinations which have been in abeyance during that period, have been resumed, much to the interest of the Craft. Many leading members of the Royal College of Veterinary Surgeons are giving valuable help by their advice and by acting as examiners for the higher Diplomas. The Masters' Association of the craft is also taking great interest in the work, while various Associations interested in the Horse are showing their active support by giving substantial financial assistance to the furtherance of the Company's efforts. It is sometimes stated that the days of the Horse are over. This is quite an erroneous conclusion, for, even in this mechanical age, there is still a very large number of horses in use. One has only to mention such activities as short haulage in and around our towns, agriculture, livery stables, hunting, racing and stud farms, to realise that an estimate of the present requirements in this country for all purposes at a million is not exaggerated.

Originally the farrier was not only a shoeing smith but also a horse doctor. Now he only deals with the shoeing, though the Company's examination requires him to have some knowledge of the anatomy of the necessary parts of the Horse; the horse's health is now, very properly, in the hands of the Veterinary Surgeon. The Court of this ancient Company feels that in continuing the Registration Scheme, it is indeed fulfilling one of the main objects of its formation, namely to assure that only good and worthy craftsmen carry on the trade.

A bad shoeing smith may do almost irreparable damage to a fine animal. Such a calamity can be avoided by referring to the Company for information as to the Certificate held. In this way the owner can ascertain definitely and quickly whether the Smith in question is properly qualified or not.'

At this point the Author cannot refrain from referring to the Minutes of 13th January 1936 for there were two entries on the same page of the Minute Book, firstly:

'Mr. Leslie B. Prince MA FCA attended the Court and made free of the Company by redemption.'

and secondly:

'The Recommendations of the Registration Committee to consider and if thought expedient to oppose the Ban on Horses being employed on the streets of London was accepted and the matter was referred back to the Registration Committee to frame a Resolution on the subject if thought advisable.'

Of these two entries, a fair amount has been heard of the first but no further reference to such a ban can be traced in the second entry.

It was in January 1940 that the following Minute appeared:

'The letter received from Mr. C. Richardson FWCF on the subject of the shortage of farriers rendered more acute by the enlistment of young farriers in the Royal Air Force was considered, but it was Resolved THAT no action be taken in relation to the matter.'

Again at the same meeting a Deficit of £15.9s.8d was shown in the 1939 accounts. The report to the Court was merely received as it had been circulated to all members prior to the meeting and it is interesting to note that the Senior Warden, Mr. F.M. Garnham particularly thanked the Master for doing so as it had given the Court ample time to consider its report. Apart from reporting deficits each year, there appeared to be very little else to report apart from appointments, resignations and votes of thanks to members who had devoted so much time to Registration Committee matters.

At this point in the story the Author can pass over the History of Craft Activities to those who have knowledge first hand, for it is those in the Veterinary profession who are to report from 1949 to 1972 – Dr. W.R. Wooldridge, MSc, DVSc, FRCVS, FRICS, Scientific Director of the Animal Health Trust; Alec Hobson, CBE, MVO who had been Secretary of the Royal Agricultural Society for many years, and the final seven years by Mr. Franklin Birch, Registrar, with a conclusion by Sir Hugh Linstead. Naturally these accounts must of necessity repeat some matters researched by the Author in his history of the sixty years and of which no record had previously been made available, and it is hoped that this repetition will give additional emphasis.

As has been stated above, in 1890, following the meeting at the Mansion House, the Worshipful Company of Farriers inaugurated its Registration Scheme for Shoeing Smiths. The duty of carrying out this part of the Company's work was delegated to a Registration Committee which has run three examinations at different levels to test the efficiency of farriers, and has awarded medals for the winners of farriery competitions at various agricultural shows. The examinations are for Registered Shoeing Smiths (RSS); the Association of the Farriers Company of London (AFCL) and the Fellowship of the Worshipful Company of Farriers (FWCF), the latter being the Company's highest award.

During the early part of this century the number of successful candidates in the examinations varied each year from around 80 to 100; but latterly the annual average has been lower. Thus during the period in which the late Professor J.B. Buxton MA FRCVS was the Chairman of the Registration Committee, namely from 1946 to 1953, the average number of candidates each year was 44. Over the same period an average of 41 medals per annum were awarded at approximately 20 Agricultural shows. Following Professor Buxton's death Mr. George Bowman FWCF became Chairman but after a year or two the Committee went into abeyance, partly owing to financial difficulties. During the earlier part of the century, examination fees, donations from the Company and specific appeals to bodies and individuals interested in the Horse were enough to finance the examinations and the awards of medals. After the establishment of the Racecourse Totalisator Charity Trust, the Company received a reasonable financial support for its work for Farriery until a doubt arose as to whether the Company was using the grant as well as it might.

In 1947 the 10th Duke of Devonshire was admitted as a Member of the Court of Assistants and his early death in December 1950 came as a severe shock to the Company. Early in 1951 it was announced that his son, the 11th Duke, had accepted the Company's invitation to join the Court. His Grace became Master of the Company in 1956 during the sexcentenary celebration of the Company's Fellowship. Realising the implication of this situation he decided that it was desirable to re-stimulate this important activity of the Company and he therefore called together a meeting of all organisations interested in the Horse with the object of discussing in the broadest way the future of Farriery.

Representatives were present from the Worshipful Company of Farriers, the Royal Agricultural Society and the Rural Industries Bureau, the National Master Farriers Association, the Hunters' Improvement Society, The National Union of Agricultural Workers, The Royal College of Veterinary Surgeons, The British Veterinary Association, The British Horse Society, The Jockey Club and the Animal Health Trust.

The Committee made an exhaustive review of the situation and set up a special sub-committee, known as the Animal Health Trust Farriery Committee, under the Chairmanship of Dr. W.R. Wooldridge, MSc, DVSc, FRCVS, FRICS, a member of the Worshipful Company's Registration Committee and Scientific Director of the Animal Health Trust.

The report of this Committee stated that the number of practicing farriers appeared to be of the order of 1,500 although the register of the Worshipful Company of Farriers showed that about 10,000 candidates had passed the examination for the Company's Shoeing Smith Certificate. Unfortunately, there was no ready means of telling how many of these farriers were still working at their craft.

The Committee found that there was no nationally co-ordinated scheme for the training of young farriers in spite of the Worshipful Company's examinations. Intending recruits either became apprenticed to established blacksmiths or attended one of the few local technical colleges which provided Farriery courses. 'The greatest difficulty' said the report, 'is that such courses give only about a third of their time to farriery, the remainder being devoted to other branches of engineering, with the result that most pupils develop a liking for other branches and do not continue with the practice of farriery.'

A further drawback to the present scheme, declared the Report, was that insufficient time was given to practical experience in 'live' farriery, and it was suggested that opportunities for this type of work could be best provided at centres where numbers of horses were still maintained, such as the Headquarters of the Royal Army Veterinary Corps at Melton Mowbray, the Equine Research Station of the Animal Health Trust, or at certain university veterinary schools.

The type of future training courses envisaged by the Report would enable three branches, i.e. a period of study at a technical college, a further period on 'live' farriery at one of the centres mentioned, and a pupilage with a registered farrier, the whole to be covered by the examinations and certificates of the Worshipful Company of Farriers.

The Committee felt that it was imperative that some form of financial assistance should be given to farriery students. On learning of the proposed scheme, the Racecourse Totalisator Charity Trust agreed to assist this work again, provided other organisations interested in equine matters would support the scheme.

This Committee then held a joint Meeting with the Registration Committee of the Worshipful Company of Farriers and it was agreed that this scheme would be carefully considered by the Registration Committee and put into effect so far as were possible. For an interim period it was arranged that the Animal Health Trust should receive moneys from the Racecourse Totalisator Charity Trust to enable the scheme to be put into operation, and the Animal Health Trust notified the Worshipful Company that it was prepared to finance its work for farriery along the recommended lines until the Horserace Betting Levy Board, the successor to the Racecourse Totalisator Charity Trust, would be prepared to make a direct grant to the Worshipful Company.

The history of the Registration Committee and the craft activities of the Company of the last two decades can best be followed by breaking it up into three periods: the Chairmanship of Past Master Dr. W.R. Wooldridge from 1960 to his death in 1966; Mr. Past Master Alec Hobson from 1966 to 1972; Past Master Brigadier J. Clabby from 1972 to date.

1960–1966 *As supplied to the Author by Dr. Wooldridge*
Towards the end of 1959 the Court of the Worshipful Company of Farriers decided to re-organise its Registration Committee and appointed Dr. W.R. Wooldridge as Chairman. The Committee met on the 19th January 1960 and immediately set to work to examine the proposals emanating from the Duke of Devonshire's Committee. It re-considered the awards of medals, the panel of Judges for these awards, and decided that such competitions should be encouraged as a way of re-creating an interest in Farriery. At certain Agricultural Shows, it made direct grants towards the cost of competitions, and it recommended the institution of certain competitions for young farriers only.

The Committee also reviewed the Company's examinations system and decided that better results could probably be achieved if the Company could play a part in the training of farriers as well as setting examinations. To this end the Committee decided to try and establish an Apprenticeship Scheme in which the Company itself could play a useful part. Quoting from the Minutes of the registration Committee held on the 2nd March 1960:

'Farriery Apprenticeship Scheme
A long discussion took place as to the best basis for such a scheme and it was agreed that the training offered to apprentices should constitute a period of technical training at college, plus apprenticeship to a working Farrier. The technical training should be confined to farriery alone and it was considered that it would be desirable if possible for such technical training to commence after the apprentice had begun apprenticeship to a working farrier. It was agreed that the initial steps to be taken before any scheme could be started would be to prepare a list of Master Farriers who were considered by the Committee to be suitable men to be Masters of Apprentices and for the Committee not only to approve these Master Farriers as individuals but also to approve their work-shops as being of a standard appropriate for an apprentice to learn the trade. Such Master Farriers would have to undertake to take these apprentices as apprentices in farriery only.
The second step would be then for the Master Farriers who had been approved as suitable to accept apprentices, to choose their apprentices from applicants, preferably in their own district, and then register those apprentices through the Registration Committee.

Training
It was agreed that the training should comprise four years total apprenticeship commencing with a minimum period of six months. During the course of the four years the apprentice should spend two months in at least three of those years at a College receiving the specialised technical training in respect of farriery only thus enabling him during the period of his apprenticeship to receive a total of six months such training. During the period of his apprenticeship the apprentice would be financially assisted and it was suggested that the wage to which the apprentices would be entitled would amount to 25% of the Master's rate at the age of 15 years and 33% of the Master's rate at the age of 16 years.'

Quoting again from the next meeting of the Registration Committee held on 16th August 1960:

'Register of Practising Farriers and Apprenticeship Scheme
The Clerk reported that he had received excellent co-operation from the Rural Industries Committee but that the task of sorting out the information forwarded by those Committees, regarding qualified and unqualified men in their respective areas was formidable and would require many hours of work. It was agreed that special staff should be engaged by the Clerk, or employed by him, to sort the lists and

prepare comprehensive lists of qualified and unqualified men and that the Chairman should be empowered to approve the expenditure of money in respect of this special staff up to a total of £100 or more, should it prove necessary for it was considered desirable that ultimately the lists should be printed.

It was agreed that when the basic lists had been prepared they should be forwarded to the National Master Farriers Association for their consideration and in particular so that details could be given if possible of Farriers practising in the larger urban areas, which areas it was known were not covered by the Rural Industries Committees.

The proposed Apprenticeship Scheme was then discussed further in detail and Mr. A.W. Williams reported that the Rural Industries Bureau had found that on several occasions an apprentice had to be sent for his training to a forge some thirty or more miles from his home and that it was necessary for him to take lodgings in the town or village where the forge was situated. The Master Farrier could not, of course, pay the apprentice a wage sufficient to cover his needs, including his board and lodging, but the Bureau had no funds with which to assist such apprentices. It was agreed that this type of case was precisely that which the Registration Committee would be pleased to help by making a payment from the funds available. Mr. Williams stated that the amount contributed in such cases was normally about 75% of the cost of the apprentice's board and lodging but was on a decreasing scale over the period of apprenticeship to offset the apprentice's own increased earnings.

It was agreed that every endeavour should be made to commence a pilot scheme operating in respect of six to ten young men who would receive financial support in the form of 'bursaries'. With a view to this object:

1   Mr. W.A. Williams would supply a copy of the small somewhat similar scheme for certain other crafts run by the Rural Industries Bureau as already approved by the Ministry of Labour.

2   At least three or four apprentices should at once be found and Masters prepared to train them.

3   Before any positive steps were taken beyond this the Chairman would approach the Totalisator Charity Trust to explain the position and to obtain written confirmation that financial support to operate the scheme in respect of these three or four apprentices would be assured for the period of the apprenticeships.

4   Following this, the number of entrants to the scheme which it was deemed necessary to maintain the trade would have to be formulated and the costs of operating a full scheme assessed.'

At the meeting of the Registration Committee on the 6th January 1961 the Apprenticeship Scheme was further considered and quoting again from the Minutes:

'The members of the Committee having received copies of the special Apprenticeship Scheme drawn up by the Rural Industries Bureau for its own purposes, the scheme was discussed as a whole. The Chairman pointed out that to operate a similar scheme for farrier appren-

128

tices would cost approximately £700–£750 per apprentice. Although the RIB Scheme was basically acceptable to the Committee certain amendments were quite obviously necessary and in particular it was suggested that the restrictive covenant contained in Clause 6 should be reduced to a five year period but that no exact radius of miles should be inserted as this would vary from district to district. References to rates of pay be in accordance with the Ministry of Labour requirements.

Consideration was then given to the question of the selection of suitable Masters for the apprentices and it was agreed that the Company's requirements in this respect should be drawn up and set out and should include in particular reference to experience, qualifications, presentability and the facilities available at their forge. It was further agreed that the Masters should normally hold the qualification at least of an RSS and must be in a position to instruct the apprentice in the making of their own shoes.

It was further agreed that there should be a restriction on the number of apprentices any Master could take at any one time and it was arranged that the Chairman should draw up a basic scheme for farriery apprentices accordingly following the lines of the RIB Scheme incorporating the above amendments.

Consideration was then given to the type of boys who should be accepted as apprentices. It was agreed that a boy need not have reached any particular standard but that he should be able to furnish two good references which it was considered might well be given by his School Master, the Vicar of his Parish, the local Youth Employment Officer or other suitable person. The financial aspect of the proposed scheme was then further discussed for it was felt that before even more work was done towards formulating the scheme it would be advantageous to find out whether there was a good chance of the necessary moneys to operate the scheme being forthcoming from the Totalisator Charity Trust or from the body to replace it in the near future or elsewhere. The Chairman agreed that he would approach the Totalisator Charity Trust advising them of the steps which the Committee had decided to take and putting forward at least an outline of the proposed apprenticeship scheme with a view to ascertaining whether we could look to the Trust for its support and that in the meantime he would apply to the Trust for a further grant of £1,000 to help set the scheme in the first instance.'

At the following meeting Dr. Wooldridge reported that the Animal Health Trust had received a further sum of £793 for Farriery and that this money would be made available to the Worshipful Company of Farriers to be put into effect these schemes to help farriery. He had also arranged for further grants to be made direct to the Company. At this meeting the Registration Committee decided to advertise grants to assist would-be apprentices.

Thus during 1961 the Apprenticeship Scheme was set in motion supported by re-vitalised examination and show competition schemes and as a result of the Committee's activities the entrants for the Company's examinations for the year ending September 1961, totalled 32 and during the same year 39 medals were awarded by the Company in Farriery competitons.

1966–1972 *As supplied to the Author by Mr. Alec Hobson*

The purport of the following pages is to describe how all the practical work developed, financially supported by the Company, the Horserace Betting Levy Board, various horse societies and by the National Master Farriers', Blacksmiths' and Agricultural Engineers' Association. It is a privilege to contribute it and to reveal how, after more than 600 years, the Worshipful Company of Farriers is outstanding among the City of London's Guilds in continuing to fulfil the objects for which it was formed.

In 1963, to relieve the then Clerk, Mr. Howard Newcome Wright, of much of the work created by the revitalized Registration Committee, Brigadier Clabby became Honorary Secretary of the Farriery Apprenticeship Scheme and Mr. C.T. Murphy, a veterinary surgeon of wide experience, acted as part time Honorary Field Office. Further evidence of progress came in 1968 with the appointment of Mr. Franklin E. Birch as Registrar to deal with the administrative work of the Registration Committee excepting the appointment and supervision of apprentices which continued to be the responsibility of Brigadier Clabby.

To conclude this brief introduction: when Mr. Birch went on to become the Company's full-time Clerk in 1971, he took over the whole of the work of the Registration Committee; but he now has Mr. R.N. Clarke, a Field Officer, to assist him.

Looking back over the decade ending in 1972, one cannot but be impressed by the volume and variety of detail dealt with at the numerous meetings held. A major operation was the setting up of two sub-committees, the first to examine the finances of the Apprenticeship Scheme and suggest how they might be strengthened; and the second to consider the modus operandi of the Company's examinations and a suggestion to establish a School of Farriery. In the light of subsequent developments the reports of these two committees are of historic interest. They drew attention to the need for more apprentices to combat the shortage of skilled farriers (there were then only seventeen lads being trained); they urged that an extension of the Apprenticeship Scheme was dependent on more money being available for grants; and they emphasized the need for more master-farriers capable of giving practical instruction on diseases of the limbs and feet of the horse and remedial and surgical shoeing. Attention was directed to the absence of precise information about the finances of the scheme, even though it was known that during 1966 there was an income of £2,800 (£2,000 donated by the Betting Levy Board) and that

£2,500 had been spent on grants. Financial aid given by the Company was for prizes for competitions and running the examination.

It was pointed out that there were four possible sources of income for the Apprenticeship Scheme:

1 The Company;
2 Charity funds of the City of London;
3 Statutory and other bodies concerned with the horse; and
4 Commercial interests.

Of these only the first and third were contributing. The Committee suggested that the registration of the Apprenticeship Scheme as a 'Charity' should be investigated. In the event a Charitable Trust was set up in 1968, which has for its objects the training and education of farriers, the promotion of proficiency and the relief of hardship. The Trust is registered with the Charity Commission. As the then Chairman of the Registration Committee I wish to be associated with the thanks due to Mr. Past Master A.J. Barsham for his invaluable services in promoting this Trust and acting as Honorary Treasurer. Also, while on the subject of finance, I must record profound thanks to Mr. Past Master George H. Smith, who succeeded me as Master, for his sponsorship of an appeal to the Livery for a capital fund designed to pay the costs of administering the Apprenticeship Scheme. There is no doubt that the splendid response of Liverymen reflects approval of the initiative of the Company in increasing the number of apprentices. £32,000 has so far been raised, which at present produces almost the whole of the overall cost of running the Apprenticeship Scheme. Any balance required is paid by the Company.

The separation of the accounts of the Apprenticeship Scheme from the Company's finances allows contributors to see how their donations are used. As apprentices are guaranteed their bursaries for four years it is now possible to build up a reserve fund to cover the liability.

The second sub-committee set up by the Registration Committee was asked to review the farriery examinations as then operating; to consider whether candidates for RSS qualifications should have served three years in the trade before taking the examination; to review the list of judges; and to consider the expenses payable to examiners. Much that has transpired since is recorded elsewhere in this survey, so it is unnecessary to detail here all the conclusions of the committee. It was thought that the Company's three qualifications – the RSS, the AFCL and the FWCF were appropriate to current needs; that the RSS should be awarded only after four years in the trade; that there should be an interval between taking the RSS and the AFCL examinations of at least six months; and that a pre-requisite for an AFCL taking the FWCF examination should be at least seven years full-time practical experience in the trade, with at least one year between taking the AFCL and the FWCF examinations.

In addition to reporting on examination procedure and fees and allowances, the committee gave an analysis of a proposal to establish a School of Farriery. It was suggested that boys should receive school training throughout their apprenticeship and that there was a need for upgrading courses for farriers seeking to improve their techniques prior to taking their AFCL and FWCF examinations; and it was thought that the most useful function of a School would be to provide the trade with a reservoir of boys who had a basic grounding in farriery. This might be done by a six-months 'basic' training course for boys who had either served a short probationary period with a master farrier, or who needed training in the rudiments of the trade. Such a preliminary course would form part of the four years apprenticeship period. After discussing various other details including site, size, staff and equipment, the Committee concluded that the cost of a School of Farriery would be not less than £25,000 and that about £5,000 a year would be needed to run it – these being pre-inflation figures. The School remains an idea; whether it becomes a reality some future chapter of the Company's History may record.

Because of the volume and variety of subjects which had suddenly emerged it was thought desirable to combine the reports of the two sub-committees for presentation to the Court. This done, the co-ordinating committee succeeded in presenting recommendations to the Registration Committee in February 1968 and the Court approved them in March of that year. It is right to acknowledge the hard and effective work done at that time. The Registration Committee not only saw the importance of building on to the foundations which had been laid, but the urgency of the problems. The fundamental conclusions were:

1   that the Registration Committee should deal with all the technical work of the Company;
2   that a Registrar should be appointed to relieve the Clerk of such work; and
3   that a new framework for the administration of the Company was necessary.

On finance it was estimated that expenses for the current year (1968) would be £5,790 and that the Company must find this. The support of the Horserace Betting Levy Board, which was of the order of £2,000 a year, was of course generous; but the hope was that it could be increased in recognition of the new drive to safeguard the future of the horse. It was then that the appeal was made to the Livery for an initial £25,000 and the Master, Mr.

George H. Smith, generously headed the list of subscribers with a contribution of £1,000. Concurrently, informal discussions were taking place with Lord Wigg, then Chairman of the Betting Levy Board, and had reached the stage where the Company had to declare an acceptable figure for sufficient recruits joining the trade and what would be done with an additional £2,000 per annum to make the Board's grant £4,000 a year. Effective replies were given to these questions after consultation with the National Master Farriers', Blacksmiths' and Agricultural Engineers' Association, and because of the success of the Appeal it was possible to tell the Betting Levy Board that if the Board increased its grant to £4,000 a year the extra money would be spent wholly on apprenticeship grants and not on administration.

Attention was then turned towards a new programme to safeguard the future of farriery. The extra money from the Betting Levy Board and from other donors enabled the Company to appoint almost as many more apprentices as were then being trained. This raised consequential problems, including a sufficiency of master-farriers capable of training apprentices, the maintenance of standards of workmanship, the enlistment to farriery of young men having a genuine interest in the craft and – still a difficult one – the need to persuade horse-owners that shoeing was a skilled craftsman's job and so justified a realistic charge for the service.

It was at this point that a fresh survey of the farriery trade was thought necessary and a Conference seemed a logical outcome. The Court gave the Registration Committee its full support and encouragement for the project. Inevitably, a great deal of the day to day work is not recorded but the minutes of meetings reveal effectiveness of the support of members of committees and the hard work of the then Clerk, Mr. Michael Burke, and the present Clerk, Mr. Franklin Birch. I greatly valued their loyal support.

Discussions began with the Technical Education Committee of the City and Guilds Institute to see whether it would be possible for the examinations for farriers to be taken over by the Institute. Eventually there was a unanimous decision that such examinations should remain the responsibility of the Company.

Due largely to the inspiration and effort of Mr. Michael Simons, MRCVS, and to a great deal of spade work by the Registrar, a Register of Working Farriers appeared in 1968.

A review of the constitution of the Registration Committee led to the appointment of Mr. M.R.C. Crawshay as a member to represent the Horserace Betting Levy Board.

An interesting sidelight on the breadth of the Registration Committee's responsibilities is a report to the Committee on the Horse-shoeing Competition and Farriery Examination held at

Cookstown, Co. Tyrone, Northern Ireland, in the autumn of 1968. The event, sponsored by Ulster Rural Industries Development Committee, was held primarily as a means of stimulating interest in the trade, and to assess the standards of farriery 'with a possible follow-up in efforts to obtain the Worshipful Company of Farriers qualifications'. One of the Company's most experienced judges, Mr. M.J. Clark FWCF, of Great Haseley, Oxfordshire, attended and was credited with a major share in the success of the event. He gave close attention to the event and interviewed every competitor 'thereby extablishing the respect for the master-craftsmen by others of his craft'. The report concluded with some observations which will always be true wherever horses need to be shod: 'A skilled farrier must . . . have a liking for both horses and metal-working, without too much regard for the heavy and often dangerous nature of this work. He must also have a knowledge of the veterinary aspects of his craft. Horse-owners should appreciate this, as in the final analysis the future of farriery must rest in a higher status and income from the trade.'

Mr. Clark went back to Northern Ireland the following year when facilities for another competition were again provided by the Rural Industried Development Committee. The Irish Olympic Horse Society lent support and Mr. Clark as chief judge and examiner was assisted by Mr. R. Chisholm, FWCF. Mr. Clark reported that he found an improvement in the standard of shoeing compared with the previous year, though he felt that 'foot preparation and elementary veterinary knowledge still needed to be improved'. To add to his practical service Mr. Clark next day met six of the farriers who had competed and gave a lecture and a demonstration on the anatomy of the horse's leg and foot.

The Registration Committee suffered a heavy loss when Mr. C.T. Murphy, MRCVS decided, in 1969, that for family reasons he had to resign his membership and give up the field-work he had been doing for the Company for many years.

Conference 1969

One of the Company's most impressive achievements was the Conference on the Future of Farriery, held in London on the 10th October 1969. It was an ambitious and practical undertaking, occupying a whole day and attracting delegates from far and wide. It was in fact unique. Officers of the Company present included 6 members of the Court and Registration Committee, 24 farriers, 8 delegates of horse societies, 10 officers of the Council for Small Industries in Rural Areas, 11 veterinary surgeons, and a number of individuals representing educational bodies, training boards, the Mounted Police, the Press, the Horserace Betting Levy Board, agricultural societies and the National Farmers' Union.

In opening Conference and welcoming those present, the chairman of the Registration Committee said the gathering represented a cumulation of years of consideration of problems surrounding farriery and its future. Without collaboration effective real progress was not possible, nor could improvements be attempted. The Conference was 'the end of the beginning' so far as the Company was concerned.

A paper on Statutory Control was presented by Mr. H.W. Dawes, FRCVS. He recommended State control of farriers through a Bill to be presented to Parliament. He suggested a referendum to shoeing smiths as a first step. It would be necessary to explain briefly that Statutory Control would lead to a register of Farriers in two parts: one, those having the Company's qualifications by examination, and the other (a Supplementary Register) those without qualifications but who practised as shoeing smiths. New registrations would be only for those who had at least passed the RSS or similar examination, so that in a few years only qualified farriers would be on the Register. There would have to be a Committee responsible for the administration of the Act and to take disciplinary action where necessary. The financing of registration and all it involved would be covered by an annual registration fee from each farrier.

Future of Farriery
Mr. M.A.P. Simons, MRCVS presented a paper on the future of Farriery. He spoke of the art of foot-preparation and the snags of 'do it yourself' farriery. Even if plastic shoes were perfected there would still be a need for the farrier to work closely with the veterinarian to prevent and cure lameness. The demand for farriers was evident by the fact that 500,000 persons per week rode for pleasure; there were 2,000 registered riding-establishments; and the horse population was of the order of 350,000 and increasing. Little was known about the economics of the trade; there should be a close study of this in order that an equitable charge could be made for shoeing.

Among the subjects raised in the ensuing debate on Mr. Simon's paper, grants and planning permission to set up forges emerged, and it was suggested that the Company should underwrite Bank loans and influence the Government Planners' towards a directive to local planning authorities who were not sympathetic to the setting up of forges. This led on to a discussion on travelling forges versus shops and to a submission that horse-owners were not encouraged to ride on the roads; therefore the travelling farrier was essential.

Training, Education and Examinations
Brigadier Clabby, CBE, MRCVS spoke on the Apprenticeship

Scheme and suggested that some recompense should be made to master farriers for training apprentices (eg £100 in the first year, £50 in second year, £25 in third year and a bonus of £50 when the apprentice passed his RSS). He emphasised the lack of training facilities and asked for more help from veterinary schools.

Mr. Kemp (Vice-Principal, Herefordshire Technical College) suggested a six to eight week pre-entry course at a school before or just after entering a farrier's shop. It was necessary to have knowledge of blacksmithing in rural areas. Not only was this a useful attribute but it was a safeguard against lack of employment due to scarcity of horses to shoe. The craft should be more generally taught in technical schools.

Encouragement of the Craft
Mr. G.J. Stevenson, FWCF talked of his personal experiences. The following discussion elicited that although shoeing-competitions were costly, they enabled young men to make comparisons of workmanship and thereby encouraged them to improve their standards.

Conclusion of the Conference
Mr. J. Stan Cosgrove, MRCVS (Bloodstock Breeders' and Horse Owners' Association of Ireland) pressed for farriers to receive adequate payment and to have their status acknowledged. Whilst a veterinary surgeon would not be allowed to stick a needle into a horse within two weeks of a race, farriers could put a nail in five minutes before the 'off'. He had never known a farrier to 'lame' a horse in such circumstances, which reflected both competence and integrity.

The Duke of Beaufort expressed appreciation of the Conference. He said he had enjoyed the discussions and had learnt a great deal. He would do all he could to further the cause of farriery, especially in educating horse owners to appreciate their services. He considered that a new vista had been opened for farriers by the Conference.

Without doubt the Conference was successful through its discussion of current problems and in bringing together so many individuals who, in one way or another, were interested in farriery or looked to it to contribute to their way of life.

The Registration Committee lost no time in examining and assessing the results of the Conference. Within weeks four Working Parties were set up:
1 To prepare for Statutory Control and Registration of Farriers;
2 To weigh the considerations involving the future of farriery as a craft necessary to the welfare of the horse;

3   To review the training necessary for the Company's examinations, the framework of the examinations themselves, and the Company's proficiency grades in farriery;
4   To consider steps necessary to encourage and give practical training to would-be entrants to the craft.

Mr. Past Master E.H. Newcome Wright, Mr. M.A.P. Simons, Dr. A.C. Fraser and Mr. J.R. Attfield agreed to act as Chairman respectively of the working parties. I cannot thank them enough for their support and practical contributions.

It was found expedient to fuse the two working parties concerned with the future of farriery and the encouragement and training of farriers under the chairmanship of Mr. Simons.

At a meeting of the Court on 21 September 1971 Mr. J.R. Attfield AFCL (President, National Master Farriers Association), Dr. A.C. Fraser and the Registrar were invited into the Courtroom and considered the combined report of the working parties which was presented to the Court by Past Master Hobson the Chairman of the Registration Committee.

The Chairman pointed out that two reports were then being considered, the report on statutory control having yet to be presented to the Registration Committee. The Report on the examinations working party had already been considered by the Court and they were asked today to consider the report on the future of Farriery and the encouragement of the craft.

The problem was to ensure the continuance of the craft which at the present time was subject to exceptional difficulties. Many Masters were unwilling to train apprentices and were content to tempt trained men with higher wages. Because of this practice other masters were reluctant to take apprentices who might be persuaded to leave them as soon as they had acquired what they considered to be adequate skills.

The adoption of the report was approved by the Chairman and seconded by the Middle Warden, Brigadier Clabby as Deputy Chairman of the Registration Committee. Mr. Michael Simons, Renter Warden, then spoke of the future of Farriery and the encouragement of the craft. He pointed out that it was only racehorse Farriers who did nothing else but Farriery. Most Farriers were obliged to engage in other activities in order to supplement their income. The present economic basis was therefore ludicrous and he pointed out that the present policy of planning committees which regarded a Forge as light industry, meant that no new forges could be started in residential areas where recreational horses were used. Mr. J.R. Attfield then spoke in support of the motion. As a practising Farrier he felt he could say that the craft needed a considerable impetus which the Company was providing. There then followed a discussion on the relationship between Blacksmiths and Farriers and the Chairman pointed out that the National Master Farriers' Association, who should take more responsibility for the future of the Craft, also represented working blacksmiths. Past Master Deputy Walker pointed out that a Farrier was also able to do general smithing, but a blacksmith was not necessarily able to shoe horses. Dr. Fraser then spoke on training and education and briefly outlined the history of the examination system. He praised highly the Farriery Training Department of the Hereford Technical College and all that it was doing to assist in the Company's aims.

In summing up the discussion the Chairman said that the Court should bear in mind three things:

1   Statutory registration which must be prosecuted vigorously.

2   The Company must secure greater acknowledgement by the horse world of the services of Farriers. This could best be done by paying a more realistic price for shoeing.

3   The Company must develop the Apprenticeship Scheme and improve and develop the examination system.

The report was carried unanimously.

Conference 1971

The Registration Committee having decided to hold a second Conference in December 1971, the invitation referred to

1   the success of the previous gathering in focussing attention on the problems of the trade,

2   summarised what had been done since and

3   suggested that the two reports of the working parties which were available deserved to be brought to the attention of farriers and the horse-world, and especially those who had generously supported the Company's appeal for funds.

The second conference was held in London on 6th December 1971. The Chairman of the Registration Committee presided and was supported by the then Master of the Company Sir Hugh Linstead, Brigadier J. Clabby, Honorary Secretary of the Apprenticeship Scheme, Mr. M.A.P. Simons, chairman of the 'Future of Farriery Working Party', and Dr. A.C. Fraser, chairman of the Examination and Training Working Party.

Dr. Fraser and Mr. Simons having introduced their reports, Brigadier Clabby dealt with the Company's Apprenticeship Scheme. Initially he said, the Scheme catered for only three or four apprentices, but it had extended to 80 boys thanks to the generosity of the Horserace Betting Levy Board and other donors. This signified an output of about 20 qualified farriers per year, which seemed about what was needed.

Mr. J.R. Attfield (President National Master Farriers', Blacksmiths', and Agricultural Engineers' Association) referred to the need to make known to horse-owners the importance of good shoeing by skilled craftsmen and regular attendance to the horse's feet. To this end his Association had offered the British Horse Society a panel of practising farriers to give talks to riding schools and pony clubs.

Mr. J.A. Ibbotson, FWCF spoke on grants to masters who trained apprentices. The basic question was whether it was worthwhile to take apprentices. Initially they were something of a liability. The Company's grants to apprentices were for board, tools and such like. He was sympathetic towards grants to masters but care should be taken that they took apprentices for training and not only to get a grant.

Mr. G.W. Kemp (Vice-Principal and Head of Engineering Dept., Herefordshire Technical College) outlined the courses in farriery available at his college for both apprentices and those already in the trade wishing to take higher examinations. The courses included general blacksmithing, as it was considered a necessary adjunct to the farriers trade. The College found instruction in farriery very rewarding. Many of the boys who had decided to specialise in it became dedicated.

Major Davies (RAVC Training Centre, Melton Mowbray) said at each course they included courses of two weeks duration for 10 or 12 apprentices in the Company's Scheme. The training at the RAVC Centre was for Army personnel with this one exception; it was not possible to extend the service to civilians generally. It was important that people were given RSS status and registration only when they had reached the appropriate standard and had passed the equivalent Army examination.

Mr. H. Wilkinson (CoSIRA, Suffolk) said the Suffolk Small Industries Committee had made a study in depth of farriery. This confirmed the Worshipful Company's findings of what was needed to be done. He thought there must be financial assistance for masters training apprentices.

Mr. H.J. Cooper, FWCF(Hons) said there was a lack of communication within the trade. The Company's Apprenticeship Scheme deserved more publicity, particularly from those in the trade. The shoeing of horses was a service and it was up to the trade to find out what horse-owners wanted and then provide it. In his opinion the farrier should go to the horse and not vice versa as in the past; the travelling forge was the thing of the future.

Conclusions of the Conference

In summarising the Conference the Chairman said the time must come when many of the problems that had been raised must be tackled by the trade itself. The Worshipful Company of Farriers was not a trade organisation and while it was proud of the service it rendered to the trade, it was still a City of London Livery Company, which meant that many of its members inevitably lacked technical knowledge. Many of the questions raised at the two conferences were, in his view, the concern of the National Master Farriers' Association. That said, the Company was enthusiastically behind the trade and looked forward to securing statutory control to complete the major reorganisation and development of farriery which had taken place during the past few years.

Conclusions of Ten Years Work

In this survey of the affairs of the Company for the Supplementary History 1962–72, there have inevitably been many references to the financial support given to the Company's Apprenticeship Scheme, and to the need for bringing together master-farriers capable of imparting knowledge and would-be farriers who are capable of absorbing that knowledge. The Farriers Company was by no means a wealthy Company; hence the support of the Horserace Betting Levy Board and of other organisations concerned with the horse, along with the generous donations of individuals, was vital. Early in 1972, a tremendous fillip was given to the Company's efforts by the agreement of the Horserace Betting Levy Board both to increase its annual grant for the Apprenticeship Scheme from £4,000 to £6,000 and to give an additional £2,500 a year for a three-year period to provide the fees and expenses of a Field Officer. That this coincided with the availability of Mr. R.N. Clarke, one who was singularly fitted to work in the field, was not pure chance; but it was certainly very fortunate. The pattern of field-work set by Mr. Murphy was being followed with the additional advantage that Mr. Clarke's long service with the Rural Industries Bureau and the Council for Small Industries in Rural Areas provides the Company with the best possible introduction to the facilities available from CoSIRA.

Statutory Registration and Control of Farriers was a complex subject and could not be hurried. There had been significant progress; an operational plan had been drawn up involving consultations with a Parliamentary Agent and a Draft Bill had been approved by the Registration Committee and the Court. After further consultation with organisations and individuals and with the Government departments likely to be involved, the Bill will be presented for consideration of Parliament, probably during 1973.

There remains the following report on the Apprenticeship Scheme by Brigadier J. Clabby, CBE, MRCVS, who generously acted as Honorary Secretary during the time when the scheme expanded to provide in each year enough new entrants for the trade.

140

Apprenticeship Scheme 1962–1972

During 1961 the Apprenticeship Scheme was set in motion supported by re-vitalised examination and show competition schemes.'

Following advertisement, 16 young men applied for apprenticeships from whom, following interviews in their own homes, five were selected and suitably qualified masters as near the apprentices home districts as possible were requested to accept the apprentices. A form of Apprenticeship Deed was agreed upon and the scheme now became a practical reality, albeit on a scale limited by the funds available.

Having established a satisfactory administrative machinery for the scheme and set it in motion the Clerk, Mr. Howard Newcome Wright, handed over its management in July 1963 to Brigadier J. Clabby, CBE, MRCVS, who became the Honorary Secretary. Another member of the Livery Mr. C.T. Murphy, MRCVS, acted as Field Officer interviewing prospective apprentices and their masters and keeping an eye on the progress of the boys under training.

The scheme was made known to the public through the friendly columns of 'Horse and Hound' and other periodicals and applications for apprenticeships steadily mounted. Thanks to the additional financial help from the Horserace Betting Levy Board the number of boys under training was increased to 10 in 1965 and to 15 during 1966.

However, it was clear that a mere handful of apprentices could not make good the great and growing shortage of farriers throughout the country. Consideration was therefore given to the possibility of creating a school of farriery and this led to the conclusion that a comparatively short school curriculum could not replace the four-year 'on the job' training of an apprenticeship. And then, among other drawbacks, there was the great initial cost of building and equipping a school and the high annual cost of running it. Nevertheless 'on the job' training has its limitations. To be fully effective it requires supplementation with theoretical knowledge, instruction on the finer points of shoe making and other details likely to be missed in the rush of a busy farriery practice. To this end, the Royal Army Veterinary Corps provided our apprentices with short intensive annual courses at its School of Farriery, Melton Mowbray, and later, as the number of apprentices grew beyond Melton's capacity, the Herefordshire Technical College also accepted Worshipful Company of Farriers' apprentices both for basic training in the elements of the craft and for regular annual courses. The success of the scheme owes much to these two organisations who have given their services freely and willingly.

In January 1968 the Horserace Betting Levy Board agreed to double its annual grant for apprenticeships to £4,000 per annum conditional on the Company being responsible for the administrative costs of the scheme. New support was also received from the British Horse Society, the British Show Jumping Association and the Pony Club as well as continued backing from the Jockey Club, the Thoroughbred Breeders' Association, the National Master Farriers', Blacksmiths', and Agricultural Engineers' Association, the Ponies of Britain, the Coaching Club, the Hackney Horse Society and other well wishers. To supplement these donations and to meet administrative costs, the Company appealed to its Liverymen for financial help and met with a gratifying response.

At this period of expansion it was particularly unfortunate to lose the services, on retirement abroad, of Mr. C.T. Murphy, who had been a mainstay of the scheme since its inception.

It would have been difficult to continue the work efficiently if the CoSIRA had not permitted their Rural Industries Organisers to carry on Mr. Murphy's work at a local level; interviwing prospective apprentices and their parents, arranging suitable masters for selected candidates and dealing personally with the problems that inevitably arise between master and apprentice.

During the next two years the scheme maintained its momentum so that in 1971 the Hon. Secretary could report that 83 boys had been under training during the year, eight of whom had successfully completed their four year apprenticeship and entered the trade. He warned, however, that the scheme was once again nearing its financial limits and that the present trend could not be sustained without increased financial support.

On learning of this situation the Horserace Betting Levy Board not only most generously increased its annual contribution but also agreed to provide for the fees and expenses of a Field Officer for a period of three years, so as to form a closer link between the Company and its apprentices and Masters.

Owing to the ready response of the Board, the co-operation of the horse world and the support of the Livery the scheme grew during the ten year period under a review into an organisation which could claim to be making worthwhile contribution towards revitalising the craft of farriery. From a small beginning in 1962 of just a few apprentices working in a fairly localised geographical area the scheme had expanded to 90 apprentices scattered all over the United Kingdom from Scotland to Devon and had added 31 trained craftsmen to the trade. It was therefore with a feeling of some satisfaction that the Hon. Secretary could hand back the responsibility for the scheme to the Clerk of the Company, Mr. Franklin Birch, and to the Field Officer.

1972 to March 1979 *As supplied to the Author by Mr. Franklin Birch*
At the conclusion of the very active period of the Registration
Committee under the Chairmanship of Mr. Past Master Alec
Hobson there remained the implementation of the reports of
three working parties set up as a result of the 1969 conference on
the future of farriery. The appointment of Brigadier J. Clabby,
CBE, MRCVS, as Chairman of the Committee ensured that the
hard preparatory work done by his predecessor and the members
of the working parties would not go in vain and the following is a
report of the events in the spheres affecting the Worshipful Company and the position at the end of March 1979.

Statutory Control and Registration of Farriers

Having held a referendum to determine the attitude of practising
farriers towards the proposed control of the trade and found the
vast majority in favour, the working party set to work to prepare a
draft Bill to go before Parliament. The vicissitudes that beset this
Bill during its compilation and passage through Parliament need
not be gone into and suffice to say that it became Law with the
Royal Assent on 22nd May 1975. Under it, a Farriers Registration
Council was set up, the Chairman of which was Past Master Sir
Hugh Linstead, OBE, LLD, FPS, and appointment the preroga-
tive of the Company as defined in the Act. It is worthy of note that
the choice of Sir Hugh Linstead as the first Chairman of the
Council was an admirable one and nobody could have excelled
the expertise with which he steered the Council to implement the
various Sections of the Act, compiled Standing Orders, saw
through Parliament in 1977 an Amending Act to rectify certain
anomalies in the original, and negotiated a date with the Home
Secretary for the bringing in of Section 16 (the Penalties Clause)
without which the Act had no meaning.

At December 31st 1978 Sir Hugh resigned as Chairman of the
Farriers Registration Council and the Court of the Company
nominated Past Master Brigadier J. Clabby to succeed him. In his
first report to the Court in March 1979 as Chairman of the Council,
Brigadier Clabby said that 'Past Master Sir Hugh Linstead had left
matters in such excellent order that he had had little to do since
taking over as Chairman of the Farriers Registration Council!'

At this point it might be appropriate to note a change in nomen-
clature as a result of the Act, for in September 1975 the Court
accepted the recommendation of the Chairman of the Registration Committee that 'in view of the possible confusion with the
Farriers Registration Council, he proposed that the name of the
Company's Registration Committee be changed to Craft Committee.'

Examinations

In 1971 as a result of the working party's report, an Examination Board was set up to consider and to implement, if though fit, the working party's findings and recommendations and to remain in being to advise the Company through its Craft (formerly Registration) Committee on all aspects of examinations in farriery; in fact, to be the examinations authority.

The Examination Board lost no time in re-organising the examinations on a sound basis and revised syllabi; examinations were to be held twice a year on specific dates at specific centres, instead of in ones and twos at any place, often without prior knowledge of the Registrar that an examiner was going to take an examination. A panel of competent examiners was formed and they were well primed on the new procedures and the standards expected for each grade of examination. The first examinations under this new system were conducted in March 1973 when two examiners took them in collaboration, instead of one previously; in the cases of the higher grades a Veterinary Surgeon was also in attendance. When the new system had been in operation for two years, it was decided to hold a conference of examiners to ascertain their views on how it was working and whether improvements could be made. The conference took place in September 1975 and as a result of discussions and suggestions the Examinations Board decided to have another look at the syllabi and conducting of the examinations in farriery.

The Examinations Board did a tremendous amount of work and had the expert help and advice of Professor C. Formston, FRCVS, Emeritus Professor of the Royal Veterinary College, whose knowledge of compiling syllabi and the conducting of examinations is vast.

With the passing of the Farriers (Registration) Act, the Company was given the statutory duty of securing standards of competence and conduct among persons engaged in the shoeing of horses (*vide* Clause 1 of the Act). So farriery examinations took on a new significance, especially as the Farriers Registration Council had accepted that the Company's RSS as the 'prescribed' examination under the Act, was for the purposes of registration. The Board bore this in mind in its deliberations and produced entirely new details and a revised syllabus for each grade of examination. New and uniform methods of examining were tabled at a meeting of examiners held in September 1978 to lead to a uniformity of standard in examining and the new syllabi gave in more detail what was espected of a candidate. The revised procedures came into force on January 1st 1979. Details of the syllabi and methods of examining will be academic so far as readers of this book are concerned and need not be tabled here. Suffice to say that at the initiation in 1979 they have proved more than satisfactory in practice.

The three grades remain as initially instituted in the late 19th and early 20th Century, namely the RSS (Registered Shoeing Smith), the AFCL (Associate of the Farriers Company of London) and the FWCF (Fellow of the Worhsipful Company of Farriers). For the record, just over 10,760 have passed the RSS; 750 the AFCL, and 156 awarded the Fellowship. The highest honour, the Fellowship, can be bestowed by the Court of the Company *honoris causa*, but as far as can be traced there have been less than half a dozen so honoured in the last 50 years and it is thought there is only one of them alive today.

There is some great doubt as to whether the Company is now entitled to issue Registered Shoeing Smiths certificates as, under the Farriers (Registration) Act, the Farriers Registration Council have the sole responsibility of giving certificates of registration. It is highly possible, therefore, that the name of the Company's first grade of examination will have to be changed to, perhaps, Diploma of the Worshipful Company of Farriers (DipWCF). With the historic significance of RSS this is a pity, but inevitable and the examination will remain the same and the Diploma issued will have equal importance.

Farriery Apprenticeship Scheme

The Company's Farriery Apprenticeship Scheme and Training Scheme continues to flourish, thanks to the annual financial support from the various organisations connected with the horse and particularly the Horserace Betting Levy Board which grant now stands at £10,750 per annum. The Capital Fund of the Charitable Trust has reached the figure of over £50,000, the investment income from which, some £4,500 a year, goes towards the costs of the training of, and bursaries to, apprentices the total amount for which in the year 1977–78 was £15,163. A separate Fund subscribed by the Livery of the Company stands at £39,000, the income from which is used to finance the administration of the scheme, the balance being found by the Company except that £4,250 is given by the Horserace Betting Levy Board towards the fees and expenses of a Field Officer.

The success of the Scheme can be judged from the following table:

Year	Apprentices under Training	Number successfully Completed Training
1962–63	5	–
1963–64	7	–
1964–65	10	–
1965–66	15	–

1966–67	16	3
1967–68	29	1
1968–69	46	5
1969–70	54	6
1970–71	83	8
1971–72	90	8
1972–73	118	16
1973–74	127	22
1974–75	162	21
1975–76	183	23
1976–77	174	35
1977–78	169	35
1978–79	136	33
(as at 31st Mar)		
		216

The demand for apprentices was so great that, in 1977, a review of the Company's finances to cover regular fixed grants, which had been given automatically on enrollment under the Scheme, was made; in addition the cost of apprentices of attending courses was causing concern. It was decided that the amount available could be more equitably deployed by cutting out the basic or regular bursaries and awarding grants only in cases of financial hardship, sympathetic consideration being given to those who had to live away from their employment; each case to be considered on its merits. In place of these grants it was decided to meet all expenses of attending courses, course fees, board and lodging and travelling costs, and arrangements were made with the Herefordshire Technical College, where all courses were now taken, for them to pay these charges and the Company reimburse them; in addition each new recruit was given a set of farrier's tools, a tool box in which to keep them and two standard text books. Also when on his first course examinations were to be subsidised, this subsidy did not wholly cover the fees payable by the apprentices. The new financial arrangements, now in effect, appear to be satisfactory to all concerned.

At the same time as financial aid was considered a revision of the system of recruitment and training was made by the officers of the Apprenticeship Scheme and an approach was made to the Training Services Agency for the financial aid to put the proposals into effect. In the meantime, Mr. W.G. Trust, Senior Crafts Officer of CoSIRA was making great efforts to get an apprenticeship scheme for farriery, based on the Company's accepted scheme and financed from public funds, keeping in touch with the Company on his progress. At the beginning of 1978 he reported that he had been successful in having funds allocated by the Development Commission and CoSIRA and a new Farriery

Apprenticeship Scheme, embracing all existing schemes, was born (At a later date Wales and Scotland were included through the interest of the Welsh and Scottish Development Agencies). A stipulation was that the scheme would be controlled by a Committee to be called the Farriery Apprenticeship Scheme Regulating Committee the Chairman of which was to be Past Master Brigadier Clabby and on which the Company would have other representation.

The new scheme was to be welcomed for it was to run on the same lines as that of the Company's, but with two improvements which had been the aim of the Company but which had not been achieved due to insufficient finances. One was the increase in time spent on courses – 36 weeks against only 11 weeks under the Company's scheme – and the other being grants to master-farriers towards the cost to them of training apprentices.

What the position of the Company will be in relation to the new scheme only time can tell. For the immediate future, the Company has an obligation to see all the 136 apprentices enrolled under its scheme through to the end of their apprenticeships which will take up to the next four years. In addition, the Company has undertaken to keep its own scheme in being to oversee those apprenticeships of persons over 19 years of age, in order to release more places for school-leavers under the new scheme; to supplement the tool allowance under the new scheme; to supply apprentices with stick-pin badges, which had been found most popular with apprentices under the Company's new scheme. No doubt other deficiencies in the new scheme will appear with which the Company can concern itself.

To a certain extent it is the closure of another successful chapter in the annuls of the Company which has achieved the original intent of rectifying the shortages of competent farriers so evident in 1950's. The Company can now concern itself with its Statutory obligation of 'securing adequate standards of competence and conduct among persons engaged in the shoeing of horses' and 'promote, encourage and advance the art and science of farriery and education in connection with the said art and science', as outlined elsewhere in this volume.

Acknowledgement must be made to the invaluable work done by the Company's Field Officers. As stated in a previous section of this chapter, Mr. Robert Clarke was appointed Field Officer in April 1972 and his retirement in May 1978, due to increasing bad vision which made travelling difficult, was accepted with regret. There is no doubt that much of the success of the Company's Farriery Apprenticeship and Training Scheme has been due to his industry and interest. Mr. Cyril Cooper, AFCL was appointed to succeed him and is keeping up the tradition laid down by his predecessor; he spends much time interviewing apprentices and Masters under the new scheme in addition to looking after those under the Company's scheme and is a member of the Selection Committee set up by the Farriery Apprenticeship Scheme Regulating Committee.

Mention must also be made of Mr. George W. Kemp with whom the Company dealt for many years in his capacity of Vice-Principal and Head of the Engineering Department of the Herefordshire Technical College up to his retirement in the Summer of 1978. His interest in the Company's apprentices and traknign and his counsels on, and arrangements for, courses at the College will be sadly missed. Tribute must also be paid to the late Mr. Bill Watts, FWCF, who did so much for apprentices under training as senior Farriery Instructor at the College, his untimely death was most regrettable. His successor, Mr. Tom Williams, FWCF, is grasping the reins most successfully and the Registrar of the Company is indebted to him for the expert way with which he acts as organiser for the Company's examinations that are held at the College.

The New Farriery Apprenticeship Scheme
The new scheme approved by the Manpower Services Commission and the Development Commission was introduced by CoSIRA in 1978. CoSIRA's Farriery Apprenticeship Regulating Committee, which was appointed to manage the scheme, produced its first annual report in April 1979. The report was well received and in June 1979 the Development Commission approved a third intake of 28 apprentices bringing the number under training in the scheme in 1979 to 58. The Commission further approved an annual intake of 28 apprentices each year thereafter.

Competitions
There is no doubt that shoeing competitions have a great appeal not only for the farriers who participate, but also for the public, which is evident by the crowds that congregate round the forges at Agricultural Shows when shoeing competitions are in progress. The competitions have, therefore, a dual purpose: firstly to raise the standard of farriery and, secondly to publicise the skill needed for the competent shoeing of horses. The Company has always considered it worthwhile to encourage these competitions and has allocated medals for the winning farriers. Unfortunately, due to lack of funds, facilities and organisers for staging shoeing competitions, they are not so abundant as they used to be; nevertheless in 1958 the Company gave three silver-gilt 17 silver and 19 bronze medals for 19 such competitions held.

George III Silver Gilt Loving Cup presented to the Company to celebrate
the 600th Anniversary of its Fellowship in 1956.

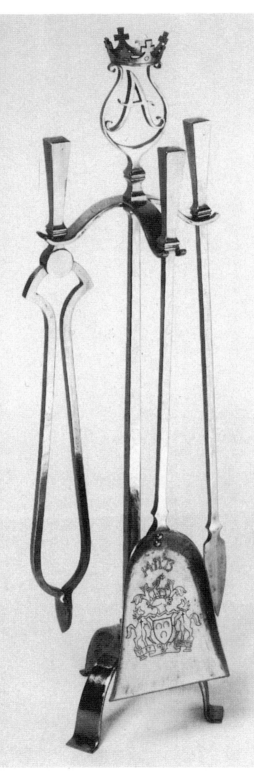

Wedding Gift from the Company to HRH Princess Anne and Captain Mark Phillips, being a hand-made set of Fire Irons and Stand.

In 1970, as a result of Mr. Past Master M.A.P. Simons' working party's report after the 1969 Farriery Conference, it was decided to encourage best-shod horse competitions at horse and agricultural shows and the Company offered a bronze medal for the farrier responsible for the feet and the shoeing of the winning horse and eight such medals were awarded in 1978. It is rightly thought that such competitions call attention of horse owners to the need for correct and competent shoeing of their horses by skilled craftsmen.

Due to the ever-increasing cost of medals in precious metals (and even bronze is becoming 'precious' in these days) there has been a review of the allocation by the Company and the Examination Board, comprising, as it does mainly of practising farriers, recommended to the Craft Committee that silver-gilt medals be no longer given, being replaced by silver that silver medals be continued for the winners of Open Classes, but that Bronze medals be allocated only to Apprentices' Classes. As far as best-shod horse competitions are concerned, the members of the Board did not think that bronze medals were appropriate and recommended something that could be nailed up in a winner's forge, such as a plaque, would be more acceptable and that horse-owners should also receive some such recognition. The Craft Committee accepted the Board's recommendations and there is no doubt that the Court of the Company will agree and that they will be put into effect from 1980.

Many references have been made to the financial assistance given to the Company by the Horserace Betting Levy Board and the part it played in the success of the apprenticeship scheme; not only by providing much of the financial backing but also by showing a friendly understanding of the Company's purpose in a way that obviated many difficulties. Lord Wigg, who was Chairman of the Board during the period of the scheme's development, was never an easy man to please but once he had satisfied himself as to the integrity of the Company and the value of its work to the horse-world he proved a staunch supporter. His successor, Sir Desmond Plummer, has continued this policy of co-operation which has been made even more effective by being channelled through the hands of the Secretary to the Board, Miss Margaret Meade, and of Mr. Martin Crawshay.

The Author is indebted to Sir Hugh Linstead for the following article on the responsibilities of the Worshipful Company of Farriers for the Maintenance of Standards by Practising Farriers after the passing of the Farriers (Registration) Act 1975:

'The Brotherhood of Farryers within our Citties of London and Westminster' petitioned King Charles II for incorporation into 'a Body Politique and Corporate' invested with power 'for the well ordering and governing of (their) Art and Trade within (the) Citties of London and Westminster and the liberties thereof and within seven miles distant from the same'. The King granted them a Charter of Incorporation in 1674 in which were included certain powers for the enforcement of standards of good practice among farriers working in the prescribed area. In particular, power was granted to the Master, Wardens and Assistants, 'or any three or more of them . . . having first obtained a warrant from the Lord Chief Justice . . . in that behalfe, with a constable or other lawfulle officer' to enter premises 'to search for, seeke, and finde out all and every misdemeanour and defective workes and medicines to the intent that due and legall prosecution may be had and taken against all and every such offenders'.

The Charter remains in force as the instrument of incorporation of the Worshipful Company of Farriers, but its disciplinary and penal provisions have long since ceased to be invoked and any residual authority that might be claimed for them at the present time could reasonably be said to have been replaced by the disciplinary and penal provisions of the Farriers (Registration) Act 1975, extending as it does to the whole of Great Britain. Indeed it could be argued that the Farriers Registration Council set up by the Act has taken over whatever powers and responsibilities granted by the Charter still rested with the Company for the governance of the craft, the conduct of its practitioners and the education of its apprentices within the London area. On this basis the Company could have retained, for reasons of history, an interest in the well-being of farriery, but could have closed a distinguished chapter in its history as the active sponsor of the progress of the craft. It would then have limited its main current activities to its functions as a Livery Company of the City of London.

Such a natural evolution has however been complicated by the insertion into the Act, on the intiative of the Company, of Section 1, which imposes certain functions, albeit defined somewhat vaguely, on the Company without geographical limits. The Section was drafted and inserted in the Bill with a minimum of discussion, mainly to ensure a continuing place for the Company in the farriery field in consideration of its historical role. It runs:

'1. The Worshipful Company of Farriers (hereinafter referred to as 'the Company') shall have the general function of securing adequate standards of competence and conduct among persons engaged in the shoeing of horses (hereinafter referred to as 'farriers') and shall promote, encourage and advance the art and science of farriery and education in connection with the said art and science.'

The remaining twenty sections of the Act (Section 15A was added to the original nineteen in 1977) spell out the functions of the Registration Council which could be summarised if need be in the words used to describe the functions of the Company in Section 1: that is to say both Council and Company are allotted identical functions by the same Act, the difference being that those of the Council are spelled out in considerable detail and funds (however inadequate) allocated for them, whereas the Company is handed a set of general responsibilities and offered no resources to finance them. Clearly anything the Company can do the Council can do, if not better, at least as well and if the Company is to pursue the opportunities of serving the craft conferred upon it by Section 1 it must be on a highly selective basis, avoiding those matters such as the registration and discipline, for which the statute has provided the Council with specific powers in considerable detail.

The sort of thing that it would be appropriate for the Company to undertake, which would supplement but not overlap the activities of the Council, could include the continuation of its examining functions, the award of scholarships and prizes and the organising of competitions and demonstrations. Whether 'the general function of securing adequate standards of competence and conduct among persons engaged in the shoeing of horses' confers on the Company the right to initiate prosecutions for offences by unregistered persons under Section 16 of the Act would require examination: it is clear that no other body is specifically given the duty of enforcement of that Section. Certainly the Company is entitled, indeed is probably required, to bring to the notice suggesting that a person registered by the Council may have been guilty of serious misconduct in a professional respect, so that the Council's disciplinary machinery may be set in motion.

These matters apart, there is one proposal which has been outlined from time to time which, if careful examination confirmed that it could confer benefits on both farriers and the horses they serve, might well become a focus for the energy and experience which the Company has accumulated in craft matters over the last century. Certainly there is no other body better placed than the Company to take the lead in exploring and sponsoring the conception.

This is the setting up of a National School of Farriery or National Farriery Centre.

At present the craft lacks any agency through which research can be undertaken and new materials or techniques can be examined. What can the sciences of genetics and nutrition contribute to the growth, health or development of the equine hoof? What new materials or amalgams or plastics are adaptable as horse shoes? What new tools, machines or techniques could be applied in farriery? These may not be the best questions to ask,

151

but every living craft needs its growing point if it is not to become moribund.

The need and possibilities of such a national development centre require examination in depth. Not least important is the ambience within which it could best flourish: within a faculty of veterinary surgery? within the British Equestrian Centre? How can the essential autonomy be assured to it within a larger organisation? How is it to be financed? The Worshipful Company of Farriers achieved the goal of statutory registration after some hundred years of endeavour. This new concept, if it is to be pursued, should be realisable within a less generous time scale.

A start should probably be made by finding the answers to the questions,

What is meant by a National Farriery School or Centre?
What functions is it to perform?
In what ambience is it to operate?

Those answers could well provide the answers to some of the other questions posed above.

Here then is one development for the benefit of the craft which might well form a new objective for the Company in furthering the responsibilities which it took upon itself in sponsoring the inclusion of Section 1 in the Farriers (Registration) Act, 1975.

H.L.

Epitaph on a Smith
in Nettlebed Churchyard

My sledge and hammer lie declin'd,
My bellows, too, have lost their wind;
My fire's extinct, my forge decay'd,
My coals are spent, my iron's gone,
My nails are drove, my work is done.

The Farriers Registration Council in consultation with The Worshipful Company of Farriers, The National Master Farriers Blacksmiths and Agricultural Engineers Association and The Council for Small Industries in Rural Areas, issued in 1979 a pamphlet entitled HOW TO BECOME A FARRIER, which gives full particulars of the Schemes of Training offered by the Worshipful Company and those offered by the National Association and the main Scheme called the Farriery Apprentice Scheme.

This pamphlet can be obtained from The Farriers Registration Council, 4 Royal College Street, London, NW1 0TU.

Composition of the Craft Committee as at 31st March 1979

The Master and Wardens, *ex officio*
Chairman: Past Master Brigadier J. Clabby, CBE, MRCVS
Vice-Chairman: Mr. Past Master Arthur G. Smith
Honorary: Mr. Past Master Alec Hobson, CBE, MVO
Court: Mr. Past Master G.B. Garnham
   Mr. Past Master John Stroud
   Mr. Past Master M.A.P. Simons, MRCVS
   Mr. Assistant H.J. Cooper, FWCF(Hons.)
Livery: Mr. E.P. Stern, FWCF
CoSIRA: Mr. W.G. Trust
British Horse Society: Mr. John Stevens MBE
Horserace Betting Levy Board: Mr. M.R.C. Crawshay
The Jockey Club: Lt. Colonel J.E.S. Chamberlayne
National Master Farriers', Blacksmiths' & Agricultural Engineers' Association: Mr. W.T. Hinchliffe, Mr. E. Martin, AFCL
Royal Agricultural Society of England: Captain C.G.E. Barclay, MA
Thoroughbred Breeders' Association: Mr. J.S. Delahooke
Scotland: Professor G.S. Ferguson, BSc, MRCVS
Examinations Board: Mr. J.R. Attfield, FWCF
Honorary Treasurer, Charitable Trust: Mr. Past Master A.J. Barsham, BCom., FCA
Farriers Registration Council: The Registrar
Field Officer: Mr. Cyril Cooper, AFCL
Registrar to the Company: Mr. F.E. Birch

Composition of the *Examinations Board* as at 31st March 1979

The Master, Chairman and Vice-Chairman of the Craft Committee, *ex officio*
Observer: The Registrar of the Farriers Registration Council

Mr. J.R. Attfield (Chairman)	Mr. D.F. Oliver, BSc, MRCVS
Brig. J. Clabby, CBE, MRCVS	Mr. Colin Smith, FWCF(Hons)
Mr. H.J. Cooper, FWCF(Hons)	Mr. D. Symons, FWCF(Hons)
Mr. A. Duff, FWCF	Mr. S.F. Varnam, AFCL
Mr. W.J. Grantham, FWCF	Mr. T.F. Williams, FWCF
Mr. T.F.M. Head, FWCF	Mr. Cyril Cooper, AFCL (Field Officer)
Mr. E. Martin, AFCL (representing the NMF, B & AE (Association)	Mr. F.E. Birch (Registrar)

Composition of the *Farriers Registration Council* as at 1st March 1979

Nominated by The Worshipful Company of Farriers:
 Past Master Brigadier J. Clabby, CBE, MRCVS (Chairman)
 Mr. Past Master E.H. Newcome Wright
 Mr. Past Master M.A.P. Simons, MRCVS
 Mr. Assistant H.J. Cooper, FWCF(Hons)
Nominated by The National Master Farriers', Blacksmiths' & Agricultural Engineers' Association:
 Mr. W.T. Hinchliffe

Mr. E. Martin, AFCL
Miss Ruth Rowley
Mr. E.G. Plant, FWCF(Hons)
One vacancy – a farrier employee – to be appointed
Nominated by the Royal College of Veterinary Surgeons:
Mr. S.L. Hignett, CBE, BSc, MRCVS
Mr. P.N. Hull, BVSc, MRCVS
Nominated by the Jockey Club:
Major W.D. Gibson
Nominated by The Royal Society for Prevention of Cruelty to Animals:
Mr. R.J. Cox
Nominated by The Council for Small Industries in Rural Areas:
Mr. W.G. Trust
Nominated by the Scottish Development Agency:
Mr. J.L. Carruthers
Nominated by The British Equestrian Federation:
Major D.S. Allhusen, DL, MA

CHAPTER 5

Administrative

Finance: Relentless Pursuit of Riches

The title of this Chapter on Finance has been chosen for the reason that throughout the Company's history there has been the constant reference to the lack of funds, which has prevented the Company from doing what it wanted to do – in particular the furtherance of the promotion of the care of its trade. In the Chapter on Craft Activities will be seen the paucity of the Company's Funds which were required to look after the Registration Scheme inaugurated in 1890 at the meeting at the Mansion House presided over by The Lord Mayor. Appeal after appeal to members of the Company, to all Horse Societies, to the Horse-owning public, and to the Livery Companies were made with very little success for the Company has always been in great financial straits and continued over the centuries to have no moneys, no land or endowment of any kind, relying for its Income from the quarter-age and fines payable by members. It was not till 1965 that a legacy from Past Master Robert Buckingham amounting to £13,000 increased the finances of the Company.

In the introduction to this Volume reference was made to Inflation and the Appendix on 'Value of Money' gives an explanation.

This Chapter has not dealt with the General Appeal made in 1969 – known as 'No Foot No Horse' – for this has been covered elsewhere, in particular in the Chapter by Past Master Barsham on the Company's Charitable Trust, and in the Chapter on Craft Activities where it will be seen that due acknowledgment has been paid to the enormous financial help from the Horserace Betting Levy Board.

In September 1975, following the adoption of the Accounts, the

Court decided that steps must be taken to ensure that the annual Costs of the Company must be covered by Income so that reliance should not be almost solely on the receipt of Fines and Fees of new Liverymen, which were an unknown amount each year and, in any case, part of the Fines and Fees should be added to Capital.

The Author, in writing the chapter on Finance and Accounts, has, so to speak, begun at the end, for what happened in 1975 resembles the exact position appertaining to the eighteenth and nineteenth centuries – an analysis of the financial state of the Company; the same references, possibly in different language, that expenditure must not exceed income. This problem, similar to that of every organisation or institution in the world, was discussed and was the subject of many Minutes in the Company's history and examples will be found throughout this volume even to the extent of the resignation of a Mr. Gower in 1872 for over-spending.

In 1961 Quarterage was abolished due to the amount of work in collecting such small sums from an increasing number of members by Redemption of the liability for the payment of Six Guineas and to call on the existing Members of the Livery to redeem their liability on the basis of 30 years purchase with adjustments for the period of their membership. It was decided to make redemption of Quarterage compulsory for new members of the Company but voluntary only for existing members and notice was given for the necessary and appropriate amendment of the Ordinances. It is interesting to read that the question of commuting quarterage had been raised sixty years earlier, for it was in June 1900 that a letter was received from Sir Ernest Clark, a Liveryman, suggesting that an arrangement should be made for members to commute their Quarterage if they so desired, but at the next meeting the Master (Arthur Gerald Smith) reported that he and the Wardens had considered the matter but were not in favour of making any change in the present position.

However, in 1975 the Company found it necessary to increase its Income by subscriptions (Quarterage) and that for the future all new Liverymen should pay an Annual Subscription of £10 and that all existing Liverymen be voluntarily invited to pay a similar subscription. It is interesting to note that the word 'Annual Subscription' was used instead of 'Quarteridge', but in 1978 it was agreed that the word 'Quarterage should be substituted to conform with the Ordinances, for 'Quarterage' was contained in the Orders, Rules and Ordinances of 1678 in the sum of 'fower shillings a piece yearely by twelve pence a quarter' and many references to 'quarterage' (the modern equivalent) are contained in the early Minutes.

And now to begin at the beginning.

Quarterages were due at the meeting of the Court at Midsummer and the Minutes each year give a list of all quarterage collected during the year. The list of names has enabled the Author to trace when a member joined and when he retired. In the meeting following, there appeared the Audit Certificate which showed 'amounts due from members'. The list of quarterages in the Minute book was also an approximate guide to the numbers in the Livery at particular dates.

Since 1899 the Record Book contains all the names of the Livery and Freemen admitted.

Admissions to the Livery
1890–1979

1890–99	16
1900–09	8
1910–19	13
1920–29	40
1930–39	40
1940–49	130
1950–59	101
1960–69	103
1970–79	156
	607

Livery 1890	81	(as per account of quarterage collected Lady Day 1890)
Livery 1979	383	(Freemen 5)

In the eighteenth and nineteenth centuries and up till 1944, the size of the Livery was between fifty to sixty members. In 1936 when the Author became a Liveryman, approximately 130. In 1961 the number had increased to 252, hence the reason for discontinuing the collection of 4/– per annum from each Liveryman (supra). In 1979 the number in Livery is 383 members. The Accounts in June 1979 show Quarterage received amounted to £2,265.

This chapter on Finance is but a fragment of 260 years (1718–1978). The information has been obtained from the Auditors' Reports entered annually in the Minute Book.

It is in the Orders, Rules and Ordinances of 1678 that is found the first reference to the audit of Accounts:

'Alsoe it is ordayned that within twenty dayes after the election of a new Master and Wardens, the last Master and Wardens and every of them respectively shall give a true and perfect accompt in writeinge unto such persons as shall be appointed auditors for that purpose by the Court of Assistants or the major part of them for the concerneinge all moneyes, plate, goods and writeings that shall come to his or theire hands or custody belonginge to the said Company, and shall upon auditing of such accompt, pay and deliver the same monys, plate goods, chattells and writeings remaineing in his or theire hands to the Master of the Company, for the tyme beinge for the use of the Company, upon payne that every person and persons refusing soe to doe shall forfeite and pay to the Master, Wardens Assistants and Commonalty, the sum of forty shillings of lawfull mony of England for every weeke that he or they shall detayne any of the premisses in his or theire hands or custody over and aboue the full value of the things detayned'

The reference to the penalty 40/– per week has a resemblance to penalties today payable under the Company's Act. So be it, the Audit Certificate has regularly been in the name of the members appointed by the Court. However, there are two references to the manner in which the Accounts should be prepared. In fact, an account of the Receipts and of the Payments has and still is the basis – perhaps over the last thirty years a little modernisation, e.g. a Balance Sheet – but no inflation accounting! It is quite clear from the Minutes that the Master was, so to speak, the Treasurer. He kept the moneys in his own hands – not always too accurately according to the following Minute:

2nd July 1770

'The Master handed over the Cash to the new Master when the latter took office just after Midsummer. At this date the outgoing Master, Mr. John Kennett was apparently in a muddle; the Auditors certified that £24. 6s. 9d. was to be handed over to Master John Bunnell, whose account opens as follows:

Received of Mr. John Kennett, the late Master,
the balance of his Account..£24. 6. 9.
    do. do.   Overplus Money
not accounted for...£7. 7. 4.'

The Minutes do not refer to the 'Overplus' – as to whether it was recovered from the Master or written off! (The Author has a fellow feeling in his many Treasurerships)

In some Livery Companies the Master or Wardens are expected to give a Bond, e.g. the Renter Warden of the Poulters – but there are no references to Bonds given by the Masters or Wardens of the Farriers Company!

It is seen that it was necessary to appoint Auditors and these were duly appointed each year.

The earliest reference in the first minute book extant was in 1719:

'This Court Doth agree now to proceed to the Choise of Mr. Daniell Williams Mr. Robert Cranston Mr. Thomas Potter Mr. George Hall Mr. John Wackett and Mr. Samuel Pullen or any ffour of them with the Clerk are appointed to Audit the Late Masters Accounts.'

The above extract regarding the appointment of Auditors is an example which was followed each year and the Minute Books contain a lengthy certificate from the auditors containing details of the Cash balances, that they have inspected the conveyances of any property held by the Company, and details of any Government Stocks.

Today the Auditors Report that they are satisfied that the accounts are in order is still shown in the Minute Book and the detailed accounts are furnished to the Members of the Court. The Auditors' Report is almost in the same form, though somewhat modernised – but there is no mention of possessions. In 1977 it was decided that a summary of accounts be inserted in the Annual Record so that Liverymen could be informed of the finances of the Company. See Introduction for another example of informing Liverymen.

Readers may find the following extracts of interest – although possibly irrelevant in a history of six centuries – nevertheless it shows not only the paucity of the Company's funds but the care and attention with which the Court dealt with its moneys – although the investment policy did not create much wealth.

The earliest reference to the investment of moneys was in 1723 when it was ordered that One hundred pounds out of money remaining in the Master's hands at the time of the audit, be invested in South Sea Stock.

The reference to 'South Sea Annuities' only five years after the 'South Sea Bubble' may need a little explanation. The original South Sea Bubble occurred in 1711–1720 with a Company formed to take over the National Debt in 1719 for Seven million pounds in return for a South Sea trading monopoly. Subsequently, speculation brought a rush of companies for the wildest aims. South Sea Stock went over £1,000 per £100 Stock before a catastrophic fall, although, strangely enough, never below £132. One of the few men to buy and sell at the right time to make a fortune was Sir Robert Walpole, later England's first Prime Minister, and the Earl of Orford.

The Audit Book of 1725 shows that balance in the hands of the Master was £62. 16s. 2d, whilst the Company held £100 of South Sea Annuities. In addition, there were 18 Notes in hand totalling £89. 18s. 0d. It is clear from the Minutes that the Notes were moneys due previously from members of the Livery. In fact in the Inventory of 1726 there is a list of the Notes which were for 'Livery and other Fines, which it was not convenient to pay on entering Some Notes were never met and as they drop out of the list in later years were probably considered 'bad'.

Obviously, the 'Funds' was the only type of investment the Court favoured although at the end of the eighteenth Century and beginning of the nineteenth consideration was given to investing in Freehold Property.

In fact, in 1793, the Court considered

'the propriety of selling out the money belonging to the Company now in the ffunds and applying the same to the purchase of Freehold Estate',

but no action was taken.

In the Records of the Company there were Audit Books containing records of the Masters' Receipts and Payments with the Auditors Certificates and annual inventories. An example of the Certificate by the Auditors is taken from the Minute of the 21st July 1726 –

'We whose names are hereunto subscribed Auditors of The Receipts and Payments made by Mr. John Wackett as Master of the Company for the year last do find that he hath received for the use of the said Company £197. 4. 2. and that he hath paid £71. 12. 8. and that there resteth due to the Company £125. 11. 6. Also the Swear Notes. Following Mr. Raynor's Noate £5. 0. 0. (here follows five more Gentlemen's Notes each for £5. 0. 0.).

In the Chest: A Silver Salt, the Charter, the By-Laws, the Pedigree, the Common Seal, the Streamers and Banners, Coates and Capps, 48 yards of blew and white Ribbon, twenty-one yards of bays.

In the Clerk's hands – the Staffe and Head, twelve Books great and small. Mr. Sole's Gift was received and given away to the Poor as the Will in that case directs.

Given under our Hand the 21st Day of July 1726
(signed by six Gentlemen)'

'Which Report was now read and approved of and the Ballance paid and the Noates delivered up and It is Agreed and Ordered that One Hundred pounds South Sea Annuities be forwith purchased'

'In 1733 the fees paid by every member coming into the Company by redemption increased from 3s. 4d. to 13s. 4d. and that the premium to be given for the procuration of Redemptioners be £1 1s. 0d. instead of 10s. 6d.'

There are numerous references to the charges, fines and quarteridge being forgiven and there were numerous references to Penalties and Summonses issued. It is clear that the Company was worried by its lack of finances. However, in 1751 the Company's South Sea Stock must have issued some new stock, which was undersubscribed, to the Company ordered its stock, now amounting to £250, to be sold and in the following year there is a reference in the Minutes:

'Ordered that Mr. Deane do Transfer the Capital Sum of Two

Hundred Sixty One pounds Thirteen Shillings and Eight pence South Sea Stock unto and for the Use and in the name of this Company in its Corporate Capacity.'

and later in the same year:

'Ordered that the Company's South Sea Stock be for the future in the name of the Master for the time being if the same be approved by the South Sea Company.'

Whilst there are many references to moneys received and expended, the Minutes do not contain a single reference to the South Sea Stock until nearly a century later in 1848 when there appears the following:

'Stock of the Farriers Company –
£2050 3 per cent South Sea Annuities of 1751

Divd due 5th July 1847	£30	15	0	
Divd due 5th Jan 1848	30	15	0	
	61	10	0	
	1	15	10	Propy Tax – 17.11
				Propy Tax – 17.11
	59	14	2d	

One of the earlier references illustrating the length the Company went in collecting the sums of 'fower shillings a piece yearly by Twelve pence a quarter' appears in the Minutes:

25th October 1764

'Ordered that the Honorary Members and others of this Company that have not paid their Quarteridge to the Company due at Lady Day Last be summoned to the different Courts of Request in the Districts they Live in for the payment of such Quarteridge, and that the Beadle of the Company be Employed to attend the different Courts and Recover the said Quarteridge for which attendance and Recovery of Quarteridge the Beadle is to have six pence each Man Exclusive of the fees of the Court, And It is furthered Ordered that the Beadle do attend the Several Courts in his Gown and Staff.'

It will be noted that the Beadle played an important part in the collection of moneys and he was also a canvasser for he was 'Intitled to ten shillings and sixpence for every Farrier that is Compelled by Caveat from the said Beadle to be a Member of the said Company'.

In fact, any means were adopted to chase members to pay their Quarteridge.

In 1818 'Mr. Gardner (Middle Warden) offered to permit his

Traveller who goes to Oxford and Lowestoffe to call upon such persons indebted to the Company for Quarteridge as live in these places, which offer was accepted by the Court'.

To-day there are many treasurers of Clubs and Societies who could no doubt use this method!

Again, in 1810 a resolution was that £1500 South Sea Stock be sold and invested in the purchase of Landed Property. Two years later, this resolution was rescinded. Instead, a Committee be appointed to purchase Freehold Ground Rents. It was sixty years later, in 1878, that a property in Hackney was purchased for £1,090.

1775

It is interesting to see a reference to Cheque Books, but it is assumed from the following minute that it was probably a Receipt Counterfoil Book:

> 'Ordered that for the future all Receipts for the Business relative to the Company be given from a Cheque Book to be provided for that purpose. And that Mr. Thos Whitehorn, Mr. John Spicer and Mr. Henry Thorowgood provide the Cheque Books and Cheque Plate for the use of the Company'.

A few more extracts from the Minutes reveal that the same state of poverty still existed. It was in 1844 that Mr. Sherwood the Clerk had resigned (reference is made in the Section on Clerks on page 181) but in 1850 Mr. Witton, one of the Assistants, reported that the Company's Stock showed £2050 but when Mr. Sherwood was elected in 1795 there was only £350. There was the following note:

> 'Mr. Higgs (The Master) also mentioned that if Mr. Sherwood had done his duty during his 49 years Clerkship, the Company would now be in possession of £2050 a year or upwards instead of a Lousey £59 11s. 2d. by taking a circumference of 7 miles round St. Paul's which the Charter had . . .'

The last few lines were badly rubbed and illegible. The reference to the circumference meant that the Company had the right to procure all working Farriers to be free of the Company within 7 miles.

1833

In October 1833 the Clerks laid before the Court a letter from Sir Francis Palgrave, one of the Commissioners appointed to enquire into the existing state of the several Municipal Corporations in England and Wales enclosing a statement of the various points on which he required information and requesting the attendance of the Clerk at Guildhall to give information and furnish such documents as might be required relative to this Corporation.

Whereupon Resolved 'That this Court is not desirous of throwing any obstacle in the way of the proposed enquiry and that the Clerk attend in pursuance of such requisition and act therein as circumstances may require.'

9th November – The Clerks reported that they had . . . attended several times on Sir Francis Palgrave . . . and had furnished him with such information and copies of such Documents relative to this Corporation as he had required and that he had expressed himself gratified by the promptness with which the information had been furnished.'

In 1834 it was reported that 'The Commissioner expressed entire satisfaction in the ready full and satisfactory answers which had been given to the requisitions of the Commissioners. But they had also requested to be furnished with an Account (on an average of the last four or five years) of the permanent income, and also of the expenses of the Company. But the Warden also reported that the Master and Wardens altho' they presumed that there would be no objection to their furnishing such an Account thought it not proper for the Clerk to furnish the Account without the Consent of the Court.

Ordered that the Clerk furnish such Accounts accordingly.'

It may be that annual accounts had to be produced each year but no evidence can be found that this was so.

This was an era of reform and already of consistent attacks on tradition, and fifty years later, in 1884, came another onslaught led by the Liberal Minister of Parliament for Chelsea, James Firth Bottomley Firth, a demagogue who became one of the Commission headed by the sadly slighted Earl of Derby. Again, the Farriers co-operated, answering fully eight Returns on Foundations and Object, one on Charities, and a six-part Return on Constitution and Privileges of Membership, not without accompanying these replies by a protest, showing the strength of their feelings against 'an infringement of the rights, liberties and privileges of the Company enjoyed by ancient charter'. The Companies were completely vindicated and one result was the setting up of the City and Guilds (sometimes better thought of as Guilds and City) Institute, which flourishes to-day.

It appears that Property Tax was deducted from the dividends. It was in 1842 that the extracts show that . . .

'inasmuch as the Income of the Company does not amount to £150 per annum Mr. Edwards be (and he is hereby) requested in conjunction with the Clerk to take the necessary measures to obtain a return of the Sum deducted for the Property Tax, and exemption from any future payment.'

However, the Tax Office in Somerset Place, after much enquiry had been told that as the Farriers are a Corporation and not an individual, the Commissioners would not be likely nor perhaps warranted in ordering a return of Duty. Accordingly no further steps were taken in regard to the Application for a Return of Duty.

In 1853 the following Minute had appeared:

'In consequence of the Orders made by the Government in relation to the South Sea Stock in which the sum of £2050 the funds of the Company are at present invested It was moved that the Trustees with the consent of the Master do transfer or otherwise deal with the said fund in such a manner as they shall think proper.'

In June of the same year:

'The Trustees of the Company reported that they had sold the South Sea Stock of £2050 and invested the money arising from such sale in the 3 per cent consolidated Bank Annuities and there is now the sum of £2258 19s. 1d. standing in such Fund in Trust for the Company.'

Once again the finances of the Company was in question for in 1866 it was reported that:

'the Clerk had felt it his duty to bring before the Court the fact that for some years past the necessary expenses of the conduct of the Business of the Company have exceeded the Income of the Company and in order to pay such excess the Court has been occasionally obliged to resort to a sale of part of the invested Funds. The Clerk has therefore advised that the Court should take such matter into its serious consideration and adopt such course as the Court in its judgement may deem expedient and necessary taking into its consideration the inability of some of the Members of the Livery when elected on the Court having refused to accept and serve such Offices.'

and in 1867:

'The Court having maturely and deliberately considered the question of excess of Expenditure over the Income of The Company directed the Clerk to lay a Case before some eminent Counsel for his Opinion as to the legality of expending the Company's funds in the manner they have been accustomed to do and what course he would advise the Court to take having regard to the Charter and By-Laws of the Company.'

In 1872 Mr. Gower (he had been Master in 1864–65 and 1865–66), in tendering his resignation from the Company wrote as follows:

'I cannot register my vote to sanction the continuous drawings from the principal, there being to my certain knowledge many poor connected with the Company who have a legal right to the moneys now unnecessarily expended in banqueting and of which I do not feel justified in being a participant.'

Mr. Gower's resignation was accepted without comment. The Company's stock by that time had been reduced to £1852. In 1873

the Stock had diminished to £1765.
In 1874:

> 'Resolved) That with the exception of the fines and fees payable by the Freemen on joining the Company the fines and fees payable by persons on joining the Company and on their subsequent steps up to and including the Mastership be doubled from the date of this Resolution.'

In 1875, £1624 2s. 1d. Stock 3% Consul was the sole asset of the Company, other than it possessions.

The following extracts from the Minutes disclose what happened at Court meetings and the interest shown by members of the Court to the financial details of the Company:

> 'Clerk to keep a Cash Book and balance it with the Bank Book. All monies received or paid to go through the Bank'.
> 'Special Account of the Poor Fund to be kept. Distributions to be as far as possible on the first Thursday in each year'.
> 'Inventory to be submitted on first Thursday in July as well as Account of receipts and payments.'

In 1879 a Committee had been set up to report on the Expenditure of the Company on Dinners etc. The cost of entertainments had risen from £34 in 1869, to £170 in 1877, and £162 in 1878. This was partly accounted for by the rapid increase in membership and the Livery having been invited to the November Dinners. The Committee made various recommendations in a long Report fully entered on the Minutes, including the raising of fees – On joining the Court from £20 to £50. On any member of the Court (other than the present members) taking Office as Warden £10 and as Master £25. The fee for Freedom remained at £1 4s. 0d. and for Livery £10. Sums paid for Apprentices to be invested as Capital. Quarteridge in arrear. If unpaid for two years, after a written demand in writing, the member and his widow and children to be ineligible for relief. Such members also shall not be invited to dinners of the Company.

Visitors Book to be kept with names of all Diners, both members and visitors.

> 'That at the Court on 24th June in each year, not less than two nor more than six of the Members of the Livery (such Members to include those who have during the preceeding year paid the Steward's fine) shall be called upon to fine for Steward at the next Court. In default such persons shall be liable not to be invited to any Livery Dinner of the Company and shall be ineligible to attend any Court Dinners'.

Beadle to be paid for each attendance not an annual salary. Beadle to collect the Quarteridge.

As to audit of Accounts at least two days before the Master is to be appointed.

In 1881 there is the first mention of a Finance Committee being appointed, but they do not appear to have done very much for there are no references in the Minutes of their reports. Meanwhile, throughout the latter part of the nineteenth century and first half of the twentieth, there are constant references to the state of the Company's finances in the Court Minutes.

(In 1956 the Finance Committee was reconstituted and is now a very active Committee and is combined with the Social Committee to advise the Court on the arrangements for Social functions).

But to continue with the financial record of the Company –

As has been said, the Auditors' Reports contained particulars of the Company's 'wealth'. The following table gives readers an idea of the Company's financial state –

	Cash at Bank	Government Stock — Consols	Income from Property	Quarterage owing from Members
1890	£ 99. 1. 8.	£1096. 11. 10	£ 53. 12. 8.	£ 10. 0. 0.
1900	153. 3. 6.	891. 14. 7.	53. 12. 8.	2. 12. 6.
1910	305. 15. 0.	891. 14. 7.	161. 10. 0.	8. 2. 6.
1920	78. 11. 6.	530. 0. 0.	32. 0. 0.	4. 2. 6.
1930	192. 1. 11.	1150. 0. 0.	32. 0. 0.	7. 10. 6.
1933	136. 1. 4.	1097. 0. 0.	32. 0. 0.	

In 1934 the Company altered the form of the Auditors Report and the Minutes show the details of a Receipts & Payments Account and the surplus/deficit in the year.

The 1935 Accounts showed a deficit of £174. 13s. 2d. brought forward from 1934 and a surplus for 1935 of £235. 12s. 1d. Thus the Company's funds show a credit of £60. 18s. 11d.

The following years' Accounts sometimes show a small deficit, sometimes a small surplus. In 1939 there appears in the Minutes a survey of the Company's future finances, which showed an annual deficit of approximately £47. 0s. 0d.

During the next ten years, as shown elsewhere, there were large numbers of admissions to the Company and fees were increased – the Capital Fund showing a balance of over £9,000.

The Company was still not 'wealthy' but it had certainly improved its position. The Author will not weary readers with any more details – suffice it to say the 'the Relentless pursuit of Riches' finds the Company to-day in a satisfactory position but with the present inflation a close watch is still needed.

In covering the financial situation of the Company for 260 years, the Author would like to mention a few of the recent Liverymen who have been responsible for the financial and accountancy services. First and foremost, George Garnham – for not only has George been Auditor since 1949, he has been the financial adviser to the Company for the last thirty years.

When in 1958 Edward Newcome Wright was appointed Clerk, he notified the Court that he felt unable to act as Accountant and the Court invited the Author's Accountancy Firm to look after this part of the Clerk's duties. The Author's son, Michael Prince, FCA, a partner in the firm and a member of the Livery, undertook the work till the appointment of Arnold Scott, FCA, as Clerk, who naturally undertook the accountancy as part of the Clerk's duties. As explained elsewhere, on his retirement as Clerk, he continued to be the Honorary Accountant to the Company until his retirement from Practice in 1975, when Past Master Barsham, FCA, kindly accepted the office of Honorary Accountant; of whom much appears elsewhere in this volume.

The Ordinances

In 1953 the Court decided that the Company's Bye-Laws should be recodified. After the Great Fire of 1666, when the Company lost practically the whole of its property, it sought, and in 1674 obtained, a Royal Charter of King Charles II which, in the cumbrous language used in legal documents of the times, sets out the powers and government of the Company, including certain matters such as regulations regarding the control of the trade and apprentices. It was appreciated that the Bye-Laws had been largely out of date and inoperative.

The new Ordinances approved by the Court on 10th March 1953 do not form a new Constitution but are a codification of the Rules and Regulations of the Company applying to modern times as settled by the Charter and the Bye-Laws above-mentioned, modified and added to by Orders and Resolutions of the Court of the Company from time to time from the eighteenth century onwards. The Ordinances amended to 1979 follow.

The Ordinances of the Worshipful Company of Farriers
1953 (Amended to 1979)

The Court

1 The Court of the Company shall consist of the Master, three Wardens and not less than ten or more than twenty Assistants.

The Master and Wardens

2 The Master and Wardens shall be elected by the Court annually on Midsummer Day, being the Feast of the Nativity of St. John the Baptist; or, if that day be a Sunday, then on the following day. They shall be installed in their respective offices at the Quarterly Court next following. Unless the Court otherwise decides their election shall be by ballot.

3 The Master shall be a person who shall have previously

served as a Warden. The Wardens, known as Upper, Middle and Renter Wardens respectively, shall be persons who have previously been elected Assistants.

4 A Master who has served his term of office and any Warden who having served his term of office is not elected to higher rank shall again immediately become Assistants.

5 The Master and Wardens shall upon taking office make and sign their Declarations in the customary form before the assembled Court, such Declarations taking the place of the Oaths prescribed in the Charter and Bye-laws.

6 Casual vacancies in the office of Master and Wardens, by death, retirement or removal from office, shall be filled for the remainder of the year by the Court.

7 If any person shall be elected and chosen by the Court to be Master or a Warden of the Company and shall refuse to take upon him the office to which he has been so elected he shall pay the Company a fine of Ten pounds.

The Assistants

8 The Assistants shall be elected (subject to Ordinances Nos. 11 and 12) for life by the Court from the Livery of the Company and upon election shall make and sign the customary Declaration, such Declaration taking the place of the Oath prescribed in the Charter and Bye-laws.

9 Unless there be special circumstances to be taken into consideration, vacancies on the Court shall be filled by the election of members of the Livery of some years standing, provided that they have the necessary qualifications and are willing to serve.

10 No person shall be elected as an Assistant at the same Court as that at which he is appointed to the Livery. This ordinance may be waived in any special case by a Resolution carried by a three-fourths majority of the members present at the Court, provided that due notice of motion has been given.

11 Procedure for Election of Assistants

(i)   The Clerk to circulate the Court asking for nominations. Such nominations to give relevant details of the candidate such as age, Company activities, connections with the City and/or farriery craft and a precis of why the nominator considers the candidate would make a good member of the Court.

(ii)   The Court Vacancies Committee to consider Liverymen in order of seniority and put forward any they think suitable for membership of the Court. In making this selection, the Committee should take into consideration (a) that the Company is a City Guild and, as such, should have a good proportional representation of the City on its Court; (b) the active state of a Liveryman and not necessarily his age;

(c) that, save in exceptional circumstances, a Liveryman should have been a member of the Company for at least ten years. In putting forward candidates the Committee should give reasons for doing so.

(iii)   The list of candidates submitted by the Court Vacancies Committee should include all those nominated by members of the Court. The list so submitted to be notified to the Court with the Agenda for the meeting at which an Assistant is to be elected; it should give against each name the name of the nominator and the qualifications for membership of the Court as supplied by the nominator and/or the Court Vacancies Committee.

(iv)   The voting for election to the Court should be a straight vote, i.e. one name only appearing on the ballot paper if there is one vacancy, two names if there are two vacancies and so on.

(v)   The Clerk to approach the candidate obtaining the largest number of votes (or the first two if more than one vacancy) asking officially if he is willing to fill the vacancy on the court.

(vi)   In the event of the elected candidate not wishing to become an Assistant another ballot on the same candidate (excluding the one refusing to take office) to be held at the next convenient meeting of the Court.

(vii)   In the event of the second selection by ballot not wishing to take office as an Assistant, a ballot shall be held at each subsequent meetings of the Court on the same candidates until the vacancy is filled, unless the Court decides by a three-fourths majority of those present that the list of candidates be abandoned and a new one compiled.

Removal from the Court

12 Any member of the Court may be removed by the Court for any just and reasonable cause on a resolution carried by a three-fourths majority of the members present at a Court and of which due notice of motion has been given. The voting on such Resolution shall be by ballot.

Resignations fromthe Court

13 Honorary Assistants. On the Court's initiative, or at his request, a member of the Court can be designated an Honorary Assistant.

An Honorary Assistant will cease to be a member of the Court, but will receive notice of meetings of the Court and all relevant papers, can attend such meetings and by leave of the Court may speak thereat. He will not be entitled to vote.

Court Meetings

14 The Court may meet at any time within the City of London or the Liberties thereof and make ordinances and regulations for the rule and government of the Company and for other general business of the Company. Four Quarter (or Quarterly) Courts shall be held on convenient days, one of which shall be Midsummer Day. If Midsummer Day falls on a Sunday the Midsummer Court shall be held on the following day.

15 The days and times for the holding of Courts shall be settled by the Court. Failing such decision by the Court the days and times shall be settled by the Master who may also call Special Courts to be held when need arises.

16 The order of precedence at Courts shall be as follows: (1) The Master; (2) The Upper Warden; (3) The Middle Warden; (4) The Renter Warden; (5) The Immediate Past Master; (6) Other Past Masters in order of seniority; (7) The Assistants who have not passed the Chair in order of seniority.

17 The Court may appoint Committees from among their number to consider any special matters with or without power to act without reference to the Court. The Master and Wardens shall be *ex-officio* members of all Committees.

18 Not less than fourteen days' notice shall be given by the Clerk of any meeting of the Court or any Committee thereof; the notice calling the meeting shall include the agenda to be taken thereat.

19 The Quorum for meetings of the Court shall be five members, and for meetings of Committees (other than the Committee referred to in Ordinance No. 55) one third, or the number nearest one third, of the Committee appointed but not less than two.

20 Any member of the Court intending to propose a motion shall give notice thereof at the Meeting of the Court immediately preceding that at which it is intended to be moved, or supply the Clerk in writing with the words of the intended motion not less than fourteen days before the Meeting at which it is to be moved.

In the latter case the full terms of the motion shall be sent to each member of the Court as soon as may be possible and not less than seven days before the meeting.

21 Voting at Meetings of the Court shall be by show of hands except where in these Ordinances a ballot is required. The Master or other Chairman of any meeting shall be entitled to vote on any Resolution, and in case of equality of votes he shall also have a casting vote.

Gowns, Badges, etc.

22 The gowns of the Master, Wardens, Clerk and Beadle and the Company's Mace shall be kept in an airtight box at the Clerk's

office or at the customary meeting place of the Court.

The Gold Chain and Badge of the Master shall be lodged at the Company's Bankers for safe custody; but, if he so desires, the Master's Badge may be retained by the Master during his term of office on his own responsibility.

The Badges of the Wardens and the Clerk shall be kept in the Company's safe.

All other members of the Court shall hold their own Badges or medals or those provided for them by the Company.

All badges and medals provided by the Company shall be returned to the Clerk when the person holding them ceases to be entitled to wear them.

23 Gowns, Badges and Medals shall be worn at all Courts of the Company (other than Special Courts held at the Clerk's office) and at dinners or similar occasions.

The Colours of ribbons which will be provided by the Company for badges and medals shall be as follows: Member of the Court who has not passed the Chair (other than Wardens), Light Blue; Wardens, Clerks and Chaplain, Red; The Master, Red; Past Master, Red with White edging; Twice Master, Two red stripes on White, and for each further period served as Master, an additional red stripe. The Chairman of the Registration Committee, Dark Blue.

24 Any member of the Court not wearing his Badge or Medal on any proper occasion shall be fined 15p. Such amounts shall be credited to the Poor Fund.

25 In the event of any jewelled Past Master's Badge coming into the possession of the Company, such badge shall be offered to Past Masters who do not possess such a badge in order of seniority, and the recipient shall be asked to hand back his unjewelled badge and make a contribution of Ten Pounds to the Poor Fund.

Admission to the Freedom and Livery

26 The Court may grant the Freedom of the Company to such persons as it may decide and whether they be members of the Farriers' Trade or not. The application for the Freedom shall be proposed by a member of the Livery and supported by a member of the Court.

27 The Court may appoint to the Livery of the Company any person who is a Freeman of the Company (whether by Patrimony, Servitude or Redemption) and of the City of London.

28 If any Freeman shall accept nomination and be called upon by the Court to take upon himself the Livery of the Company and shall refuse so to do he shall pay to the Company a fine of Ten Pounds.

29 Fellows and Associates of the Company, being Master Men or retired Master Men, may be admitted to the Freedom and Livery of the Company at reduced fines. Their application for such admission shall be supported by a member of the Council or Executive Committee of a Society or Association approved by the Court and by at least four other members of such Society of Association.

30 No member of the Company shall be called upon to act as a Steward of the Company (as required by the Charter) but every person appointed to the Livery shall be required at the time of his admission to pay a fine of such amount as the Court may from time to time decide in lieu of serving that office.

31 The application of any person desiring to take up the Freedom and/or Livery of the Company shall be submitted to the Court as soon as may be convenient, but prior to such submission each applicant shall be interviewed by the Master and Wardens.

32 The admission to the Freedom of the Company of persons approved by the Court may take place immediately, but admission to the Livery shall not take place until the applicant has been granted the Freedom of the City and has produced to the Clerk the certificate thereof.

The Fee Farm Rent

33 The Company shall pay 67p annually to the Exchequer, and if unpaid for forty days after demand the Company's right under the Charter shall cease. (NOTE: This amount is in modern times paid to The Crown Estate Commissioners).

Property and Investments

34 The Company's silver and all deeds and securities shall be lodged with the Company's Bankers for safe custody.

35 All investments of the Company shall be made in the name of the Company or in the joint names of three members of the Court as Trustees.

36 No investment shall be made or sold except pursuant to a Resolution of the Court.

37 The term 'Investment' in Ordinances Nos. 36 and 37 shall be deemed to include Stocks, Shares, House or Landed Property and money placed on deposit with a Building Society or the like, excepting a deposit made temporarily on the order of the Master pending permanent investment.

Banking

38 The Company's Banking Account shall be operated by the signatures of the Master and the Clerk for the time being; the Master and the Clerk shall also be authorised to sign any docu-

ments required by the Bank, including any orders for the temporary removal when necessary of any property in the hands of the Bank for safe custody.

The Company's Seal

39 The Seal of the Company shall not be used except by Order of the Court and shall be witnessed by the signatures of the Master and the Clerk.

The Auditors

40 Two or more of the Assistants shall be elected at each Midsummer Day Court to act as Auditors of the Company's Accounts for the year then ended. Such Auditors shall have the right of access to the books of Account and other records of the Company at any time during the year following their appointment.

Poor Fund

41 A special account shall be kept in the Company's Books of Account of all moneys received for the benefit of the poor. Such moneys shall be distributed as the Court may direct among distressed Freemen or Liverymen of the Company of Farriers, their widows and orphans, or other needy persons or charities.

42 The distribution of such moneys shall be decided upon at the Court next before Christmas and the distribution shall be made shortly before Christmas Day. Any special cases of need may, however, be considered and assisted at other times.

Honorary Chaplain

43 The Court may appoint an Honorary Chaplain.

The Clerk

44 The Court shall appoint a Clerk to hold office during the goodwill and pleasure of the Court; he shall be elected annually at the Midsummer Day Court. On his first appointment he shall make his Declaration before the assembled Court; his duties and remuneration shall be settled by the Court. The Court may also if thought fit appoint an Assistant (or Deputy) Clerk.

The Beadle

45 The Court shall appoint a Beadle to hold office during the goodwill and pleasure of the Court; he shall be elected annually at the Midsummer Day Court and his remuneration shall be settled by the Court. On his first appointment he shall make his Declaration before the assembled Court.

46 The Beadle's duties shall be to attend at all meetings of the

Court and upon such other occasions as the Master or the Clerk may direct; he shall also attend at every Common Hall summoned by the Lord Mayor.

Dinners, Luncheons, etc.

47 The Court may hold such Dinners, Luncheons, Entertainments and Meetings as it may deem fit, and either for the Court or for the Livery.

48 Unless it decides otherwise the Court shall lunch together on the days of the Quarterly Court Meetings; the expense of such Luncheons being defrayed by the members of the Court attending. Each new Liveryman shall be invited to lunch with the Court on the day of his appointment at the expense of the Company.

49 The order of precedence set out in Ordinance No. 16 shall be observed (except as to the Wardens) at all functions other than those declared by the Master to be informal occasions. The Wardens shall at Luncheons and Dinners sit either among the company or at the end of a table as may be convenient. The Clerk's seat shall be at the end of the table.

50 The expense of Court Dinners, Livery Dinners or Livery Luncheons shall be defrayed in such manner as the Court may decide.

51 Visitors may be introduced at any Luncheons or Dinners. The number of visitors and the charge to be made for them shall be in accordance with the accommodation available and the cost of the function.

52 The arrangements for any Court or Livery Dinners, Luncheons or other Entertainments shall be under the joint control of the Master and Wardens for the time being.

Registration of Farriers, etc

53 In view of the spirit of the Company's Charter, the Company shall do all possible to improve the standard of the Art of Farriery in London and elsewhere, whether by the holding of examination, the giving of prizes, or by other means considered by the Court to be convenient or advisable.

54 The Court may also, in similar manner, seek to improve the standard of work in other rural industries and crafts usually carried on in conjunction with farriery.

55 For the carrying out of any schemes the Court may appoint a Committee to be known as the Registration Committee, consisting of the Master and Wardens, other representatives of the Court and Livery of the Company, Veterinary Surgeons, practical members of the Farriery and allied trades, and any other persons considered by the Court to be suitable for such service.

56 The Registration Committee shall have such powers as are delegated to it by the Court, including the appointment of Examiners and any other schemes for encouraging the Craft.

57 Unless the consent of the Court has been first obtained, the Registration Committee shall not have authority to expend more than Twenty-five pounds on any one project, and its total expenditure in any one year (ending 24th June) shall not exceed One hundred pounds.

58 The Quorum for meetings of such Committee shall be decided by the Committee.

59 The Diplomas in Farriery to be granted after examination shall be 'Registered Shoeing Smith' (RSS), 'Associate of the Farriers' Company of London' (AFCL) and 'Fellow of the Worshipful Company of Farriers' (FWCF). The Syllabus and requirements for such examinations shall be decided by the said Committee.

60 The Court, on the recommendation of the Registration Committee may admit to the Honorary Fellowship of the Company (FWCF) a limited number of Farriers already on the Company's Register and in exceptional circumstances may admit to such Honorary Fellowship persons who, in the opinion of the Court, have rendered exceptional services to the Company or to farriery in general, even though the names of such persons shall not already be on the Company's Register. The number of such Honorary Fellows shall at no time exceed twelve in addition to those who were appointed prior to the year 1932. The nomination papers to be submitted to and considered by the Registration Committee shall be supported in such manner as the Court may direct.

61 The Fees chargeable to candidates and all matters of expense and finance of such schemes shall be decided by the Court who shall, however, take into consideration any recommendations made by the said Committee.

Apprentices and their Masters

62 The fees payable by a Liveryman of the Company on binding an Apprentice shall be as follows:

	£
Contribution to the General Funds	2.10
Poor Fund	0.15
	2.25

The Liveryman shall in addition pay the cost of preparing the Articles of Apprenticeship in a form approved by the Court of the Company and of the stamp thereon.

Fines and Fees Payable on Admissions

63 Save as provided in Ordinance No. 65, the Fines and Fees payable by persons made free of the Company and upon appointment to the Livery shall be as follows:

Servitude or Redemption

	General Funds	Poor Fund	Total
	£	£	£
Freedom	2.00		2.00
Livery	443.00	5.00	448.00
	£445.00	£5.00	£450.00

Plus Quarterage of £10.00 p.a. renewable 1st December

Patrimony (Sons, Sons-in-Law, Daughters)

	General Funds	Poor Fund	Total
	£	£	£
Freedom	2.00		2.00
Livery	243.00	5.00	248.00
	£245.00	£5.00	£300.00

Plus Quarterage of £10.00 p.a. renewable 1st December
Fee payable to the Chamberlain for the Freedom of the City £4.00

64 Of the above mentioned amounts payable to the Company's General Funds on joining the Livery such proportion shall be carried to Capital Account as the Court may from time to time determine. The remainder of such amounts shall be considered to be Income.

65 The Fines and Fees payable by persons who hold a Diploma as a fellow or Associate of the Company who are made free of the Company (whether by Patrimony, Servitude or Redemption) and upon appointment to the Livery shall be as follows:

	General Funds	Poor Fund	Total
	£	£	£
Freedom	2.00		2.00
Livery	145.00	3.00	148.00
	£147.00	£3.00	£150.00

Plus Quarterage of £10.00 p.a. renewable 1st December.
Fee payable to the Chamberlain for the Freedom of the City £4.00.

66 The whole of the amounts payable to the General Funds under Clause 65 shall be considered as Income.

176

Fines and Fees Payable on Court Elections

67 The Fines and Fees payable on elections to the Court and offices thereon shall be as follows:

	General Funds £	Poor Funds £	Total £
As an Assistant	124.00	1.00	125.00
Renter Warden	24.00	1.00	25.00
Middle Warden	24.00	1.00	25.00
Upper Warden	24.00	1.00	25.00
Master	49.00	1.00	50.00

68 One half of the amount payable to the Company's General Funds on election as an Assistant shall be carried to Capital Account or as the Court may direct. The other half of the said amount and the whole of the fines payable on election as a Warden or Master shall be considered to be Income.

Fines on Taking Office a Second Time

69 Any member of the Court remaining in the same office as Master or Warden for a further term in consecutive years may not be required to pay a second time the fines and fees set out in Ordinance No. 67 at the discretion of the Court.

Alterations in these Ordinances

70 No alteration in these Ordinances shall be made by the Court save by a Resolution of which notice of motion has been given and which is passed by a three-fourths majority of those present at the Court.

Minutes Rescinded

71 All Resolutions on the Minute Books of the Company prior to the Tenth day of March, 1953, which are repugnant to the terms of these Ordinances shall be deemed to be rescinded.

The above Ordinances were considered by the Court and finally approved on the Tenth day of March, 1953 and have since been amended pursuant to Ordinance No. 71.

Charitable Trust

by A.J. Barsham, FCA, Hon. Treasurer

In his review of the work of the Registration Committee during the decade 1962 to 1972 Mr. Past Master Alec Hobson referred to the growing need for more money to extend the Apprenticeship Scheme and the offer of the Betting Levy Board in 1968 to double its grant provided that the Company paid all the costs of administration of the scheme. When this was reported to the Court the obligation was willingly accepted and it was decided to make an Appeal to the members of the Livery to raise £25,000. It was also decided to set up a Charitable Trust to Administer the appeal funds and the money donated for the Apprenticeship Scheme.

The Livery Appeal was initiated by Mr. Past Master George Smith and continued by me when I succeeded him as Master in September 1968. The Livery Appeal was successful, soon passing the initial target of £25,000, and it was then decided to set up a National Appeal for the future of horse-shoeing. The Duke of Beaufort, KG, PC, Master of the Horse, kindly agreed to become President and the Appeal was launched by Past Master R.W.V. Neathercoat at a Cocktail Party held at the Cutlers Hall on the 30th October 1969. The theme was 'No Foot – No Horse' and over 35,000 copies of a pamphlet, drawn up by Mr. Past Master Michael Simons, explaining the need for trained farriers, were distributed to all societies connected with the horse, to race-courses, hunts, owners, trainers, veterinary associations etc. The members of the Committee all made valuable contributions in publicising the appeal and were greatly encouraged by the excellent response. We were fortunate to receive the support of Her Majesty The Queen and Her Majesty The Queen Mother. Donations or Deeds of Covenant were received from individuals, firms and associations anxious to support the training of more farrier. Whilst it is obviously impossible in this short review to deal to any extent with individual contributors I should like to mention the great help given by Mr. G.C. Gibson, the father of the Present Master and by two American owners, both of whom had Derby winners and the saddlers Company.

Ten years after the initial Appeals the funds stand as follows:

Livery Appeal	£ 4,400	annual income	£3366
National Appeal	£54,000	annual income	£4362

The income from the Livery Appeal has covered the Administration Costs while the income from the National Appeal has made an important contribution to the Apprenticeship Scheme funds.

The achievement of the Registration Committee in increasing the number of apprentices is referred to elsewhere in the History, and the financial support given by the Charitable Trust to the Committee has been an important factor in its success.

Both the Livery Appeal and the National Appeal are still open and I hope that when the next history comes to be written the funds available will have shown a considerable increase.

February 1979

The John Soule's Charity, 1572

The Soule's Charity arises out of the Will of John Soule (or Sowle) dated 28th March 1572, the Farriers' Company being entitled to an amount of 13s. 4d. per annum charged upon property in West Smithfield and payable to the Company by the Churchwardens of the Parish of St. Sepulchre, Holborn. The Charity passed out of the hands of the Parish to the Trustees of the London Parochial Charities under the City of London Parochial Charities Act, 1883.

In 1907 The Charity Commissioners for England and Wales made an Order whereby the charge upon the Smithfield property was redeemed by the transfer in trust for the Charity of an amount of New Consols, the dividends on which are payable to the Farriers' Company; the Investment stands in the name of 'The Official Trustees of Charitable Funds'.

Miss Sarah Smith

1882

'The Clerk reported that Miss Sarah Smith of No. 34 High Street, Islington (whose Father and brother were Farriers) had presented the Company with the sum of £250 for Investment, the Interest to be applied as the Court should at their first meeting in each year determine, with Power to the Court to spend the principal if they in their absolute discretion should at any such Meeting determine'.

In 1884 the Master reported a further gift of £250 by Miss Sarah Smith on the same terms as the previous gift. At the same meeting 'The Freedom of the Company to be conferred on her'. This was subsequently declined by Miss Smith, but an Address on Vellum was sent to her.

In 1884 the Capital sum of £500 was invested in £496 11s. 10d 2½% Consolidated Stock and the Income was paid to the Poor Box Fund.

In each annual report of the Auditors the Company's amount of Consolidated Stock was mentioned (approximately £900) and then appeared the phrase 'of which £496 11s. 10d is Miss Smith's gift to the Company'.

In 1911 the amount of Consolidated Stock (£891 14s. 7d), including Miss Smith's gift, was sold and the proceeds (£683 17s. 2d) were invested in Ground Rents. No mention was made of Miss Smith's gift or of its income. Obviously the Court had taken advantage of the Clause in the 1882 gift 'with Power to the Court to spend the principal if they in their absolute discretion should at any such Meeting determine'. So Miss Smith's gifts were absorbed in the Company's Capital Account.

William Yuill Memorial Fund

In 1966 his son, Mr. A.E. Yuill, in memory of his father, presented the Company with £500 to be constituted as a fund the income of which to be distributed annually on St. Andrew's Day as the Company in its discretion should think fit but paying due regard to the wish of the donor that it should benefit farriers blinded or injured in the course of their trade or too sick to carry on their trade.

The Poor Fund

The earliest reference appears in 1789 that the sum of £1 1s. 0d. should be paid to Mr. Layton (formerly one of the Assistants) when he requested the Court to grant him a Letter of Recommendation as a fit person to be chosen Beadle of the Parish of St. Andrew's Holborn. In the Minutes granting such recommendation, the sum of £1 1s. 0d. from the Poor Box was mentioned.

Obviously there had been a Poor Box − for later on in the extracts there are references to the state of the Poor Fund not having sufficient money in hand to pay the persons.

The Poor Box had a lock and key and the Minutes disclose in the 18th and 19th centuries that 'the Poor Box was duly produced and unlocked by the Master, opened and found to contain . . .' and the Clerk informed of the collection. It appears that the collection was made in the Court Room and not, as to-day, at the Court Luncheon or Dinner. (On one occasion the key was mislaid and a locksmith was called in).

In 1804; 'It was Resolved that a ffine of 1/− be paid by every member of the Court who attends without wearing his Medal and that such ffines be for the use of the Poor'. (To-day such fines as are collected are paid into the Poor Fund).

And in 1805: 'Resolved that in future no Member of the Court shall be exempt from payment of his ffine for non-attendance in Case he leaves the Court without leave of the Master.'

In 1808 an extract shows 'It appearing to the Court that the Poor's Money in Hand is not sufficient to pay the annual Sums usually given to the Poor. Resolved that the Court have no Public Dinner at the next April Court and that the sum of six pounds allowed towards such Dinner be applied in Aid of the Poor's Fund.'

In 1812 reference was made to the allowances that the Court made for a Dinner was increased to Ten Pounds except for the July Court which was to be £12 − but if the whole should not be expended, the surplus should be applied in aid of the Poor Box. (If such sums were exceeded the Master should pay the excess out of his own pocket).

The Minutes give us further information about the Poor Box or Poor Fund when in 1878 Mr. George Burt who was Sheriff in 1878–79, and Master in 1889, presented the Company with a Poor Box (See Gifts Section).

The Box is still in existence and is handed round the Table at each Court Luncheon or Dinner and the contents are paid into the Fund. In 1978–79 the collection received was £332 and in 1943 it was £5.

Possibly the best way to conclude this Account of the Poor Box is by quoting the paragraph contained in the 'Record', published in 1976:

> 'Thanks to the generosity of those attending the Quarterly Court lunches and dinners when the 'Poor Box' is passed round and the Fines on admission to the Livery and on members of the Court, Christmas gifts were made to four needy farriers and three dependants of recently deceased farriers and donations were made to the Riding for the Disabled Association and the London Harness Horse Parade Society, to a total of £245.'

Clerks

On page 188 appear the names of the Clerks from 1613–1972. It is pleasing to record that Franklin Edwin Birch is still the Company's Clerk, but it should be added that whilst the word 'Clerk' still exists as it did in 1674 in the Charter, the responsibilities and duties are hardly the same, for the Farriers Company has expanded enormously since the early days and members of the Livery who will have read of our Company's activities in this volume, will appreciate the work that the Clerk does today. However, the Clerk will be the first to agree that there are far less squabbles or friction in the Livery or in the Court than in the past. Perhaps today the members are far too busy with the activities of the Company to have time for the personal troubles as recorded in the last three centuries.

The Clerks of the 17th, 18th and 19th centuries were very much occupied in collecting fines. Today, whilst our Clerk has to collect a far greater sum of money each year, it is hoped 'Bad Debts' are few and far between!

The first reference to a Clerk was in the 1674 Charter, although the List shows three previous names. Then followed George Daggett, Clerk of the Company, who in 1691 gave evidence of the existence of the Company and, as referred to elsewhere, the Court of Aldermen on 23rd June 1692 'found by the oath of George Daggett the late Clerk of the said Company that most of the said Company's books and records were burnt in the dreadful fire of 1666'. From this evidence the Court of Aldermen 'hath sufficient grounds to pray the favour of this Court to re-establish this as a convenient Livery according to this humble petition'.

The Ordinance of 1356, to which reference is made elsewhere, makes no mention of a Clerk although no doubt Richard de Hertele and John de Oxenford, whom the Mayor chose from all the farriers in the City of London, 'the most sufficient men and the best knowing' and gave them full power to oversee and govern the said trade and to espy into the defaults thereof, required someone in the Company to help them keep records and accounts and also to see that those doing 'false work in shoe and nails or works of false metal shall pay 40 pence to the Chamber of the Guildhall.' The first election of a Clerk appears in 1726 when Mr. Thomas Jackson died and a ballot took place for the two candidates and 'upon casting up the votes or scratches then made that Walter Hutchins had sixteen votes and that the said Thomas Jackson fourteen votes.' (A curious coincidence that one of the candidates bore the same name as the late Clerk – possibly his son). Mr. Hutchins was elected . . . 'To have Hold exercise and enjoy the said place with all ffees proffitts and advantages there-unto due and of right belonging so long as he shall well and honestly use and behave himself therein, and was sworn for the Due execution of the said place accordingly.' Presumably his remuneration was fees collected from the fines.

'In 1731 Mr. Hutchins' health was questioned in Court, a vote taken whether he should continue as Clerk, resulting in the negative and arrangements were made for an election of a new Clerk. To be held at the Crown Tavern.' (A debate took place as to whether the vote recorded above was legal and a further vote was taken with the result that the Master was ordered to apply a fit person to transact the business of the Company). Nevertheless Mr. Hutchins appears to have continued in office, for two years later the minutes show that 'The Court having received a Letter from Mrs. Catherine Hutchins, Wife of the Mr. Walter Hutchins the present Clerk praying the Company to elect a Clerk in his stead he being not in a capacity to act for the Company and that the Company would be pleased to allow unto the said Walter Hutchins what they should think proper during his life.'

'Resolved that the said Mr. Walter Hutchins be discharged from his said Place or Office of Clerk to this Company, and he is discharged accordingly. And it is ordered that this Company do allow unto him during his natural life all ffees usually paid at the binding or turning over Apprentices At the taking up of ffree-doms Livery or any other Office of this Company (except only the fees of those who shall hereafter become Members of the said Company by Redemption which shall be received by the Clerk for the time being for his own use) to be accounted for by the Master and Wardens and three of the Assistants to the said Walter Hutchins or whom he shall appoint to receive the same.'

Here again is confirmation that the fees form part of a Clerk's remuneration and is being used as a pension.

Mr. John Leadbeater was elected and his remuneration was

recorded as follows:

'Resolved that the ffee hereafter to be paid by every Member coming into this Company by Redemption be thirteen shillings and four pence instead of three shillings and four pence heretofore paid and that the Premium to be given for the procuration of Redemption be one Pound and one Shilling instead of ten Shillings and Six pence formerly paid.' It will be noted that the remuneration included a Procuration fee paid to a Clerk which was called a Premium.

No matter of interest appears until 1747 when John Leadbeater died and his son, bearing the same name, was elected 'nemine contradicente'. In 1752 he received the Freedom of the Company in consideration of his faithful services.

It is of interest to note that in 1752 a Committee of the whole Court of Assistants were summoned' to attend the Popes Head Tavern in Cornhill on Tuesday next at 4 o'clock in the Afternoon to Examine and settle the late Master's Accounts. And that any seven of the said Court shall be a Court for that purpose And if in case the Clerk do not then attend he is ordered to be suspended for one month.' Clerks in those days were apparently a little more independent or casual than at present!

According to the list of Clerks, Mr. John Leadbeater retired in 1755 and Mr. Samuel Coates was elected Clerk. There are no references to the appointment of the new Clerk and his name does not appear in the Minutes until 1762 when a copy of a letter to the Master Farriers was written and signed by Sam Coates, Clerk of the Company – following a Committee for looking into the Charter and By-Laws of the Company. Mr. Coates' Address was St. Thomas Apostles near Bow Lane, Cheapside. A note appears at the foot of the letter in the form of a Post Script:

'NOTE: This is done at the request of Several Noblemen and Gentlemen of the First Distinction who have suffered by the Ignorance of Unskillful Quacks who Assume to themselves the Name of Farriers.' (An interesting early use of the slang term 'quacks') (see page 20).

Sam Coates was succeeded in 1776 by Benjamin Parker, he was succeeded by his son, of the same name, to serve until 1795.

Thomas Sherwood was elected in 1795 and served until 1844.

In 1814 there is the first mention of a Salary for the Clerk; previously his bill had been rendered for the work actually done by him.

In 1844 the Minutes show that tribute was paid to Mr. Sherwood, presented to him on Vellum and worth recording for its rather beautiful though perhaps over-lauditory terms:

'That in reviewing the Conduct of Mr. Sherwood their late Clerk for a period of nearly fifty years during which he held that office, the subject is one theme of entire satisfaction to this Court – for whether they look towards him as a gentleman in his manners – as a kind and affectionate Father in the advice he has at all times afforded to the Members of the Court – or as an Officer in the ever vigilant and courteous discharge of his various duties – the result in all cases is the same being such as has justly endeared him to every member of the Court; while he will carry into retirement the pleasing reflection that by those who have had most opportunities of knowing him he is the most beloved.'

Elsewhere will be found more critical references to Mr. Sherwood just six years later!

In 1844 Mr. Joseph Eldin Moulden was appointed Clerk, followed in 1850 by Sydney Smith (Father of Sidney Smith who in 1883 became Master of the Company). There were references to Sidney Smith's appointment:

'In all future elections of Officers of the Company, the Master shall in addition to his own vote be entitled to give his casting vote in the event of there being a "Tye" or equal number for any two or more candidates.' The apparent reason for this resolution was the very considerable altercation which arose following the insistence of the Master on giving a casting vote on the election of Mr. Sidney Smith as Clerk in 1850 and his subsequent re-election.

In 1856 the following appears and is interesting in regard to the altercations previously mentioned when the Master used a casting vote:

'Mr. Sidney Smith the Clerk having respectfully tendered his resignation to the Court as Clerk of the Company.

It was moved by Mr. Field and seconded by Mr. Hill that the Court retain their confidence in Mr. Smith their Clerk and request him to withdraw his resignation.

Eleven for the Motion

Contrary none

Carried unanimously

Resignation thereupon withdrawn.'

Mr. Sidney Smith appears to be a controversial gentleman for when in 1865 it was . . . 'Moved that in future after the confirmation of the minutes of any past Court; that the Master for the time being do sign his name at the foot of such Minutes and whether confirmed in part or whole.'

Previous to this no Minutes had been signed although always confirmed at the next meeting – the signing of Minutes is now normal commercial practice.

'Mr. Smith the Clerk respectfully asked permission to resign his Office of Clerk at the termination of his now year which will expire on the 24th June next.'

Did Mr. Smith object to having the Minutes signed? In fact no further Minutes were signed until May 1877. Mr. Smith however remained in office until May 1869, and was succeeded by John Rippon Heron. It is of interest to note that on the death of Mr. John Rippon Heron in 1877, a sub-committee was appointed regarding the appointment of a successor. In answer to an advertisement 29 Solicitors had applied. A short list of six was placed in ballot by the Court and Mr. Wynne E. Baxter was declared duly elected. (In 1881 he was the first Mayor of Lewes). Baxter served until 1906, then Benjamin Francis Popham until 1925, when William Robert Starkie was elected. Briefly in 1941–42 Walter Rose was acting Clerk until in 1942 Leonard Fisher Robson was appointed and it was Robson who compiled the History referred to elsewhere.

When the Minutes of 1942 were examined, the real story of Robson's History became clear. The Court meeting of 22nd July 1941 sets out in great detail that the then Clerk, William Robert Starkie was appointed in 1925. Owing to a disolution of partnership and the loss of his clerk and to his health he was not only unable to continue the Clerkship but further, had to vacate his office, and was forced to ask the Court to take charge of its activities and all books and papers, as the matter was urgent. It will have been seen that the Company had never had a Hall or any place to store its Minute Books and other records which had from 'time immemorial', to use a City of London phrase, passed from Clerk to Clerk.

A sub-committee was immediately set up by the Court under the Chairmanship of Past Master Mr. F.J. Robinson (Master 1923–24) 'To examine and schedule the position of the Company and to report to the Court their recommendation for the future organisation and administration of the Company'. The Master, Mr. R.W. Buckingham, had approached Mr. Walter Rose, FCIS a member of the Common Council, a member of the Needlemakers Company, but not a Farrier, who consented to give what assistance he could. (Rose became a Farrier in June 1942) In the meantime, the Clerk, Mr. Starkie, had arranged with a friend, Mr. Leonard Robson, an Incorporated Accountant, to assist him in bringing the books of accounts up to date. Eventually, Leonard Robson became the Clerk of the Company and presented to the Court in October 1942 a 'Record Book' containing matters ancient and modern and a file containing the all-important Minutes from 1718–1889. Thus, it can be seen that when Robson published his History in 1948 it was in fact based on the file which had been ordered to be printed – (3 copies presented to the Court in March 1943 at a cost of £17 11s. 3d). This file is no longer in existence but it is in fact the basis of Robson's History.

In 1949 Leonard Robson compiled an account of the Worshipful Company of Farriers which was printed by Order of the Court for private circulation. The Foreword read as follows:

'In this volume an attempt has been made to place before the Reader such extracts from the Records of the Company as may together form a Documentary History of our ancient Guild so far as it can be traced'.

This History has been of enormous help to the Author in writing this volume and his Supplement (1949–72) contained the following:

'At this stage it is proposed to pay a tribute to the late Mr. Robson who died on the 22nd December 1958. In September 1950 he was elected to the Court of Assistants. Following ill-health in September 1958 he retired as Clerk to the Court and as a tribute to his past services he was elected CLERK EMERITUS.

Shortly before his death he was asked 'when is the History of the Company going to be brought up to date?' He smiled in his inimitable manner and replied 'That's for the next fellow I think, I have done my bit'. How right he was, he had contributed his share in a magnificent manner. He had achieved so much in keeping alive the traditions of the Company, in writing the History of the Company which had meant many years of research into the Archives. It was his initiative that led to the idea of holding the 600th Anniversary Celebration Banquet in Guildhall which meant a great deal of extra work making all the necessary arrangements, including the designing of the Souvenir Menu. It was Mr. Robson who made all the arrangements in connection with the first Honorary Freedom when His Grace the Duke of Beaufort was admitted and this has formed a precedent for all other similar occasions.

Mr. Robson was elected Clerk to the Company in 1942 and served in all under nineteen Masters, for in the years 1949, 1951 and 1953 the Masters died in office and on each occasion Mr. Frederick Malcolm Garnham, the Senior Past Master, was elected Master for the balance of the year in question. It is appropriate that this Supplement should be dedicated to the memory of the late Mr. Robson'.

In 1948 Robson suggested that in view of his age an Assistant Clerk be appointed, accordingly in 1949 one of his Partners, Mr. Kenneth George Darke MA was duly appointed.

In 1949 Robson presented the Company with an Illuminated Book containing the Orders for admission to the Freedom and Livery.

On his resignation the following Minute of 9th September 1958 appeared:

'That Mr. L F C Robson's retirement from the Clerkship of the Company owing to advancing years be regretfully accepted and that as a mark of the Company's indebtedness to him for his invaluable services to the Company during the past 16 years, he be appointed Clerk Emeritus to the Company and his remuneration be continued at the present figure.'

Robson had been elected to the Court in 1950 free of fine in consideration of the great interest he had taken in the affairs of the Company.

In 1951 he was elected President of the Fellowship of Clerks of Livery Companies.

In 1954 he was the first representative of the Company to be appointed to the Board of Governors of St. Martin in the Fields High School for Girls, until the Author's appointment in March 1959.

Reference is made elsewhere to Robson's services in connection with the 600th Anniversary Banquet in 1956.

Leonard Robson, Clerk, Clerk Emeritus, Assistant and Historian, will long be remembered by those members of the Company who knew him for his extensive Minutes and for being the first Clerk who indexed every Minute!

Robson died in 1959. The Court granted his widow the sum of £250 as a token of regard for his valuable services.

In September 1958 a Sub-Committee had been appointed to discuss with Robson the desirability of an Assistant Clerk being appointed to help him with his work. Robson had intimated to the Court that in view of his age he would be prepared to retire as Clerk if a successor could be found. Edward Howard Newcome Wright son of a Past Master; W Newcome Wright, had been approached but was unable to accept the appointment due to the regular date of the Installation Meetings being held on second Tuesday in September. The Court agreed that the date be altered to the last Tuesday and accordingly Mr. Howard Newcome Wright was duly appointed as Clerk at a salary of £200 per annum.

Howard Newcome Wright was Clerk for five years. A Solicitor by profession. In 1963 he had informed the Court that owing to business pressure he could not longer act as Clerk. In December 1962 he was elected to the Court. He became Master 1970–71, the first recorded Clerk ever to become Master. In 1976 he became an Honarary Assistant. Further particulars of his services will be found in the chapter on Masters.

Arnold George Warham Scott, FCA, a Liveryman in 1958, was appointed Clerk in 1963. He remained in office for three years but he too found pressure of professional work and he accordingly resigned in 1966. He continued to act as Accountant to the Company until Mr. Past Master Barsham took over in 1975. Mr. Scott was thanked for his services over a period of twelve years in his capacity as Clerk and Accountant to the Company.

Michael John Burke, LLB succeeded Mr. Scott and for six years had a very busy Clerkship. The Company, as has been referred to elsewhere, was progressing in every way. The admission of 85 new members including HRH The Princess Anne show the Company's growth. It was all too much for a part time professional Clerk and so he retired on 31st January 1972. The Court presented him with a Silver Salver to commemorate his six years of service to the Company and admitted him to the Freedom of the Livery.

The Court was much exercised throughout the year with the problem of the administration of the Company, particularly in view of the responsibilities it was being urged to undertake with regard to the Craft and possibility of statutory registration of Farriers. A number of part time officials consisting of the Clerk, the Registrar, the Secretary of the Apprenticeship Scheme, the Treasurer and the former Clerk, Mr. Arnold Scott as Accountant were running the Company all of whom were active in their own profession. It was decided that Mr. Franklin E. Birch be invited to take the Clerkship and to continue the office of Registrar and Secretary of the Apprenticeship Scheme (he had been appointed to this office in 1968). He took up the office in 1972.

During these seven years so much has happened. Readers will have read of the many hundreds of events – each and every one has been monitored by the Clerk. During the seven years 120 new members have been admitted – over one third of the Livery. He has the good fortune to have the assistance of his wife Francesa and the Company owes a great debt of gratitude to both Mr. and Mrs. Franklin Birch for the manner in which the activities of the Company are controlled.

The Clerks of the Company 1613–1979

1613 Robert Glover	1850 Sydney Smith
? date – Nicholls	1869 John Rippon Heron
1666 Robert Strugnell	1877 Wynne Edwin Baxter
1675 George Daggett	1906 Benjamin Francis Popham
1718 Thomas Jackson	1925 William Robert Starkie
1726 Walter Hutchins	For a short period in 1941–42
1733 John Leadbeater	Walter Rose was Acting Clerk
1747 John Leadbeater (son of the former)	1942 Leonard Charles Fisher Robson, FSAA
1755 Samuel Coates	In 1949, Kenneth George
1776 Benjamin Parkes	Darke, MA, ACA, was
1787 Benjamin Parkes (son of the former)	appointed Assistant Clerk
1795 Thomas Edward Sherwood	1958 Edward Howard Newcome Wright
For two years, 1832–34, Joseph Sherwood, his son, was Joint Clerk	1963 Arnold George Warham Scott, FCA
	1966 Michael John Burke, LL.B
1844 Joseph Eldin Moulden	1972 Franklin Edwin Birch

Honorary Chaplains

Whilst no doubt the Company had Honorary Chaplains in its early days, no trace of any appointments can be found before

1876. Since that date there have been regular appointments.

    1876–95 Rev J. Harris – Liveryman

    1895–05 Rev H.R. Gamble, Rector of St Botolph Without, Aldersgate

    1907–18 Ven Archdeacon Sinclair, DD

    1918–31 Rev Prebendary A.W. Gough, MA

    1931–34 Rev W.P. Besley, Rector of St Lawrence Jewry

  *1935–37 Very Rev William Foxley Norris, DD, CVO, Dean of Westminster – Liveryman

 **1937–50 Rev Canon James O. Hannay, Vicar of Holy Trinity Church, South Kensington

***1950–69 Rev Everett George Turner, MA, Vicar of St Giles Cripplegate – Liveryman

    1970– Rev Prebendary F.A.F. Poulden, AKC, Rector of St Clements, Eastcheap – Liveryman.

  * On the death of Rev W.P. Besley in 1934, there were two candidates nominated:

Rev A. Lombardini, AKC, Curate of St Botolph, Bishopsgate, and

Rev Canon J.O. Hannay, Vicar of Holy Trinity Church, South Kensington.

At the Court Meeting the point was raised that a member of the Livery should have the offer of the vacant post.

Accordingly, the Very Rev William Foxley Norris, being a Liveryman, was appointed.

  ** James Owen Hannay was an interesting national figure, because he was also the internationally famous and prolific detective story and religious author. His writing career for such leading publishers as Methuen, Arnold and Unwin covered fifty years from 'Benedith Cavanagh' in 1907 to 'Do You Know your Bible?' in 1958, and includes the classic books, 'Red Hand of Ulster', 'The Search Party' and 'Spanish Gold', together with titles as varied as 'Adventures of Dr. Whitty' (1918), 'Appeasement' (1939), 'Piccadilly Lady' (1946) and 'Two Scamps' (1950).

  *** In 1925 the Rev Everett Turner presented the Company with a Chaplains Badge.

Stewards

In the Orders, Rules and Ordinances of 1678, it was 'ordayned that every yeare yearly the Master, Wardens and Assistants of the said Company for the tyme being shall elect and chose thre fitt persons being of the livery of the said Company whoeshall for the honor of the said Company att theire the said Stewards' owne costes and charges make and provide two competent and suffi-cient dinners, one of which shall be called the Stewards' Dinner, and shall be kept on the day that the Lord Maior shall be sworne att Westminster, and shall be for the Master, Wardens, Assistants and Livery of the saide Company, and the other Dinner shall be yearely kept on the day of Election of every new Master and Wardens, and shall be for the Master, Wardens and Assistants of the said Company, unless it shall be otherwise ordered by the Master and Wardens and every person and persons soe elected Stewards that shall refuse to hold and execute the same place or faile to make the same dinners, shall forfeite and pay to the Master, Wardens, Assistants and Commonalty of the said Company the summe of twenty pounds lawfull mony of England.'

Throughout the extracts of Minutes of the Company there are numerous references to Stewards and whilst many of these are performing their proper function, there are many more references to Stewards agreeing to pay the fine for not so acting – which would appear not unreasonable, having regard to their being responsible for the 'Coste of the Dinner'.

The present Ordinances do not contain such an office, probably because it would not be possible to find any one in the Livery to undertake the duties. It is not mentioned in the Minutes when the Office of Steward was eliminated from the Ordinances. The following references do show some examples of how the Stewardship was dealt with by the Master.

The first references was in 1723 when on June 13th it states;
'This Day Mr. Richard Johnson desired that he might be permitted to ffine for the places of offices of Steward Livery Assistant Wardenship of this Company and after some consideration Had It was agreed and ordered that upon his paying to the Master for the use of this Company the sum of twelve pounds besides the Clerk and Beadles ffees which he agreed unto and Was Sworne a Liveryman of this Company also an Assistant and was admitted into the Office of Master Wardens and ffined for Steward and paid the twelve pounds and took his place at the Board accordingly.'
('Notwithstanding the above mentioned admission as Master Mr. Johnson did not act as Master and was merely an Assistant').

8th November 1725
'Att this Court Mr. Thomas Coleman appeared upon summons for Steward pursuant to a former choice but refused to hold or serve the said place. It is agreed and ordered that the said Thomas Coleman shall be one of the Stewards of this Company for the year ensuing to provide dinners as the Bye Laws direct.' (NB Thomas Coleman did not become a Master of the Company). In January of the following year, 1726,
'It is ordered and agreed that Mr. John Parsley deceased's Note for Five Pounds dated 30th July 1721 be now cancelled.'

(On the date mentioned, Mr. Parsley had appeared before the Court to take upon himself the office of Steward: his fine was £5 for which he gave his note, payable six months after the date) In 1732 four Livermymen were appointed Stewards for the ensuing year, but at the next meeting two of them refused to pay the fine which had been reduced to £5.

1743

'Mr. Luke Alder being elected and chosen Steward of this Company on the 24th day of June last appeared and promised to accept of 'a Bill of Fare and serve the said office.' But in September 1751 it states in the extracts of the Minutes:

'A Motion was made that Mr. Luke Alder be summoned before the Right Honorable the Lord Mayor to show Cause why he refuses to appear and accept the Office of Steward of this Company he having been duly served with a Bill of ffare for that purpose.'

It passed in the affirmative and later that month:

'Mr. Luke Alder desired to be admitted to ffine for the said Office of Steward which was granted and he thereupon paid the ffine of ffive pounds.'

There is no further mention of Stewards until 1761 when a Mr. James Gregory refused to serve the Office of Steward to which he had been elected and claimed exemption because he was a Yeoman of the Guard. The Clerk was then ordered to prepare a case before Counsel to decide whether the Company could by law enforce him to serve the office of Steward. (Reference to this appears on page 13).

In 1776 'Francis Blackbeard appeared, And refusing to take the Livery of the Company to which he had been elected and repeatedly summoned, was Ordered to be sued forthwith to Compel him so to do.' 14th November – 'Francis Blackbeard appeared, and having first paid the Costs of the Suit against him for not taking the Livery of the Company pursuant to Summons, was Admitted thereto, and Sworn, and paid Five pounds. He desired Also to fine for the Office of Steward of the Company which was granted for the sum of Four pounds which he paid.'

Again in the following year the Clerk reported that Edward Drew was fined £20 for refusing to take the office of Steward:

'That the extra charges of the Suite amounted to the sum of Six Pounds Eleven Shillings and Six Pence which being deducted therefrom there remains the sum of Thirteen pounds Eight Shillings and Six Pence due to the Company and was paid to the Master.'

In 1809 'It was moved and seconded and the Question being put it was carried in the Affirmative that no person shall hereafter be admitted to the Livery of the Company who does not at the same time fine for Steward.' But in 1810 this Resolution was rescinded.

In 1846, following the retirement of the Clerk, T.E. Sherwood, who had retired after 49 years service, it was resolved that a Committee be formed to examine the rights and privileges 'conferred upon this Company by the original Order by which the Company was founded in 1356, the Charter of Incorporation, the Bye Laws, and the Act of Common Council of December 12th 1758. And (have made enquiries) of the Chamberlain The City Solicitor and the Town Clerk of London.'

One of the items was to elect and choose who was to serve as Stewards.

1846 – 'The 7th Bye Law has not of late been sufficiently acted on. And therefore (we) recommend that every year yearly the Court shall elect and choose 3 fit persons being of the Livery to be Stewards. And that every person or persons so elected Stewards that shall refuse to hold and execute the same place shall forfeit and pay the sum of £20. Your committee however do not hereby mean to interfere with the fine respectively of £8 or £10 which is now generally imposed nor with the power of the Court under the 25th Bye-Law to mitigate or wholly remit such fine if the person or persons elected steward offers a reasonable excuse.'

There is no mention whether the recommendation was approved – possibly it all worked perfectly well and consequently there was no necessity to bring the matter up again in Court. It is certain however that the Bye Law still existed for in 1882 another committee was appointed to consider the Bye-Law 'in force but not now in print' and they 'presented their report (which dealt with resolutions) forming quasi Bye Laws of the Company now in force and not now in print (being those made since 24th June 1871 on which date the Charter Rules and Orders then extant were ordered to be printed) and recommended that the same be amended and circulated among the Members of the Court.'

They contained the following:

In 1874 Stewards if paid later £20. 10s. 0d. and in 1879 'That at the Court on 24th June in each year, not less than two nor more than six of the members of the Livery (such Members to include those who have during the preceeding year paid the Stewards' fine) shall be called upon to fine for Stewards at the next Court. In default such persons shall be liable not to be invited to any Livery Dinner of the Company and shall be ineligible to attend any Court Dinner.'

It appears from the above extracts of Minutes that Liverymen took the opportunity of not acting as Stewards but paid fines to be excused for not carrying out their duties. In fact, it became the practice for new Liverymen 'to pray to be permitted to fine as

Steward'; in other words, it became part of the admission fee and the Ordinances clearly showed this position. In 1935 the fine was increased from £5 to £11 11s. od. and this amount remained in force until 1972, when the Ordinances were amended. Ordinance 30 now reads –

> 'No member of the Company shall be called upon to act as a Steward of the Company (as required by the Charter) but every person appointed to the Livery shall be required at the time of his admission to pay a fine of such amount as the Court may from time to time decide in lieu of serving that office',

and no mention is made of the Stewards fine. It is now part of the Fines and Fees of the Livery. So, apart from the reference in Ordinance 30 (to comply with the Charter) the word 'Steward' has disappeared from the traditions of the Company.

Beadles

The Orders, Rules and Ordinances of 1678 refers to the election of a Beadle –

> '. . . also shall and may elect and chose one or more persons or persons of good and honest behaviour meete for that service to be theire beadle or beadles, whoe shall att all tymes be attendant vpon the Master, Wardens and Assistants, and shall take the oathes in these presents appointed, and for reasonable cause shall and may be remoued and displaced'.

His oath is included among the Declarations (Appendix).

Few Livery Company Histories have given much space to this Officer of the Company but in reading the earlier Minute Books the Author found much interest in his activities and much can be learnt from his duties. He was, in fact, responsible for the collection of the Quarterages, for the Clerks in those days do not appear to have had anything to do with collection but merely to record the receipts from the Master to whom the Beadle was responsible. However, after 1817, no further reference can be found in respect of the collection of Quarterage by the Beadle, which, in this Company, was part of the duties of the Clerk. From 1890 there appear only a few references to a Beadle – only occasionally when a new Beadle was elected following his predecessor's retirement or death.

What follows applies naturally to the Farriers Company. Other Livery Companies, as in all aspects differ, so generalisations do not apply and in particular in the case of the Beadles. In those Companies who own Halls a Beadle will no doubt have executive duties, such as the arrangements for dinners and functions and may be expected to assist the Clerk, particularly those Companies who manage Charities and Schools, e.g. the Haberdashers Company.

As has been seen, the first Minute Book available is from 1713 so there is no trace as to who was elected the first Beadle of the Company, the first reference being in 1720. –

'The Court doth now agree to proceed to the Choise of a Beadle for this Company in the Roome of William Aris Deceased. Thereupon Mr. Robert Looker and Mr. Joseph Hand was putt in Nominasion and Mr. Robert Looker was Declared Duely elected Beadle of this Company to continue so long in the said place as he should well and honestly use and behave himself therein and Was Now Sworne accordingly.

And the said Robert Looker did now quitt all his right and Claime of being upon the Assistants of this Company for the future and is Now by this Court ordered to be Discharged from the said office'.

It appears from the Minute that Robert Looker had been an Assistant of the Court.

In 1721 the following Minute shows part of the duties of the Beadle and whilst there appears to have been two Beadles, the only reference in the future are to 'a Beadle' –

'It is now agreed and ordered That one of the Beadles do attend at the Dore at all Dinners

and in 1722 his salary was £4 per annum and the ffees usually paid to the Beadle.

The Beadle was 'allowed a New Gown and that £5 10s. be allowed for the same and that the colour be grey'.

In the same year William Poole is mentioned as Beadle and in 1733 his salary was increased by seven shillings instead of his receiving 'Two Pounds sixteen Shillings once in two years for a Coat'.

Mr. Poole having died in 1743 it was –

'Ordered that the Clerk of this Company doe advertise the Beadles Staff and Gown on Saturday and Monday next and that the same be brought to Mr. Thos. Winsmore Master of this Company'.

The next mention of the Beadle was in 1762 –

'The Wardens declared the Beadle's place Vacant by the Death of Robert Carter.

In Nomination for Beadle –

    Mr. ffrancis Butler

    Mr. James Poole

Resolved on Debate that Mr. ffrancis Butler shall resign his place as an Assistant of this Company before he Shall be a Candidate for Beadle, who being called in and acquainted with the Resolution of the Court made his Publick Declaration to the Court of his Resignation of his said place of Assistant.

Whereupon the Wardens declared a Vacancy in the Court of Assistants by the Resignation of Mr. ffrancis Butler.

The two Candidates for Beadle being severally put up the Election fell on Mr. ffrancis Butler Who was thereupon Declared duly Elected and was now Sworn to the due Execution of the said Office'.

ffrancis Butler had already served as Renter, Middle and Upper Warden in the years 1750 to 1753 and Master in 1755-56. The only instance of a Beadle who had been Master of the Company.

It appears from the following Minute that the Beadle was entitled to a 'commission' if he procured a new member of the Livery:

'Ordered that the Clerk do pay to Mr. ffrancis Butler or any other person who shall procure any Redemptioners to be made free of this Company the sum of One guinea for each of them which shall be repaid to the Clerk by the Master of the Company for the time being'.

The Minute is somewhat difficult to understand for it appears that it was the Master not the Company who was liable for the procuration fee.

As will be seen in the Chapter on Quarterages (page 00) the Beadle was 'Employed to attend the different Courts and Recover the Quarteridges'.

On the 16th October the following Minute is of interest:

'This Day Mr. James Butler the late Apprentice to his ffather Mr. ffrancis Butler Citizen and ffarier of London the Beadle (late Past Master) was made free and sworn and by the favour of the Master and Wardens of the Company paid no fees'

It is supposed that Mr. Butler the Beadle found it difficult to forget his present status in the Company for in 1767 it was –

'Ordered that Mr. Butler the Beadle of the Company shall take away no Victualls (without the permission of the Master or Wardens) till the next day after the Company have Dined or Supped at the Half Moon Tavern And that he be under Inspection or orders of the Master of the House. Nor shall any person belonging to the Beadle be admitted to attend for him for that purpose at any Dinner or Supper of the Company'.

The Minutes of 1772 now mention a new Beadle, Mr. Richard Brinkworth, who was instructed to attend to the cleaning of the Colours and Poles and the Caps and Coats.

In 1789 it is interesting to find a Liveryman asking for a recommendation to be a Beadle –

'Mr. Thomas Layton (formerly one of the Court of Assistants) requested the favour of this Court to grant him a Letter of recommendation as a fit person to be chosen Beadle of the Parish of St. Andrew Holborn and it was Ordered Nem. Con. that the Clerk draw up such recommendation and sign the same as by Order of this Court. And it was further Ordered that Mr. Layton receive out of the Poor Box the sum of £1 1s. 0d'.

It is not known whether he received the appointment.

In 1794 'The Beadle (William Goodsall) was reprimanded for neglect of duty in Not Collecting the Quarterage in due time and It was Ordered that he be suspended from receiving the perquisites of Breeches and Shoes till he Collects the same more closely', and in the following year he was declared unfit to be again appointed.

In 1795 the Minutes read:

> 'Resolved that the place of Beadle is now vacant; and that the person who shall be appointed Beadle shall enter into a Bond with sufficient Sureties . . . for the due performance of the several Duties of the Office'.

This was the first time the Beadle had to give a Bond; the Master had always done so, and this year the Clerk also.

In 1796 the Minutes show –

> 'Resolved and ordered that the Clerk commence proceedings at Law against all such persons as shall hereafter refuse or neglect to attend the Court, when duty summoned for that purpose. Resolved unanimously that William Goodsall the late Beadle have a Gratuity given him of One Guinea; but that he be forbid from attending on any of the Court days in future'.

In the following year Court Dinners had been cancelled for the time being due to lack of finance, and it was –

> 'Resolved that the Beadle be allowed 5/–s for his attendance on this day and 2s/6d. for his attendance on every Court day during the next Twelve Months, as a recompence for the Loss he may sustain by the Courts not dining together on those days'.

A Bill of Messrs. Emerson & Docker, for several Actions in the Mayor's Court, brought by the Beadle, amounting to £7, was laid before the Court and taken into Consideration –

Ordered that such Bill be paid; but that the Beadle be strictly forbidden to commence any action or other proceeding whatever in future, without the express direction of the Court.

In 1808, the Beadle (Mr. William Laycock) was again in trouble for he was suspended until he had made up and delivered his account of the Quarteridges and paid over the balance due.

> 'The Clerk reported to the Court that he had drawn out the Beadle's Account by which it appears that a Balance of £8 3s. 0d. is due to the Company but which Balance had not been paid by the Beadle which Report and also a letter from the Beadle to the Court being taken into consideration – Resolved unanimously that William Laycock be dismissed from his Office of Beadle to the Company'.

Matthew Croft was appointed, his salary being Eight pounds per annum (including the allowance for Shoes and Breeches and he was required to give a Bond for £50 for the faithful discharge of his Office).

Mr. Edward Clark the next Beadle did not prove a success, for in 1812 the Minutes show –

'Resolved that the Master be requested to put on paper Three Charges wherewith the Beadle at present appears to have given offence to the Court, and that the said Beadle be directed to reply to them severally and separately that the Court may either excuse him, in part, or the whole, namely
1st. For not being present at the last Common Hall
2nd. For not attending the Court on this Day, and
3rd. For having delivered the late Summons's on a Sunday'
The Beadle being now in attendance he was called in and the foregoing Resolutions was read and he was heard in his Defence and then being withdrawn – Resolved That this Court is not satisfied with the excuse on either head.
That the Master be requested to reprimand him, and That he be acquainted that both the charges and reprimand will be entered on the Minutes, And That he be not paid for the day of the Common Hall as tho' he had been on his Duty',

but matters did not improve for later in the same year –

'The Clerk reported that it appeared by the Beadle's account that he had a Balance in his Hands of £20 18s. 8d. which he had not paid over, as he ought to have done.
The Beadle was then called in & heard in his Defence after which It was Resolved That unless such Balance be paid to the Clerk by the next Court, That proceedings be commenced against the Beadle's Surety for recovery thereof'.

It must have been very difficult for the Beadle as there appears to have been very little co-operation from Members who had been Summoned to take up their Livery.

'The Beadle reported that he had served Summons's on the several persons ordered to be summoned to take up their Livery. And it appearing that Mr. George Cooke one of the persons so summoned has not only neglected to attend but has sent a very rude message by the Beadle.
Ordered That the Clerk take the necessary measures against Mr. Cooke to compel his taking up the Livery of the Company'.

In 1818 the following appears:
'Ordered that 200 copies of the following notice be printed and that one of such Notice be left by the Beadle with every person (Liveryman or Freeman) who shall be in arrear for his Quarterings:
'Ordered that the Beadle do inform the several persons in arrear for their quarterage that inasmuch as they enjoy Pri-

vileges by being Freemen and Liverymen of the Company, This Court does expect them to pay their quarterage, otherwise they will be proceeded against for the same'.

In 1823 the Beadle reported that 'Mr. Luck in nomination for Freedom is confined in Ludgate for Debt and that one Chick carries on the business in his Stead'.

The Beadle, Francis Black, had resigned due to a paralytic stroke; his successor's name does not appear in the Minutes, but a reference three years later to the Beadle (Thomas Skirror) having carried out his duties satisfactorily was granted his fee of two pounds.

There are no further references to Beadles until 1838 and 1853. One can only presume that Thomas Skirror had been succeeded by Robert Feargus who was appointed in 1853; neither the resignation nor the appointment is minuted.

It is strange that from 1853 to 1932 the Clerk did not think it worthy of mention in the Minutes of appointments or resignations of an officer who had played an important part in the Company's affairs, for five hundred years.

In 1932 Robert Ede retired and Edward Kerry Cox was appointed. He was followed by E.J. Lambert in 1941. In the Record Book prepared by Robson, in 1945 there appears the following as guidance to future Clerks –

'E.J. Lambert, the present Beadle, is an experienced man and quite au fait with all ceremonial matter etc.

His Remuneration is for a Court & informal lunch	£1 1s. 0d.
for Common Hall (where he also acts as a Ward Beadle)	10s. 6d.
For United Guilds Service	15s. 0d.
On occasions when he also acts as Toast Master – extra	10s. 6d.'

Lambert served till his death in 1951.

During the last thirty years there have been four Beadles in office and the present holder of that office is Charles Ellwood appointed in 1979.

As a Summary of the above, the following names have been obtained from the Minutes:

–	William Aris	1823	– Luck
1720	Robert Looker	1827	John Thomas Skirror
1731	William Poole	1853	Robert Feargus
1743	William Wensman		Robert Ede
1762	ffrancis Butler	1932	E. Kerry Cox
1772	Richard Brinkworth	1941	E.J. Lambert
1794	William Goodsall	1951	Arthur Booth
1808	William Laycock	1955	Walter Long
	Matthew Croft	1964	Walter Smith
1812	Edward Clark	1979	Charles Ellwood
1817	George Cooke		

CHAPTER 6

The Company To-day

Ladies of the Company

The first reference to Ladies being admitted as Freeman was on 2nd August 1762 when Mrs. Hester Mills was made free of the Company and paid 13s. 4d. Mrs. Hester Mills kept the New Castle Coffee House at St. Mary Hill, where the meeting was held. (In 1763 Mr. Thomas Warner who had married Mrs. Hester Mills, was made free of the Company at the same cost).

The Minutes show that on 6th December 1764 –

'Mrs. Elizabeth Wells Widow (being here present and consenting) do pay two shillings per month of her quateridge due to the Company at Lady Day last until the Whole be Discharged'.

Subsequently, on the 7th February 1765, Mrs. Wells was forgiven her past quarteridge upon condition that she paid it in the future. Again, in the same year, it was –

'Ordered that Mrs. Sarah Fortescue Widow (having been summoned to the Court of Conscience for payment of her Quarteridge due to the Company) shall on Account of her Age and Infirmities and on payment of the Charges at the Court of Conscience be excused her present as well as all future Quarteridge which shall become due from her to the Company'.

In 1882 Miss Sarah Smith (referred to in page 179) was offered the Freedom of the Company, but she declined.

In 1955 Mr. Past Master Walker suggested to the Court that Miss Pat Smythe (now Mrs. Koechlin), the leading show jumper at that time, should be invited to be an Honorary Freeman of the Company (details of the ceremony will be found on page 205).

In 1971 Her Royal Highness The Princess Anne was admitted as a Freeman, and on 8th February 1977 was admitted to the Livery and elected to the Court on 6th December 1978. These ceremonies are fully described in Chapter 7.

In 1975, after much discussion, Ladies were admitted into the Livery and in September 1975 Mrs. Diana Pagan, the daughter of Past Master George Garnham, Mrs. Simon, wife of Past Master M.A.P. Simon, and Mrs. Bulfield, wife of Assistant R.W. Bulfield, made their Declaration as Freemen and Liverymen. Ladies have since been admitted and at the date of writing they number eight.

On 25th June 1975 the Court considered the report of the sub-Committee set up to review all aspects of the further association of women with the Companies activities when 'it was agreed that ladies should be considered for admittance to the Freedom and Livery. In dealing with applications at the interviews, the Master and Wardens should, bear in mind the preservation of the present character of the Company. Members of the Court acting as supporters to applications for the Freedom and Livery should satisfy themselves particularly that the bona-fides of applicants, both male and female, are such that they will make a material contribution to the activities of the Company'.

It was agreed that normally no more than 20 new applicants be admitted in any 12 months.

In connection with the acceptance of women to the Freedom and Livery, it was agreed that Ordinance No. 64 should be extended to include daughters and daughters-in-law at reduced rates of Fines and Fees.

The Arts

The Guilds do not muster many names in the Arts as Liverymen. The Poulters include the late Geraldo as an Assistant and another Band leader, Edmondo Ros, on the Livery; the Senior Past Prime Warden of the Fishmongers is Playwright Ben Travers; Actor and Author Robert Hardy belongs to the Bowyers Company and many famous musicians naturally joined The Musicians. In 1968 the Farriers welcomed a distinguished Actor with an unostentatious interest in Welfare and it is amusingly fitting that of all his Stage, Screen, T.V. and Radio work, it is for his BBC TV appearances as the son in STEPTOE AND SON that Harry H. Corbett is so well known – those two London 'totters' or rag and bone men, traditional users of the Horse, living with their Co-Star 'Hercules'.

Coincidentally, on the same day that Harry H. Corbett joined, another actor, Norman John Mann, became a member – not only is he the Author's son-in-law, but his TV appearances include the successful series ALL CREATURES GREAT AND SMALL based on a

200

Country Vet with patients from horses to pekinese, in which Robert Hardy played the masterful senior partner. Norman was in the Household cavalry and was in attendance on Her Majesty at her Coronation in 1952.

Another liveryman for a few years in the 1930's was Bertram Mills, who successfully added horses to showmanship and showbusiness. Before the first World War he was in the family coach building business, which made him a familiar figure at Horse Shows, during the war as a Captain in the RASC he was responsible for the horses' provender, then in 1919 he was challenged to produce a better Circus than that at Olympia. He succeeded to such an extent that Bertram Mills' Circus at Olympia was one of the year's highlights, and carried on by his sons till the 1950's when costs started to kill off tenting circuses, which are of course almost the greatest users for horses, whether liberty or *haute école* or for transporting. Mills himself was a great rider and driver, having ridden on the last coaches, acted as Mr. Pickwick's coachman in the famous 1936 run, maintaining a superb stables himself of hacks and hunters, and riding to win at many famous shows all his life.

Mention should also be made in this section to Dorian Williams (Master 1977–78) as a Director of Drama at Pendley Manor, Tring, and of course for his ability to keep the public fully atuned to the activities of the Show Jumping ring on the Television screen.

Farriers Lodge No 6305

On 30th July 1946 the Farriers Lodge was consecrated. All Freemasons who were members of the Company were eligible to join and they became Founder Members. The Lodge has prospered over the last thirty years. Sons and sons-in-law of members of the Company are entitled to join or be initiated into the Lodge. The first Master was R.W. Buckingham who had been Master of the Company in 1937–38 and from 1940–44.

The following have been Masters of the Lodge:

1946	R.W. Buckingham	1958	R.S. Winter
1947	G.B. Garnham	1959	H.S. Carter
1948	G.H. Fenton	1960	G.H. Smith
1949	H. Threadkell	1961	E. Charles Winn
1950	T. Sullock	1962	H.D. Sparshatt
1951	W.P.C. Tenison	1963	C.H. de Boer
1952	Vincent A. Balls	1964	J.W.E. Wormell
1953	J.E. Lines	1965	E.C. Mould
1954	L.B. Prince	1966	G.K. Findlay
1955	H. St Clare Elliott	1967	H.J. Rye
1956	K.J. Lines	1968	L.J. Stroud
1957	W.R. Wooldridge	1969	W.J. Haycroft

1970	T.L. Butler	1975	M.J.E. Gibbs
1971	E.A. Styles	1976	J.A.E. Winter
1972	S.J. Lines	1977	R.J. Rye
1973	J.G. Foley	1978	P.J. Lines
1974	A.G. Smith	1979	W.H. Ladd

The present strength of the Lodge is 54. They meet four times a year and the Masonic Meetings Places have been:

Talbot Restaurant, London Wall

Armourers Hall

Plantation House

Butchers Hall.

Farriers Golfing Society

In 1955 the idea of forming a Farriers Golfing Society was suggested by Mr. E.C.P. Whiteley, the son of Mr. C.C.O. Whiteley, Master 1946–47. Eric Whiteley, a member of the Court, later to be Upper Warden, but owing to ill health was not able to accept the office of Master. He died in 1973. Eric had played full-back for England at Rugby Football. A very keen golfer, he formed the Golfing Society. Each year a meeting is held to compete for cups and shields given by George Smith, Master 1967–68 and J.B. Hill a member of the Livery. The first Captain was L.B. Prince, Master 1955–56 and he has been followed by Arthur Smith, Master 1975–76, Antony Pagan, 1976–77, and Arnold Scott, 1977.

All members of the Farriers Company are eligible to join the Golfing Society and the present Captain and Secretary is Arnold Scott.

For some years the Farriers Golfing Society have entered for the Connaught Cup Competition for all Livery Companies. The Farriers won second place in 1958 when the team comprised L.B. Prince, E.C.P. Whitely, J. Barsham and Arthur Smith. It is of interest that the Connaught Cup Competition was started following a letter from Mr. A.F. Pollen the Master of the Coachmakers Company, and reported to the Court in 24th June 1927. It was proposed to form a Golf Competition between the City Livery Companies to compete for a cup to be known as the 'Prince Arthur Cup', presented to commemorate the honour done to the Coachmakers Company by HRH The Prince Arthur of Connaught joining and becoming an Assistant of the Company. The Farriers Company was represented by Lieutenant Colonel G.W. Parkinson (Master 1927–28) on the committee formed in connection with the competition.

St. Martin-in-the-field High School for Girls

The Foundation of the School dates back to 1699 when the Parish of St. Martin-in-the-Fields, at the instigation of the Society for Promoting Christian Knowledge, which had been founded in 1698, set up a Committee to establish a Charity School, first for boys and then for girls. The Minute Books of the girls' school Committee, dating from 1700 to 1798 and from 1873 onwards, are in the possession of the School and the association between Church and School has been closely maintained.

In 1873 the School obtained a Scheme of Government under the Endowed Schools' Act. This was amended by Acts of 1894, 1911 and 1928.

From 1873 to 1928 the School was situated in the Charing Cross Road backing onto Archbishop Tenison's Boys' School in Leicester Square. In May 1928 the present building at Tulse Hill was formally opened by HRH The Duchess of York, now The Queen Mother. The School expanded quickly and in 1938 the total number of pupils was 474, including the Junior School.

Along with other London Schools, St. Martin's was evacuated on the outbreak of the Second World War. A party of two hundred went to Leatherhead in Surrey. Although many incidents occurred in the reception area both by day and night, no girl was ever injured and only one had her billet bombed.

Early in 1940, in response to the request of many parents whose children were not evacuated, the Governors re-opened the School at Tulse Hill. In September 1945 the evacuated part of the School returned to Tulse Hill.

In March 1944 incendiary bombs set light to and destroyed the top floor of the Tulse Hill building, including the Laboratories and Art Room. More damage to the fabric also occurred three months later as a result of a flying bomb.

The Education Act of 1944 resulted in the abolition of fees and the gradual closure of the Junior and Preparatory Departments.

In 1953 Sir John Smyth, Bt, VC, MC, MP (Master 1961–62) was instrumental in arranging for the Worshipful Company of Farriers to take up one of the eight Foundation Governorships of the School under section 17(2) of the Education Act 1944. The School was to be managed by a body of twelve Governors, eight to be Foundation Governors and four appointed by the Local Education Authority. The Governorship offered to the Farriers Company was accepted and this formed a permanent link between the Company and the School. The Clerk, Mr. L.C.F. Robson, was appointed a Governor in 1954 and on his death in 1959 Past Master Mr. Leslie B. Prince was appointed. An annual prize is given by the Company known as the 'Farriers Prize'.

In April 1957 the Ministry of Education granted Aided Status and St. Martin's became, and it is still, a voluntary aided Church of England School maintained by the Inner London Education Authority.

The link with the Church and the Society for Promoting Christian Knowledge is as strong to-day as ever, a fact which has added significance at the present time since the nature of the School is undergoing important modifications. Because of Inner London Education Authority policy, St. Martin's in common with other London Aided Grammar Schools, took girls of all abilities into the first form in September 1978. It is thus gradually becoming a Comprehensive School.

It is with confidence and hope that St. Martin-in-the Fields High School moves forward into the next chapter of its history, with the support of the Farriers Company.

Honorary Freedoms of the Livery

1952 His Grace the Duke of Beaufort, KG, PC, GCVO, Master of the Horse.

This was the first time the Company had granted the Honorary Freedom so far as can be ascertained from the existing records, and also the first time that the Master of the Horse had been associated with the Company. A very beautifully Illuminated Address, bound in morocco was presented to His Grace which read as follows:

To His Grace Henry Hugh, tenth Duke of Beaufort,
Knight of the Most Noble Order of the Garter,
Member of Her Majesty's Most Honourable Privy Council,
Knight Grand Cross of the Royal Victorian Order,
Master of the Horse.

Your Grace

It was unanimously *Resolved* at a Court of The Worshipful Company of Farriers on the 24th day of June last, to request Your Grace to honour the Company by accepting its Honorary Freedom and we are most grateful to *Your Grace* for consenting to do so.

Our Craft is most ancient, our Guild almost Six Hundred Years old. During that time our predecessors and ourselves have endeavoured not only to preserve the status of our craft and its members but also to do what is possibly in every way to benefit the health and comfort of the Horse.

The Court and Livery are aware of your Grace's own desires and interests in the same direction and it is particularly for that reason that with much respect we welcome Your Grace into the Freedom of the Company.

The Seal of the Company is affixed this 9th day of September in the 596th year of the Fellowship in the year of Our Lord 1952, in the presence of

Oswald Lewis (*Master*); J.B. Buxton (*Warden*); S.R. Walker (*Warden*); L.B. Prince (*Warden*); L.C.F. Robson (*Clerk*)

On the 17th July, 1958 His Grace the Duke of Beaufort attended at the Chamberlain's Court, Guildhall and was presented to the Chamberlain of London, Sir Irving Gane, KCVO, for Admission to the Freedom of the City of London by the Master, Mr. John Stroud, the Wardens, Mr. George Bowman, Sir Leslie Hollinghurst, Mr. Deputy Allison-Beer and the Clerk Mr. Leonard Robson. His Grace made the Declaration as required by Law and was offered the right hand of Fellowship by the Chamberlain in accordance with ancient custom.

A Luncheon followed at which the senior members of the Corporation attended.

1955 Miss Patricia Rosemary Smythe, OBE

When in March 1955 Miss Pat Smythe was present at a Dinner for the Livery and their ladies the Master, Mr. Deputy S.R. Walker, C.B.E., conceived the idea of inviting Miss Smythe to accept the Honorary Freedom of the Company. The Court readily endorsed this suggestion. Accordingly at a Special Court held at Apothecaries Hall on the 28th November, 1955, Miss Pat Smythe became the first woman to receive the Honorary Freedom of the Company.

An Illuminated Address was presented to her containing the following *Resolution*:

At a Meeting of the Court held on 25th June last the following Resolution was proposed by the Master Mr. Deputy S.R. Walker, CBE, seconded by Mr. Past Master F.J. Robinson, MA, and carried unanimously:

That Miss Pat Smythe, holder of the British Horse Society's Medal of Honour and a distinguished member of the British Show Jumping Team be asked to accept the Honorary Freedom of the Company.

The Master Mr. Leslie B. Prince, MA, FCA, CC, addressed Miss Pat Smythe as follows:

The Court and Livery of the Worshipful Company of Farriers acknowledge with gratitude that you, one of the most distinguished women riders in our time, have accepted our Honorary Freedom, the greatest compliment which the Company is able to offer. We confer this upon you not only because of your outstanding achievements but also because we know that you are truly interested in the welfare of the Horse which is the predominant interest of this Company. We feel that in accepting the Honorary Freedom you are doing a very great honour to the Court and Livery of our ancient Guild.

At the conclusion of the proceedings Miss Pat Smythe was entertained at the Court Dinner.

Subsequently on 27th February, 1956, Miss Pat Smythe was

admitted to the Freedom of the City by the City Chamberlain, Sir Irving Gane, KCVO, in the Chamberlain's Court after having been presented by the Master, Mr. Leslie B. Prince, and the Wardens, Mr. John Stroud and Mr. George Bowman and the Clerk Mr. Leonard Robson.

After the ceremony the Chamberlain entertained Miss Smythe, the Master, Wardens and Clerk and a company of friends including Senior Members of the Corporation.

1958 Field Marshal The Rt. Hon. John, Baron Harding of Petherton, GCB, CBE, DSO, MC.

In December 1957 the Court decided to confer the Honorary Freedom of the Company on Lord Harding and accordingly on 11th March, 1958, his Lordship attended before the Court and made his Declaration as a Freeman. The Chamberlain of London, Sir Irving Gane, KCVO, being present invited Lord Harding to sign an Application for the Freedom of the City of London.

At the Luncheon which followed an Illuminated Address was presented which read as follows:

To Field Marshal The Rt. Hon. John, Baron Harding of Petherton.

At a Meeting of the Master, Wardens and Assistants of the Worshipful Company of Farriers held in December last, it was proposed by Mr. Past Master S.R. Walker, CBE, and unanimously *Resolved*:

That the Honorary Freedom of the Company be conferred upon Field Marshal Sir John Harding, GCB, CBE, DSO, MC, in recognition of his distinguished services to the Country and the Commonwealth and in admiration of his having risen from a Private Soldier to the highest position in the British Army (Chief of the Imperial General Staff), culminating his his outstanding services as Governor of Cyprus.

We are glad that since that time Her Majesty The Queen has been pleased to honour you with a Peerage, we desire to offer you our sincere congratulations thereon.

We also desire to place upon record our deep appreciation of your Lordship's kind expression of goodwill towards our Ancient Company and your interest in the Horse in accepting our suggestion that you should become associated with us as an Honorary Freeman which indeed is looked upon by us as a signal honour to our Company.

On behalf of the Court and Commonalty of the Company the Seal is affixed the 11th day of March, 1958, in the presence of

John Stroud (*Master*); Geo. Bowman (*Warden*); G. Allison-Beer (*Warden*); L.N. Hollinghurst (*Warden*); S.R. Walker (*Past Master*); Leonard C.F. Robson (*Clerk*)

On the 4th June, 1958, Lord Harding attended at the Chamberlain's Court, Guildhall and was presented to the Chamberlain of London, Sir Irving Gane, KCVO, for Admission to the Freedom of the City of London, by the Master, Mr. John Stroud, the

Wardens Mr. George Bowman, Sir Leslie Hollinghurst, Mr. Allison-Beer and Mr. Leonard Robson, the Clerk.

His Lordship made the Declaration as required by Law and was offered the right hand of Fellowship by the Chamberlain in accordance with ancient custom.

At a Luncheon which followed Senior Members of the Corporation including Mr. Sheriff and Deputy Walker, CBE, and Mr. Past Master Prince, attended.

1961 Colonel Michael Picton Ansell, CBE, DSO

In July 1961 the Court decided to confer the Honorary Freedom of the Company on Colonel Ansell in recognition of his outstanding services in connection with the organisation and holding of Horse Shows and Competitions throughout the country and in view of his tremendous courage in carrying on despite the loss of his sight in the second World War. Accordingly on the 26th September, 1961, Colonel Ansell attended before the Court and made his Declaration as a Freeman. The Chamberlain of London being present invited Colonel Ansell to sign an Application for the Freedom of the City of London in the Company of the Farriers.

The Address fully illuminated on parchment in book form and bound in morocco reads as follows:

To Colonel Michael Picton Ansell, CBE, DSO.
Dear Colonel Ansell,

At a Court of the Worshipful Company of Farriers held at the Tallow Chandlers Hall on the 24th day of June last, it was unanimously Resolved to request you to honour the Company by accepting the Honorary Freedom of the Company and we are most grateful to you for consenting to do so.

Our Craft is most ancient and our Guild is more than six hundred years old. During that time our predecessors and ourselves have endeavoured not only to preserve the status of our Craft and its members but also to do what is possible in every way to benefit the health and comfort of the Horse.

The Court and Livery are aware of your Great services to the Horse both in your capacity as a Director of the British Horse Society and as Chairman of the British Show Jumping Association and it is particularly for that reason that we welcome you to the Freedom of the Company.

The Seal of the Company is hereunto affixed the 26th day of September in the 605th year of the fellowship in the year of our Lord 1961 in the presence of:

J. Smyth (*Master*); F. Lord (*Warden*); J.E. Lines (*Warden*); E.C.P. Whiteley (*Warden*); E.H. Newcome Wright (*Clerk*)

On 26th January, 1962, Colonel M.P. Ansell, CBE, DSO, was admitted to the Freedom of the City of London at the Chamberlain's Court by the Chamberlain of London, Sir Irving Gane,

KCVO, after having been presented by the Master, Brigadier Sir John Smyth, Bart, VC, MC, MP, the Wardens Mr. John E. Lines and Mr. Eric C.P. Whiteley, TD, and the Clerk Mr. E.H. Newcome Wright.

Colonel Ansell made the Declaration as required by Law and was offered the right hand of Fellowship by the Chamberlain in accordance with ancient custom.

After the ceremony the Chamberlain entertained Colonel Ansell, the Master, Wardens and Clerk and a Company of friends, including Mrs. Ansell, their daughter, Mrs. Sandy Evans and the Senior Members of the Corporation.

1968 Major Derek Allhusen

In December 1968 the Court decided to confer the Honorary Freedom of the Company on Major Derek Allhusen in recognition of his Leadership of the Equestrian Team, winners of the Gold Medal in Mexico, and accordingly Major Allhusen attended the Court and made the Declaration as a Freeman on the 24th June, 1969, and the Master Mr. A.J. Barsham, B.Com, FCA, presented an Illuminated Address which read as follows:

To Major Derek Allhusen.

At a Court of the Worshipful Company of Farriers held at Tallow Chandlers' Hall on the 10th day of December, 1968, it was unanimously resolved to invite you to honour the Company by accepting the Freedom of the Company and we are very grateful to you for consenting to do so.

Our Craft is most ancient and our Guild is more than six hundred years old. During that time our predecessors and ourselves have endeavoured not only to preserve the status of our Craft and its members, but also to do what is possible in every way to benefit the health and comfort of the Horse.

The Court and Livery are aware of your great service to the Horse and salute you as leader of the Equestrian Team which succeeded in winning the Gold Medal for the Three-Day Event at the Olympic Games held in Mexico in 1968 and also as winner of the Silver Medal for individual performance. It is particularly for these reasons that we welcome you to the Freedom of the Company.

The Seal of the Company is hereunto affixed the 26th day of June in the 613th year of the Fellowship in the year of our Lord 1969 in the presence of:

A.J. Barsham (*Master*); R.W.V. Neathercoat (*Warden*); E.H. Newcome Wright (*Warden*); Hugh Linstead (*Warden*); Michael Burke (*Clerk*)

CHAPTER 7
The Royal Connection

When, in 1970, HRH The Princess Anne expressed her interest in the Company by consenting to become an Honorary Freeman, the members of the Company, and in particular, the Court were delighted to welcome her in their midst; not only as a member of the Royal Family but, as stated in the Illuminated Address handed to her in March 1971, 'one of the most distinguished young women riders in our time'. Her interest was further shown by consenting to become an Assistant of the Court in 1978. One wonders how our predecessors in the Middle Ages would have reacted if the daughter of the Sovereign had been elected to the Court!

The Author has happy memories during his year as Master (1955–56) when he had the privilege of conferring the Honorary Freedom on Miss Pat Smythe, then the first woman to become an Honorary Freeman in the Company.

Her Royal Highness is a Freeman of other Livery Companies connected with the Horse: the Saddlers, the Loriners and the Farmers, also the Fishmongers by virtue of her Father being a Freeman of the Company.

The following pages place on record the Addresses presented to Her Royal Highness by the Corporation of London and the Company of Farriers and her gracious replies.

The Author takes this opportunity of thanking Her Royal Highness for her kindness in writing the Foreword of 'The Farrier and His Craft'.

In December 1971, the Honorary Freedom of the Company was conferred on HRH The Princess Anne.

At a meeting of the Court in March 1971 a Resolution was proposed by Past Master Mr. Deputy S.R. Walker CBE, and seconded by Past Master George Garnham, to confer the Honorary Freedom of the Company on Her Royal Highness The Princess Anne in recognition of her great interest in the Horse and as one of the most distinguished young women riders in our time, and accordingly Her Royal Highness The Princess Anne attended at a Court Meeting at the Drapers' Hall on the 6th December 1971, and made her Declaration as a Freeman. The Master, Sir Hugh Linstead, OBE, LLD, FPS, presented an Illuminated Address to Her Royal Highness which read as follows:

'To Her Royal Highness The Princess Anne.

At a Meeting of the Court of the Worshipful Company of Farriers held on the 23rd day of March 1971, it was unanimously resolved to request you to honour the Company by accepting the Honorary Freedom of the Company and we are most grateful to you for consenting to do so.

The Court and Livery acknowledge with gratitude that you, one of the most distinguished young women riders in our time, have accepted the greatest compliment which the Company is able to offer. We are happy to confer on you our Honorary Freedom not only because of your outstanding achievements but also because we know you are truly interested in the welfare of the Horse which has been the predominant interest of this Company during the six centuries which our Guild has been in existence. We feel that in accepting our Honorary Freedom you are doing a very great honour to the Court and Livery of our Guild.'

The Seal of the Company was hereunto affixed the 6th day of December in the 615th year of the Fellowship in the year of our Lord 1971 in the presence of:

H.N. Linstead   Master

K.J. Lines Warden   M.J. Burke Clerk
John Clabby Warden
M.A.P. Simons Warden

Her Royal Highness's speech acknowledging her Admission, revealed great interest in the Company's activities, particularly its apprentices, some of whom she met when they presented her with a Mounted Horseshoe Pen-rack specially made by one of them for the occasion.

At the conclusion of the proceedings, Her Royal Highness The Princess Anne graciously accepted an invitation from the Company to attend a Livery Dinner attended by Members, their Ladies and Guests, totalling 230. The Dinner was a very happy occasion at which the Princess spoke graciously and accepted from the Company a Stock-Pin to mark the historic event.

On the 14th November 1973, Her Royal Highness was married

to Captain Mark Phillips and the Company gave as a wedding present a set of fire irons and stand, personally delivered by the Master, Brigadier Clabby. The set was designed and hand-made by Mr. Ken Grantham at Ashurst Wood, Sussex. He and his brother John carried on his father's business which started in about 1900. John is a Fellow of the Company and is a member of the Company's Examination Board and is very interested in the Company's Apprenticeship Scheme. The Princess sent a personal letter of thanks to the Master for the gift.

In March 1974 Captain Mark Phillips became a Freeman of the Company and in December 1975 was admitted into the Livery.

On 27th February 1976 HRH The Princess Anne, Mrs. Mark Phillips was presented by the Master, Arthur Smith, in Company with Past Master George Garnham, Past Master Deputy S.R. Walker, CBE, the Wardens, Professor Frederick Bell, Dorian Williams and David Gibson and the Clerk, for the Freedom of the City of London at Guildhall and afterwards was entertained to Luncheon by the Corporation of London at the Mansion House.

The Minutes of the Court of Common Council record the event: 'This Day Her Royal Highness, The Princess Anne, Mrs Mark Phillips GCVO, was admitted to the Freedom of the City in the Worshipful Company of Farriers, agreeably to the Resolution of the 15th January 1976, and after reading of the Resolution by the Town Clerk, Her Royal Highness made the usual Declaration. The Chamberlain, Mr. John Griggs, addressed her in these words:

'My Lord Mayor,

May it please Your Royal Highness, Your Grace, Mr. Prime Minister, Your Excellency, My Lords, Ladies and Gentlemen.

In the air today there is a feeling of spring for we are meeting together in Guildhall to welcome Her Royal Highness The Princess Anne, Mrs. Mark Phillips. The Princess has honoured the City by accepting from our Ancient Corporation the highest honour we can give and which by right she can claim.

It is my proud privilege as Chamberlain to try to put into words the pleasure we all feel in our hearts as we welcome our youngest Freeman.

From time immemorial this City and the Monarchy have enjoyed a very special relationship. It is true that many years ago there were occasions when the City was known to flex its muscles in a marginally unconstitutional manner so as to wear that relationship a little thin, but never to the point of fracture. The golden thread of absolute loyalty runs and will ever run unbroken.

The Crown has consistently recognised the worth of that loyalty by interesting itself and becoming involved in the City's

211

Institutions, Traditions and Affairs.

We live at a time when there are those who question, and try to erode, each value which experience has shown to be the bed rock upon which our greatness has been based.

"An Englishman's word is his bond": right will triumph and decency prevail. The end never justifies the means unless they be honourable too.

Those are simple expressions of simple virtues, and it is our comfort and our pride that we see them reflected in every word and deed of our beloved Queen your Mother, and Prince Philip your Father and that splendid example is clearly mirrored in The Prince of Wales. And in you Ma'am we see just the same firm strength.

Today you honour us. We confirm our loyalty and affection.'

Perhaps a measure of the affection in which The Princess is held is the immense interest her presence anywhere always arouses, and it is to her great credit that she fulfills her diverse responsibilities with an abundance of verve and charm – whether ceremonial occasions, foreign travel, social engagements, charitable functions, sporting events or anything else.

Ours is an affection and a loyalty at one and the same time impersonal and yet deeply personal.

It is impersonal because it is endemic among all Englishmen to love and honour Princesses.

It is personal because your warmth and beauty Ma'am has wooed and won us all. You must not think too hardly of us if our admiration and respect for that Officer of the Dragoon Guards who wooed and won you is tinged with a little envy. It makes today an even happier one that you, Sir, are here.

It is personal because we like what you do. Indeed we wish we could do it half as well. You should know that, however much the Crown elsewhere may have seized upon the internal combustion engine as the most convenient form of transport, we Englishmen see in our minds eye our Queens proud upon horseback or drawn along in a silent stately carriage, and so it has been from Boadicea to the second great Elizabeth. If we disregard Boadicea's disconcerting habit of using her carriage wheels for human scythes, your family's loyal subjects have long enjoyed a relatively tranquil view of the Royal Family on horseback. But you certainly changed all that. In the early days we held our breath a little at the risks you ran riding mettlesome horses in 3 Day Eventing a sport that not so long ago was regarded as so dangerous that it was thought to be a male preserve. After all there was not much of a 'stock pile' of Princesses and we feared for your safety. We would have been wiser to have preserved our sympathetic concern for the routed male opposition.

Now the Olympics threaten. If you are chosen to go there and we certainly hope you will be, you will take our best wishes for your success; and the warning that it is no less than your duty Ma'am to win.

We like what you do because you have found time in the midst of your success to notice that there are those with the heart and mind for the same thing but limbs ill-fashioned to that end. Your heart warming concern to help the disabled to ride is entirely typical of you and your whole family as is your work for the underprivileged through your continuous involvement with the Save the Children Fund.

Finally we liked your indifference and cool contempt for the armed crank who conceived and tried to execute that kidnap in the Mall. Your courage more than matched that of those around you.

It would be superfluous for me to recount even a small part of our Freeman's other wide-ranging activities. They are well known to all of us having taken place before the ever-watchful ever critical but sincerely admiring eyes of the worlds Press and of the supposedly unlying, if sometimes misleading, cameras of the world's most eager photographers.

George Linley, that great lover of mountain and stream, wrote:

> 'Among our ancient mountains,
> And from our lovely vales,
> Oh, let the prayer re-echo:
> "God bless the Prince of Wales".'

If George Linley were still alive and with us today he would have continued:

> 'And from the ancient City
> The Voice of every man
> Is heard to thunder back again
> "God Bless The Princess Anne" '

Ma'am it is with respect, pleasure and very warm affection that each of us comes here today to see you take your place as a Citizen and Farrier of this Ancient City.

Your Royal Highness, this is your copy of Freedom and this is a copy of the Rules for the Conduct of Life. Although it was written over 200 years ago I still commend it for your consideration. It is now my great privilege and pleasure, as Chamberlain of this ancient City, to offer you the right hand of fellowship and to greet you as a Citizen and Farrier of London.'

The Right Honourable the Lord Mayor having presented Her Royal Highness with a pearl necklace with a diamond and sapphire clasp, Her Royal Highness replied in the following words:

'My Lord Mayor,

On an occasion such as this, "thank you" seems rather an inadequate statement and I don't think I am the first person who has found themselves in the difficult position of trying to thank the great City of London and its people for the honour of its Freedom. I am deeply conscious of that honour and can only express my gratitude to the Worshipful Company of Farriers for presenting me, to the Ancient Corporation for accepting me; and the courtesy of my father for his patrimony. Many famous people have been honoured with the Freedom of this City and I am very flattered to be able to count myself among such a company. I confess to being rather dubious about my qualifications for being so honoured, but I hope to improve upon my so far limited experiences and perhaps eventually improve my qualification.

Trotting through the streets of London on a comparatively mild February morning in an open carriage might appear rather a foolish thing to do to some people and as a humble commuter myself on some days I can sympathise with the confused motorist, but I make no apology on this occasion because I am thoroughly convinced of the value of tradition in our modern lives and in particular when one stops to consider the important traditions enveloped in the Ancient Corporation and in the City of London. Some people might say that this ceremony has no modern significance, but I would like to suggest that they stop to think about the background to the Ceremony and the people in it. My Lord Mayor, the Aldermen, Sheriffs and all the Worshipful Companies represented here today. Now there is a history lesson in itself and not just of financial whizz kids, but of every kind of trade. Their roles have changed somewhat over the years, but in many cases they still give their help and support to the various trades that perhaps would have fallen by the way-side under the pressures of a modern world – and speaking from my experience of those Worshipful Companies who have been kind enough to accept me, I feel that they should be congratulated and encouraged in their work – after all they are only another tradition.

Going back to the carriage and more horses, another tradition, before anyone asks why we didn't ride here, I would first draw their attention to my apparel – 100% unsuitable – added to the fact, that I don't ride side saddle very well and I do draw a pretty firm line between business and hobbies – as the saying goes "there's a time and a place for everything!" and we are very sorry if we disappointed anybody and although ever since our small breakdown in the Mall on the way to the Opening of Parliament, I would prefer to have slightly more control over all those horses. It is a very comfortable method of travel – a lot of people consider anything to do with horses is uncomfortable, in which case they've never had the opportunity to see the children and adults who go to great lengths to get on a horse or pony of any description or had the privilege of seeing the delight in their faces when they get into the saddle of their indomitable sense of humour when they fall off. Nothing unusual in that you may say – there isn't – except that these people are all handicapped in some way – some normally confined to wheelchairs and would never have the opportunity of independent motion without the assistance of a separate living being that does most of the work. People may consider the horse as an over-rated luxury, but to these people it gives them a sense of Freedom they might never experience otherwise. Freedom – that word again – a symbol perhaps to me of which I am very proud, but to the handicapped, a real luxury! Thanks to the extraordinary generosity of the people of this country, I think it could also be said that the Save the Children Fund also offers Freedom to a lot of children who would otherwise suffer from fear of all sorts of deprivation – fear of hunger and all the sorts of things that you and I take for granted.

On this day when London has seen fit to confer the Freedom of the City on me, it is a pleasure to know that with a little thought one can provide a little Freedom for those who might otherwise hardly ever experience it.

I have also just read the Declaration of a Freeman and though far be it for me to hold a candle for anything like Women's Lib or equality, I'm not sure that the Corporation oughtn't to think in terms of perhaps a Freeperson. I don't really have room to talk about Women's Lib., etc., as I have been foolish enough to pick one of the few sports where men and women compete against each other on as level terms as possible – so I suffer quite enough equality without particularly wanting any more. But by courtesy of the Corporation it's always nice to be on equal terms with not only the Prime Minister, but also with one's elder brother, one's mother, father and husband as well! I only hope that I shall be worthy to follow those who have gone before and to serve the City and the people of London. And finally, My Lord Mayor, to thank you for the truly wonderful memento of this very memorable occasion.'

It was then ordered that the Address of Mr. Chamberlain and the reply of Her Royal Highness The Princess Anne, Mrs. Mark Phillips, be entered on the Journal of the Court and printed in the Minutes of the proceedings sent to every member.

The Author has reproduced the above two speeches in full – for other than those present at the Guildhall they could only be read in the Volume entitled 'London's Roll of Fame' consisting of the Presentation of the Freedom of the City and Addresses of Welcome from the Corporation of London to Royal and other Distinguished Personages. The last edition of the book (AD 1885–1959) was printed by Order of the Corporation under the Direction of the Library Committee. No instructions have been given by the Corporation as to when the next volume will be issued. It is of interest that 'London's Roll of Fame' followed a Resolution of the Corporation in 1883 that it would be desirable to print the Addresses of the Chamberlain of the City to honour those on whom the Honorary Freedom had been conferred, with the replies of the recipients. The first volume was published in 1884 commencing on 24th May 1757 with the Presentation of the Freedom to William Pitt, MP (afterwards the first Earl of Chatham) and Henry Bilson Legge, MP, later Chancellor of the Exchequer. The last Freedom in Volume I took place on 20th January 1884, the recipient being the philanthropist Anthony Earl of Shaftesbury who had devoted his life and his fortune to improving the lot of the less fortunate of his fellow human beings. On 6th May 1882 Queen Victoria was pleased to accept a loyal Address on the occasion of her visit to High Beech, Epping Forest, when she crowned the labours of the Corporation in securing this unique open space by dedicating it to the enjoyment of her people for ever.

'Among the admissions of members of the Royal Family will be found those of four Sovereigns in the persons of Prince George of Wales (King George V), The Prince of Wales (King Edward VIII), Prince Albert (King George VI), and Princess Elizabeth (Queen Elizabeth II).

The admission by Patrimony in the Company of Drapers of Her Royal Highness The Princess Elizabeth, now our gracious and beloved Queen, made history for the Corporation in that Her Royal Highness was the first Royal Princess ever to be admitted to the Freedom.'

Her Majesty was followed by her sister, Her Royal Highness The Princess Margaret, Countess of Snowdon in 1966 and now by her daughter Her Royal Highness The Princess Anne, Mrs. Mark Phillips.

The admission of our Honorary Freeman, HRH The Princess Anne, Mrs. Mark Phillips to the Livery of the Company was arranged for the 20th April 1976 at the Mansion House prior to the Company's Livery Dinner, but owing to an injury to The Princess shortly before that date, having been thrown from her horse, HRH was unable to attend. Fortunately she recovered very soon but it was a great disappointment to the fully attended Banquet.

In July 1976 the Company sent a telegram congratulating HRH

The Princess Anne on having been selected as a member of the British Equestrian team at the Olympic Games in Montreal.

A telegram of thanks had been received from the Princess for the 'kind good wishes'.

However, on the 8th February 1977 the great day arrived when Her Royal Highness, accompanied by her husband, attended the Court which was held in the evening at the Innholders Hall, and took up her Livery. Afterwards she dined with the members of the Court and their guests.

On 15th November 1977, Her Royal Highness gave birth to a son and the Company look forward to 1998 when Peter Mark Andrew Phillips will be able to join the Company by patrimony.

On 6th September 1978 the Court Resolved that HRH The Princess Anne, Mrs. Mark Phillips be invited to become an Assistant of the Court.

Her Royal Highness The Princess Anne, Mrs. Mark Phillips, having graciously accepted to fill a vacancy on the Court of the Company, attended a meeting of the Court held on Wednesday 6th December 1978, at the Innholders Hall and having made her Solemn Declaration she was formally admitted as a member of the Court of Assistants. Her Royal Highness stayed for the subsequent Court Luncheon and the Master, Major W. David Gibson in welcoming her as an Assistant, quoted from the original Ordinance of the Company that the Court 'may from time to time as occasion arises shall require, elect and choose the most able and sufficient persons of the said Company to be Assistants. and said that on this occasion the Court had done just that, for who else but Her Royal Highness was 'most able and sufficient.

This was promptly borne out by her presence at Court Meetings and her continued attendance at Company functions.

Appendices

The Six Hundredth Anniversary Banquet in Guildhall
22nd November 1956

Whilst in the Annals of the Livery Companies the Farriers are shown as having received its Charter in 1674, as has been seen it was in 1356 that in the records of the Corporation the Mayor summoned the Farriers of the City because many offences and dangers had been committed against the Commonalty of the City and the Realm by 'people not wise therein' who kept forges in the City and intermeddled with works of farriery which they did not understand, with the resultant loss of many horses. The Mayor ordered the choosing of two Wardens the most 'sufficient and best knowing' men; these men were then sworn and given full power to oversee and govern the trade and to espy into the faults thereof and thus was first established by the Court of Mayor and Aldermen the Fellowship by the name of 'MARSHALLS OF THE CITY OF LONDON'.

The Court of Assistants in March 1955 decided that the Foundation of the Fellowship should be celebrated in the 600th year of its existence and plans were laid accordingly to hold a Banquet in Guildhall. Permission was readily given by the Corporation. His Grace the Duke of Devonshire was then the Renter Warden and by the kindness of John Stroud, the Middle-Warden, it was arranged that His Grace should be Master in 1956 in order to preside at the Banquet. Twenty months of hard work then ensued in making all the necessary arrangements. Their Royal Highnesses the Duke and Duchess of Gloucester accepted the Company's invitation to be present. The Lord Mayor, Lt-Col. Alderman Sir Cullum Welch, OBE, MC, and the Sheriffs, Alderman Frederick Hoare and Sir James Miller signified their willingness to be present.

While this purports to give a description of the Banquet it is not possible to set out all the names of the Guests and other details which are so well described in the beautiful Menu and Brochure so ably prepared by the late Mr. Robson. Suffice it to say that in all 639 ladies and gentlemen were present. This number included 150 members of the Company, 412 personal guests and 77 guests of the Company. Among the latter were:

The Right Honourable the Lord Mayor, Lt-Col Sir Cullum Welch, OBE, MC

The Lady Mayoress
His Royal Highness The Duke of Gloucester, KG, PC
Her Royal Highness The Duchess of Gloucester
Alderman and Sheriff Frederick Hoare
Sheriff Sir James Miller, DL, LLD
Their Excellencies the Swedish and Belgian Ambassadors
Her Grace Mary, Duchess of Devonshire, GCVO
The Lord Bishop of London
Earl de la Warr, PC, Trustee of the Royal Agricultural Society
Hon J.J. Astor
Lord Willoughby de Broke, MC, Senior Steward of the Jockey
Club
Lord Digby, DSO, MC, Hunters' Improvement Society
Lord Birdwood, MVO
Sir Dingwall Bateson, CBE, MC, Chairman, The Racecourse Betting Control Board

The Olympic Equestrian Team was represented by:

Major A. Lawrence Rook, MC
Miss Patricia R. Smythe, OBE
Lt-Col F.W.C. Weldon, MVO, MBE, MC
Mr. Wilfred H. White

The Civic Toast was proposed by the Earl de la Warr to which The Rt Hon The Lord Mayor replied. The Toast to the Guests was proposed by the Immediate Past Master Mr Leslie Barnett Prince and the response was made by Lord Willoughby de Broke. The Toast of the Company was given by HRH The Duke of Gloucester and replied to by the Master, His Grace The Duke of Devonshire.

As soon as the Company was assembled at the table the ceremony of the presentation of the Loving Cups took place. The Master presented the Cup subscribed by the Court of Assistants whilst Mr. George Smith who had organised the subscription, presented the Cup subscribed by the Livery.

The beautiful souvenir programme contained a brief account of the condition of the Fourteenth Century as it affected the Horse, and read as follows:

'The middle of the Fourteenth Century. What a different world we live in today! Printing from movable type was not yet invented, there was no machinery, few roads, no proper drainage, none of the amenities of modern life; little learning, the vast majority of folk quite unable to read or write; little knowledge of medicine, no "social services"; the poor, on the whole content to stay in the position to which they were born. "God Bless the Squire and his relations and keep us in our proper stations" seems to sum up the general position.

'It was the time when our great Chaucer was born. What a marvellous picture of the times he has given us in the wonderful Prologue to the Canterbury Tales. It was the time of the Hundred Years War; the Battle of Poitiers was fought in the year of which we are thinking at this celebration, 1356.''

The Days of the Farriers
Professor F.R. Bell, BSc, PhD, FRCVS
Master of the Worshipful Company of Farriers

(A paper given at the joint meeting of the Veterinary History Society and the Association of Veterinarians in Industry on 8 February 1977, at the Wellcome Institute for the History of Medicine, London)

The term farrier, according to the *Shorter Oxford English Dictionary*, came into general usage in 1562, probably derived from Old French *ferrier* and Latin *ferrarius*, formed from *ferrum* meaning horse-shoe. A farrier, however, was not restricted to the shoeing of horses but became concerned with the treatment of the general ailments of horses and thence of other animals. We all know that in this broad sense the farrier was superseded at the turn of the 19th century by the veterinary surgeon especially in military circles, and the farrier then reverted to the more restricted activity of shoeing smith. The veterinary surgeon during the 19th century evolved into an equine physician and later took up preventive medicine when controlling the plagues which attacked agricultural animals. Only fairly recently has the veterinary surgeon assumed the general mantle of physician administering to the health of all the domestic animals.

Rise of craft guilds
Interest in agriculture and consequently animal diseases has shown a number of surges since medieval times. In Chaucer's England, mainly because of the success of the continental wool trade, the feudal manor and serfdom were beginning to make way for a merchant class and urban population. In order to maintain trade, standards were set up such as 'the Staple' to safeguard the quality and therefore the value of wool. At the same time trade associations were established to protect the newly emerging classes of leasehold farmers, merchants and craftsmen while at the same time social justice became more effective with the concentration of legal power in the Lower House of Parliament and the institution of justices of the peace. These changes were consolidated by the holocaust of the Black Death and the subsequent demands from a markedly depleted labour force. As the merchant developed wealth and power, craftsmen also began to organise themselves to improve standards of workmanship

225

and to provide proper training through apprenticeship. The time of Edward III was the heyday of craft guilds in many trades and they received letters patent as royal charters. In this way the forefathers of the Worshipful Company of Farriers were established in 1356 by the Court of the Mayor and Aldermen of the City of London by the name of 'Marshalls of the City of London'.

At the time of the Renaissance a second surge of craftsmanship arose and a renewal of interest in animal medicine occurred. This period of resurgence was associated again with a consolidation of the power of the great merchant companies as they became enriched by the Indies trade. In agriculture the horse was becoming more closely allied to cultivation and transport, relinquishing its role as a single transport animal for the single rider. At the same time, especially in the Stuart era, Arabian and Barbary stallions were imported to upgrade the native riding horse and to produce the thoroughbred and to establish horse-racing as a national sport. Books on farriery began to appear emphasising the care of the foot and the treatment of lameness. There can be no doubt that the tremendous interest in equestrian skills must have kindled an interest in the diseases of horses and their treatment. It was during this period that the influence of the great Italian anatomists and physicians was spreading all over Europe.

Mistery of the farrier

After the fire of London most of the ancient companies and fellowships of the 14th century sought to renew their letters patent by petitioning King Charles II. A great incentive was the need to re-establish the guilds since most of the records had been lost in the Great Fire of 1666 which destroyed the halls of the companies. On 17 January, 1674, under Privy Seal, the masters and wardens of the Farriers' Company were given 'the power to impose fines, pains, penalties and forfeiture upon breach of rule and government of the Company'. Further restrictive practices were reinforced for it was laid down that 'no person other than persons free of the Company should practice or exercise the Art or Mistery of a Farrier unless he had served as an Apprentice to the said trade for seven years'. Members of the livery could, when armed with the proper documents, 'enter shops, cellars, stables and other suspected places within an area of seven miles around the Cities of London and Westminster' to search for misdemeanours and defective work and medicines with a view to prosecution. Accounts of the activity of the Company for the first time, although it had been in existence for 300 years, mention its interest in medicines. There is no doubt, however, that farriers, marshalls, horse keepers, grooms and others, 'doctored' horses long before this. In classical times, Xenophon, Virgil and Pliny alluded to the treatment of animals and the Roman essayist,

Martial, composed the tag *venienti occurite morbo*, which loosely translated conveys his meaning that it is better to go out and prevent disease than to treat the established condition. It is also worth noting that the idea of control, search and standards of the 17th century is now re-established today in the Medicines Act of 1968.

Quacks and cow-leeches

The main body of farriers in the late 17th century, however, did not prosper and their activities were infiltrated in urban and rural society by quacks and cow-leeches. It should be noted that there were probably as many cows in cities as in rural areas so the cow-leech was both a rural and urban character.

Because of this unsatisfactory state of affairs a number of treatises on farriery were produced about this time to enlighten owners of horses, 'never to suffer his groom or any other person to administer any medicine by drench or with their corn, in a mash, or by other means, without first being informed what is to be used and for what purpose'. That is surely sound advice and applies equally today, for the Medicines Act states clearly its concern with both the efficacy and proper usage of medicines. In the early 18th century some writers said that 'carters gave antimony and sulphur almost constantly with every feed of corn to sweeten his blood and make his skin sweet'. A plea was made to regulate such medicines and it was pointed out that liver of antimony is detrimental to young horses, making them incapable of converting 'what food is taken, into proper nourishment'. Sir Paulet St. John exhorts that 'medicines should never be administered but when disease or some fault in the constitution require them, and these medicines should always be of the best sort and quality'. Henry Bracken, a surgeon practising as a farrier, in his treatise upon the *Art of Farriery* (1750) has a section on 'drugs and compound medicines with remarks, discovering whether genuine or adulterted and their several prices'.

Rowelling, oiling and firing

These treatises are rather like earlier pharmacopoeias and judging from some of the prices quoted, prescriptions must have been quite expensive. For example, inspissated oil of cinnamon cost £1 16s 0d per lb and Glaubers salts 1s 6d per lb. Bracken states that certain 'New-England traders have got a way of imitating or coming very near to the finest turpentines and balsams of the East from trees of their own growth'. Bracken was very definite in many of his statements, for example, when discussing surgical treatment of rheumatism and sciatica, which he called hip-gout, he states that the poor creatures (horses) undergo all the most painful and ill-contrived operations of rowelling, oiling and firing which farriers could invent. He states that he is satisfied that a different method should be practised because 'the *nervus sciaticus*, lies so very deep and close to the joint that outwards applications are not of much service unless we were to bore holes very deep into the muscular parts near to the nerve according to the practice of the Arabians'. He was presumably advocating that these holes should be filled with some stimulating lotion such as alcohol, vinegar or vitriol. I was amused to read that although Bracken commended Dr Sydenham's (the renowned physician of the mid-18th century) views on medical treatment as deserving ever-lasting remembrance he thought that 'Sydenham was no conjurer in Mathematics or Mechanics'. Perhaps Bracken's views were those typical of a surgeon towards a physician.

Jeremiah Bridges was not only a farrier but also gave a course of lectures in anatomy in the first half of the 18th century. He had a list of remedies too, with their prices. Fever balls cost 4s 0d per lb and strong poultice 2s 0d per lb. Although he gave excellent descriptions as to how to use the remedies he was very discreet as to the ingredients.

Good and sensible men

Captain William Burdon, writing in 1732, stated that 'a farrier is as useful a trade as any other in His Majesty's Dominion; we commonly call him Doctor because he professes Physick and Surgery among horses; and some are good and sensible men; but people who are able to give their sons learning seldom bind 'em to that trade, so that farriers are obliged to take such Apprentices as they can without regard to their education'. He is equally outspoken on overseas authors, saying in commending his own book 'what a splutter has Mons. Sollyfell made in his works, where is costs you as many pounds to cure a distemper as it does shillings in this. Besides the Difficulty and Loss of Time'.

Royal Veterinary College founded

All was not well with the craft of farrier in the mid-18th century and the Worshipful Company of Farriers attempted to put their house in order by a series of prosecutions of farriers who had not taken the livery. The Company records show that in 1762 action was demanded by 'several Noblemen and Gentlemen of the 1st Distinction who have suffered by the Ignorance of unskillful Quacks who assume to themselves the Name of Farrier'. In spite of their efforts the Company was overtaken by events which arose with the attempts of the Odiham Society to set up a school of scientific farriery. A powerful group of landowners, horse owners and agriculturalists formed a lobby which in 1791 brought about the inauguration of the Royal Veterinary College. The farrier was now relegated to the craft of shoeing horses and the new educational establishment took on the role of training veterinary surgeons for the cavalry as well as giving training in the diseases of farm animals. A great deal of attention was given to materia medica and pharmacognosy and a herb garden was established at the new Veterinary College in Camden Town. The early 19th century was a turbulent time for both veterinary surgeon and farrier alike but with the 1844 Royal Charter for the Royal College of Veterinary Surgeons the treatment of all animals by veterinary surgeons was advocated. The Worshipful Company of Farriers once again adopted its craft role towards the end of the 19th century and an examination scheme for shoeing smiths was introduced.

With regard to medicaments little progress was made from medieval times until the 1930s when chemotherapeutics began to expand. The first *British Veterinary Codex* 1953, contained many drugs which were commonplace in the year of the Company's first Charter in the 14th century. Only in recent years have many of these medicines been removed from veterinary practice and even today certain kinds of bitters are still advocated as rational treatment. It is apparent that only when the Medicines Act is fully supported by the veterinary profession will the quacks and cow-leeches who bedevilled the farriers for so long cease to debase and disbar their modern successors from the ethical and professional practice of veterinary medicine.

The Rights of the Liveryman

The City of London was unique in evolving a separate electoral assembly, known as the Common Hall, for the choice of important municipal officers. Originally all freemen were entitled to attend such assemblies but apparently the concourse became too large for Guildhall. Even in the thirteenth century attendance depended on individual summons and constant orders were issued for enforcing the rule that only those summoned on the advice of the Mayor and Aldermen should attend. This enlarged assembly was designated a Congregation.

In 1467 the assembly was reinforced by the addition of the Masters and Wardens of the misteries or companies. This was the first step in the direction of organizing the assembly on the basis of the guilds. It was followed in 1475 by the inclusion of the Liverymen of the companies. Thus the original right of all Freemen to attend came to be limited to those Freemen who were able to assume, or later to be elected upon, the livery of their companies. This privilege of the Liverymen was confirmed by statute in 1725 (II Geo. 1, c.18, sec. 14) which requires that electors at meetings of Common Hall shall be Freemen and Liverymen of at least one year's standing.

The Congregation was, and the Common Hall still is, the largest gathering of citizens for any muncipal purpose and such an assembly places the election of mayor on a far wider basis than the usual appointment by a council.

A Common Hall is summoned by precept from the Lord Mayor to the Masters and Wardens of the Livery Companies, requiring them to give notice to their Liverymen to attend at Guildhall on a certain day. Another precept requires the attendance of the Beadle of each Company at the entrance to Guildhall to prevent any other than Liverymen from entering. The members of each Company enter by a particular wicket guarded by their Beadle, and the Common Cryer opens the proceedings by directing all who are not Liverymen to depart on pain of imprisonment. This assembly elects the Lord Mayor annually on 29th September and the Sheriffs, Chamberlain, Bridgemasters, Aleconners, and the Auditors of the Chamberlain's and Bridgemasters' Accounts on 24th June.

All Liverymen of the City's Livery Companies of one year's standing, irrespective of their address or residence have a right to vote in Common Hall, and the common weal, good goverment and the future of the City depend on every qualified Liveryman exercising his right whenever possible.

L.B.P.

Abstract of the Charter of the Farriers' Company
By Letters Patent under the Privy Seal, 17th January 1674

Note: The Word 'Court' is not to be found in the Charter but is used in this precis in place of the words 'Master, Wardens and Assistants'. The word 'area' here used means 'the Cities of London and Westminster or within seven miles thereof.'

After reciting the petition of the Brotherhood of Farryers of London and Westminster for a Charter because of the damage done by unexpert and unskilfull persons.

It was ordained that 49 named persons and all others than then professed the said Trade, Art or Mistery of a Farryer and had used the same by the space of three years last past within London and Westminster and seven miles thereof and all others that should thereafter exercise the same and should have served as apprentices within those limits for seven years should be one Body Politique and Corporate in the name of the Master, Wardens, Assistants and Comonalty of the Farryers of London with perpetual succession capable of holding land not exceeding the yearly value of £100 besides their Hall and all things personal to any amount with power to sell and deal with the said land as fully as any other subject and to sue and be sued in respect thereof.

Power for the Company to have a Common Seal and to alter it.

There should be a Master, three Wardens and not above twenty nor under Ten Assistants, the first Master to be Gregory Costen to hold office until the Feast of the Nativity of St John the Baptist (i.e. Midsummer Day) 1674, and thereafter Andrew Snape (who was Sergeant Farrier to the King) for one year or until another of the Company should be chosen, the Master in each case taking his oath for the due and faithful execution of the said office, the first Master before a Master of the High Court of Chancery and succeeding Masters before the Court or any five of them.

Andrew Snape, Samuell Mabbs and Samuell Dickons to be the first three Wardens to continue to the Feast of the Nativity of St. John the Baptist 1674 and thereafter Thomas Halfpenny, Samuell Dickons and Robert Snape for a year and thenceforth until others should be elected, they taking the oath as to the first Wardens before a Master of the High Court of Chancery and as to succeeding Wardens before the Master of the Company.

Twenty persons were named as Assistants during their lives or until the removal for just and reasonable cause, to assist the

Master and Wardens, for the better rule and direction of the Company and to take their oaths before the Master and Wardens or any two of them.

The election of Masters, Wardens and Assistants to take place on the Feast of the Nativity of St John the Baptist yearly for ever unless on a Sunday and then on the Monday following at a meeting of the Court after notice in the Company's Hall or place of meeting.

The Master should be someone who had been a Warden and should hold office for the ensuing year. The three Wardens to be elected and hold office for a year, the last Master and Wardens (unless removed for just and reasonable cause) at the end of their term becoming Assistants.

The Masters and Wardens to be removable by the Court for just and reasonable cause.

Power for the Court to fill from among themselves a vacancy caused by death or removal of a Master or Warden until the next election. Similar power in respect of Assistants to fill a vacancy from the Commonalty.

Power to impose fines on persons elected to office and refusing to accept it, not exceeding in the case of a Master, £20, of a Warden, £15, and of an Assistant, £10, such fines to be recoverable by action of debt or by distress.

Power to choose one honest and discreet person to be Clerk.

Robert Strugnell to be the first Clerk for Life or until removed for just and reasonable cause. After his death or removal the Clerk to be appointed by the Court to hold office during their pleasure and to take oath before the Court.

Liberty for the Court to make constitutions, ordinances etc., for the good estate, rule and government of the Company and in what manner the Master, Wardens, Assistants and Commonalty of the Company and all other persons exercising the art and mistery of a Farryer within the Area should demean and behave themselves in all matters appertaining to the said Art or Mistery and imposing fines, pains, penalties and forfeiture upon breach thereof.

Power to recover by action of debt or distress.

No laws to be made by the Company repugnant to the laws of the realm or prejudicial to the customs of the Cities of London or Westminster.

No person other than the Master, Wardens, Assistants and Commonalty and persons free of the Company should within the Area practice or exercise the Art of Mistery of a Farryer unless he had served as an Apprentice to the said trade for seven years upon such penalties as can be inflicted for contempt of our Royal will and pleasure.

Power for the Master, Wardens, Assistants or any three of them, of whom the Master or a Warden should be one, with a Warrant from the Lord Chief Justice of the Court either of King's Bench or Common Pleas with a constable to enter shops, cellars, stables or other suspected places within the Area aforesaid to search for misdemeanors and defective works and medicines with a view to prosecution.

All apprentices to be bound to a free Farryer member of the Company in accordance with the ordinances of the Company under penalties to be enforced by all Mayors, Sheriffs, Justices of the Peace, Chamberlains and other officers whom the same concerns.

Liberty to purchase lands to the yearly value of £100 without licence under the Statute of Mortmain and for other persons to sell or bequeath the same to the Company.

Direction to the Lord Mayor of London and other officers of the Cities of London and Westminster and mayors, sheriffs, justices of the peace, constables, bailiffs, head-boroughs and other officers within the Area and elsewhere in England and Wales upon request to assist the Court and Commonalty of the Company in the execution of these Letters Patent and all ordinance made thereunder.

Covenant by the Court and Commonalty of the Company to pay into the Exchequer at the Feast of St Michael the Archangel the yearly sum of thirteen shillings and four pence for ever.

Proviso that if the said rent should be unpaid for forty days after being lawfully demanded then the Letters Patent would be void.

Proviso that if these Letters Patent should be not enrolled with the Clerk of the Pipe within six months from the date thereof the Court and Commonalty should pay a penalty of Ten Pounds for every six months of such default.

Proviso that the Masters, Wardens and Assistants should before admission to office take the Oath of Allegiance.

Declarations

By a Master

I do solemnly and sincerely declare that I will be good and true to our Sovereign Lady the Queen's Majesty and to her Heirs and lawful Successors that I will be faithful and true unto the Company of Farriers now incorporated, and that I will as Master of the Company keep maintain and execute or cause to be kept maintained executed and observed all the lawful ordinances and orders of the said Company, and of all goods, plate, writings, sum and sums of money and every other thing and things whatsoever in anywise belonging to the said Company which shall come into my hands or possession I will render a good and faithful account to the best of my skill and knowledge.

By a Warden

I do solemnly and sincerely declare that I will be good and true to our Sovereign Lady the Queen's Majesty and to her Heirs and lawful Successors and I will be faithful and true unto the Company of Farriers now incorporated and that I will as Warden of the said Company, to the best of my skill, so far as I lawfully may observe and keep, all the lawful and laudable acts, ordinances, and order of the said Company now made or hereafter to be made, I will do my best endeavours to receive or cause to be received to the use of the said Company all fines and amercements imposed upon any offenders by the order and by-laws of this Company, and of all goods, plate, writings, sum and sums of money and every other thing and things whatsoever in anywise belonging to the said Company which come into my hands or possession I will render a good true and faithful account.

By an Assistant

I do solemnly and sincerely declare that I will be good and true to our Sovereign Lady the Queen's Majesty and to her Heirs and lawful Successors that I will be faithful and true to the Company of Farriers now incorporated. I will in all things relating to the said Company of Farriers deal justly and indifferently without partiality, and all the lawful counsel and secrets of the Company of the Trade, Art and Mystery of Farriers I will faithfully and truly keep. I will readily attend the Master and Wardens upon summons by their Beadle or other officer, unless I shall be reasonably hindered, so long as I shall continue an Assistant.

By a Clerk

I do solemnly and sincerely declare that I will be good and true to our Sovereign Lady the Queen's Majesty and to her Heirs and lawful Successors and in all matters and things lawful and reasonable I shall be faithful and obedient unto the Masters and Wardens of this Company for the time being and their successors and that I shall keep all the lawful Councils and secrets of this Company. I shall not deliver a copy of any books concerning the said Company nor of any act or ordinance made or to be made or ordained within this society whereby the Company may receive any hurt or prejudice nor will I show the same books to any person without the knowledge of the said Master and Wardens or two of them. I shall not embezzle any manner of writings books scripts scrolls or evidences belonging to the said Company. I shall give my best counsel and advice unto the Master Wardens and Assistants for the time being in all things concerning the common weal and profit of the said Company. I shall diligently and truly according to my best skill and knowledge inform the Master and Wardens for the time being of all acts orders and ordinances of the said Company. So that errors may not by my silence or negligence be committed I shall carefully register all orders made from time to time by the Master Wardens and their Assistants and I shall behave myself well and truly towards the said Company in all things according to my best judgement.

By a Liveryman

I do solemnly and sincerely declare that I will be good and true to our Sovereign Lady the Queen's Majesty that now is and to her Heirs and lawful Successors; and in all matters and things lawful and reasonable I will be obedient to the Master, Wardens and Assistants of this Company for the time being and readily attend them in my Livery Gown upon all Summonses by their Beadle or other Officer except I have sufficient cause to be absent.

By a Freeman

I do solemnly and sincerely declare that I will be good and true to my Sovereign Lady the Queen's Majesty that now is and to her Heirs and Lawful Successors. In all matters and things lawful and reasonable relating to the said Company I will be obedient to the Master, Wardens Assistants and Governors of the Company for the time being and their Successors, and will readily appear upon all summonses by their Beadle or other Officer (except I have sufficient cause to be absent). All the lawful Acts Ordinances and Orders made or to be made for the weal, rule and good government of the said Company I will to my power observe and keep or else forthwith pay such Fines and Penalties as I shall according to the said ordinances forfeit by reason of my disobedience and breaking the same. I will not do any wrong to any Member of this

Company in relation to the said trade, but will behave myself in my said trade well and honestly.

By the Beadle

I solemnly and sincerely declare that I will be good and true to our Sovereign Lady, The Queen's Majesty that now is, and to her heirs and lawful successors. I will be obedient to the Master, Wardens and Assistants of the Worshipful Company of Farriers of the time being, in all matters and things Lawful concerning my place and office of Beadle, and I will behave myself well and orderly so long as I shall continue in my said office.

London Livery Companies
In Order of Precedence

Mercers*
Grocers*
Drapers*
Fishmongers*
Goldsmiths*
Skinners*[3]
Merchant Taylors*[3]
Haberdashers*
Salters*
10 Ironmongers*
Vintners*
Clothworkers*
Dyers*
Brewers*
Leathersellers*
Pewterers*
Barbers*
Cutlers*
Bakers*
20 Waxchandlers*
Tallowchandlers*
Armourers &
  Brasiers*
Girdlers*
Butchers*
Saddlers*
Carpenters*
Cordwainers[4]
Painter Stainers*
Curriers[5]
30 Masons
Plumbers
Innholders*
Founders*
Poulters
Cooks
Coopers
Tylers &
  Bricklayers
Bowyers
Fletchers[6]

40 Blacksmiths
Joiners
Weavers
Woolmen
Scriveners
Fruiterers
Plaisterers*
Stationers and
  Newspaper Makers*
Broderers
Upholders[7]
50 Musicians
Turners
Basketmakers
Glaziers*
Horners
FARRIERS
Paviors
Loriners[8]
Apothecaries*
Shipwrights
60 Spectaclemakers
Clockmakers
Glovers
Feltmakers
Framework Knitters
Needlemakers
Gardeners
Tinplate Workers
Wheelwrights
Distillers
70 Pattenmarkers[9]
Glass Sellers
Coachmakers & Coach
  Harness Makers
Gunmakers
Gold & Silver
  Wyre Drawers
Makers of Playing
  Cards
Fanmakers

241

Carmen[10]
Master Mariners*[11]
City of London
  Solicitors
80 Farmers
Air Pilots &
  Air Navigators
Tobacco Pipe Makers
  & Tobacco Blenders
Furniture Makers
Scientific Instrument
  Makers

Chartered Surveyors
Chartered Accountants
Chartered Secretaries
  & Administrators
Builders Merchants
Launderers
90 Marketors
Actuaries
Insurers'

* These Companies now have Halls

1 There are also two ancient companies, the Watermen and Lightermen's and the Parish Clerks' that have never had a Livery.
2 The Weavers and the Saddlers claim to have the longest history.
The last fifteen in the list are twentieth-century creations.
3 The Skinners and the Merchant Taylors take sixth and seventh place in alternate years.
4 Shoemakers
5 Leather-dressers
6 Arrow makers
7 Upholsterers
8 Harness-makers
9 Pattens were overshoes with wooden soles
10 Carters
11 The first grant of livery since Queen Anne was to the Master Mariners in 1932; they have a floating hall in HQS Wellington.

The official number of each company was 'Sette, ordeyned and agreed' by an act of the Court of Aldermen in 1515 starting with the Mercers and the 'twelve Great companies'.

Value of Money

In writing the history over six hundred years, it is clear that any mention of expenditure or income must have reference to the value of money at the date of the transaction. Whilst this value did not vary annually as it does to-day, known quite simply as inflation, nevertheless over the centuries there was a very great difference in the value of the £1.

In order to give a guide to readers – if 1 is 1979, then the multiplier for:

$$1700 \text{ is } 25$$
$$1800 \text{ is } 20$$
$$1900 \text{ is } 19$$
$$1939 \text{ is } 12$$
$$1972 \text{ is } 2\tfrac{1}{2}$$
$$1979 \text{ is } 1$$

These few figures may help readers to appreciate the present day value of such sums as four shillings as the quarterage, and fines of £20 on any member who refused to undergo and accept the office of Master, £15 for a Warden and £10 for an Assistant, etc. as were laid down in the 1674 Charter. The comparison with tradesmen's wages in the eighteenth and nineteenth centuries would be even more dramatic.

Calendar ofDocuments available for reference at the Guildhall Library

Ms. 5522
Masters' account books. 1725–1878
Paper, 3 vols., sm. fo.
vol. 1. 1725–1768; vol. 2. 1768–1818; vol. 3. 1818–1878. Each vol. described on cover as an 'Audit book'.

Ms. 5523
Court minute books. 1718–1890.
Paper, fo. and sm. fo., 6 vol.
vol. 1. 1718–1747; vol. 4. 1776–1806:
vol. 2. 1747–1760; vol. 5. 1806–1847;
vol. 3. 1760–1776; vol. 6. 1847–1890;

Ms. 5524
Register of freedom admissions (stamp duty book). 1755–1820.
Paper, 1 vol., sm. 40.

Ms. 5525
Register of freemen, arranged alphabetically, giving dates of admission to the freedom and election to the livery, offices served, trades and places of abode, 1731–1869; and list of freemen according to seniority, commenced c. 1777 and continued until 1795.
Paper, 1 vol., fo.
Described on cover as 'Freedom book'.

Ms. 5526
Registers of apprentice bindings. 1619–1811
Paper, 2 vol., sm. fo.
vol. 1. 1619–1744; vol. 2. 1744–1811.

Ms. 5527
Register of apprentice bindings, with account of orphans' duty paid into the chamber of London. 1694–1862.
Parchment, 1 vol., fo.

Ms. 5528
Register of freemen, arranged alphabetically, giving dates of admission to freedom, places of abode and offices served. 1709–1776.
Paper, 1 vol., sm. fo.
Described on cover as 'Alphabet book'.

Ms. 5529

Register of assistants, arranged chronologically by date of election to court of assistants recording dates of offices of master and warden served, trades and places of abode. 1749–1868.

Paper, 1 vol., sm. fo. obl.

Ms. 5530

Register of members of the livery, arranged alphabetically who served the office of steward, also recording trades and places of abode. 1739–1864.

Paper, 1 vol., fo.

Ms. 5531

Quarterage books. 1794–1802.
Paper, 2 vols., sm. fo. (1) and sm. fo. obl. (2).
vol. 1. 1794–1798; vol. 2 1798–1802.

Ms. 5532

Book of fines for non-attendance of the master, wardens and assistants at meetings of the court of the company. 1825–1876.

Paper, 1 vol., sm. fo.

Ms. 5533

Clerks' out-letter book. 1846–1877.
Paper, 1 vol., sm. fo. Indexed.

Ms. 5534

Volume containing: copy of the charter granted to the company by Charles II, 17 January 1673/4; copy of the ordinances made 23 June 1675 and ratified 29 January 1675/6; copies of documents relating to the re-establishment of the livery, 1692–1724, and to various legal points arising from the charter and ordinances, 1758–1867.

Paper, 1 vol., fo.

Ms. 5535

Blacksmiths' company

Volume containing *inter alia*: memorandum concerning lease by mayor and aldermen of London to the company of a tenement in Lambeth hill in the parish of St. Mary Magdalene Old Fish Street, 26 September 1494; memorandun concerning the appointment and duties of John Walter, beadle, 29 September 1569; calendar of saints' days and holy days, undated; copies of the ordinances in Latin and Norman-French of the Blacksmiths' company, 25 January 1372 ad 22 September 1395, with English translations and sixteenth century marginal annotations; copy of an order of the court of aldermen relating to the union of the Blacksmiths' and Spurriers' companies, 5 March 1561/2; copy of the will of John Whorton, citizen and blacksmith, 20 February 1497/8; copy of the ordinances of the fraternity of St. Eloy (Blacksmiths, Farriers and Loriners) with list of members, 1424; copy of the ordinances of the Blacksmiths' company, 1426; copy of the ordinances of the fraternity of St. Katherine the Holy Virgin (Spurriers' company) with a list of the livery, 1421; memorandum concerning the regulation of spur manufacture, 18 October 1534; various oaths of the Blacksmiths' company; extract from the ordinances of the Farriers' company 1556; extracts from a statute concerning foreign artificers (1 Ric.3, c.9).

    Vellum and parchment, 1 vol., sm. fo.

    Found amongst the archives of the Farriers' company.

Ms. 2890

    Volume containing: oath of a freeman; copies made c. 1600 of two orders of the court of aldermen relating to the company, 27 March 1356 and 17 March 1599; calendar, extracts from the gospels; contemporary copy of act of common council concerning employment of foreigners, 1 August 1557; copy of the will of John Sowle, made 28 March 1572 and proved 7 June 1572; (? late 15th century) copy of the ordinances of 1356; and general memoranda. c. 1400–1619.

    Vellum and parchment, 1 vol., sm. fo.

    Found amongst the archives of the Blacksmiths' company.

Ms. 8035

    Masters, wardens and assistants declaration book. 1884–1930.

    Paper, fo.

The Livery and the Royal College of Veterinary Surgeons
Present Day Links

As readers of the main text will have noted there has been a close and continuing relationship between the Worshipful Company of Farriers and the veterinary profession over the years – particularly after the creation in 1844 by Royal Charter of the Royal College of Veterinary Surgeons. Such co-operation has continued to the present day and, indeed, the last decade has seen as much contact and consultation between the bodies as ever before, as progress was made towards the statutory registration of farriers. The start of this era was marked by the Livery holding a conference on the future of farriery on the 10th October 1969, and inviting the Royal College to send representatives to it. Shortly afterwards the President of the Royal College agreed to be one of the patrons of the Livery's National Appeal for the Future of Horse Shoeing.

In December 1969 a meeting was held at the Royal College between representatives of the Livery and the College to discuss formal regulation of the training of farriers and their ultimate statutory registration. This led to the Royal College participation in the deliberations on the training of farriers by the Livery's Registration Committee and in the autumn of 1971 the first meeting was held of the Sub-Committee appointed by the Livery to consider the statutory control of farriers. All the subsequent meetings of the sub-committee were held at the Royal College, and the Registrar of the College sat with the sub-committee throughout to provide guidance based upon the statutory registration of veterinary surgeons in terms of the Veterinary Surgeons Act 1966, and the rules, regulations and procedures relating thereto. As early as February 1972 the Royal College Council gave its official support to the promotion of a Farriers Registration Bill and in December of that year agreed to the inclusion of two representatives of the Royal College on the eventual Farriers Registration Council.

As the Bill began its passage through Parliament in the Spring of 1974, close contact between the Royal College and the Livery was maintained and indeed the Master, Brigadier John Clabby, himself a distinguished veterinarian, held the Master's Reception at the College on the 9th July 1974.

With the passing of the Act, some consideration was given to housing the administrative offices of the new Council within the

Royal College. This proved impracticable, however, and the Royal Veterinary College – the veterinary school within the University of London – provided accommodation instead. Mr. S.L. Hignett and Mr. P.N. Hull were appointed as the first Royal College representatives on the Farriers Registration Council, and they have continued as such to the present time – thus maintaining the age-old links between the Livery and the veterinary profession.

A.R.W.P.

Bibliography

In addition to those histories mentioned in the text passim by Robson and the two Supplements by the present Author, the following selected list gives further data on some of the persons and events mentioned:

CITY OF LONDON DIRECTORY AND GUILDS GUIDE (City Press).

DISCOVERING LONDON'S GUILDS AND LIVERIES, John Kennedy Melling (Shire Publications, 2nd ed. 1978).

FARRIERY, Lt. Col. J. Hickman.

THE GUILDS AND COMPANIES OF LONDON, George Unwin (Frank Cass, 1966).

THE HISTORY OF THE RAVC 1919–61, Brig., J. Clabby (J.A. Allen, 1978).

PRINCESS ANNE, A GIRL OF OUR TIME, Anne Matheson and Reginald Davis (Frederick Muller, 1973).

THE SHIRE HORSE, Keith Chivers (J.A. Allen, 1976).

THE SOUL OF THE CITY, LONDON'S LIVERY COMPANIES, Colonel R.J. Blackham (Sampson Low, Marston, 1931).

VILLAGE BLACKSMITH, Roy Webber (County Book Club, 1972).

MASTER OF ONE, Dorian Williams (J.M. Dent, 1978).

FIFTY YEARS A VETERINARY SURGEON, Sir Frederick Hobday, CMG, FRCVS, FRSE (Hutchinson, 1938).

FROM FARRIERY TO VETERINARY MEDICINE, 1785–1795, Professor L.P. Pugh (R.C.V.S., 1962).

READ ABOUT BLACKSMITHS' SHOPS (Colourmaster International).

THE WAX CHANDLERS OF LONDON, John Dummelow, MA(Cantab), C.ENG. (Master 1960–62) (Phillimore, 1973).

LONDON'S ROLE OF FAME (Corporation of London, 1959).

THE CITY OF LONDON, A RECORD OF DESTRUCTION AND SURVIVAL, C.H. Holden, FRIBA, and W.G. Holford, FRIBA, MTPI (Corporation of London, 1951).

GENERAL INDEX

253

INDEX OF PEOPLE AND PLACES

254

255

Loveday, William Thomas, 100
Lovegrove, Colonel, 57
Lovell, R.A., 106
Lowestoft, 162
Loweth, Walter, 17
Lucas, Jonathan, 54, 55
Lucena, 33
Luck, 198
Ludgate, 198
Ludgate Hill, 14
Ludgate Street, 12, 14
Lyle, R.C. 106
Lacy, John George, 29

McCauley, Charles, 17
McConnell, Robert, 63
Mabbs, Samuel, 233
Mall, The, 88, 214
Mann, Norman John, 76, 200, 201
Manville, Sir Edward, 70
Marden, George Ernest, 102, 104
Marden, John Louis, 104
Margaret, Princess – Countess of
  Snowdon, 216
Marlborough House, 34
Marsh, Ernest John, 63
Masters, Miss Betty, 2, 4, 67
Martin, E., 153, 154
Mary, H.M. The Queen, 57
Mates, Michael, 111
May, William, 97
Meade, Miss Margaret, 149
Melling, John Kennedy, (Editor), 58, 106,
  110
Melton Mowbray, 117, 139, 141
Merrick, William, 52, 53
Methuen, 189
Mexico, 208
Midlands, 33
Miles, W.J., 106
Miller, Hemsley, 17
Miller, Sir James (Lord Mayor), 39, 41, 42,
  221, 222
Mills, 33
Mills, Bertram, 201
Mills, F.B., 102, 117
Mills, George, 100
Mills, Mrs. Hester, 199
Montague, Hyman, 56, 101
Montreal, 217
Moore Brabazon, Miss, 9, 102
Moreton, Lord, 113
Morgan, Veterinary Lieut., 57
Mould, Eric Cecil, 201
Moulden, Jospeh Eldin, 184
Mulvey, Veterinary Lieut., 57
Murlock, Miss Frances, 59
Murphy, C.T., 130, 134, 140, 141, 142

Neathercoat, Ernest T., 70, 71, 81, 104
Neathercoat, Russell William Vernon, 47,
  70, 81, 94, 104, 178, 208

Newell, Lord, 87, 111
Newgate Street, 12, 108
Newington, Fred, 106
Newmarket, 47, 90
New Zealand, 118
Noble Street, 64
Norfolk, 25
Northampton, 117
Norwood, 78
Notte, John, 50
Nottingham, 38
Noyon, Bishop of, 48

Odber, William, 98
Oldfield, Herbert Rooke, 64
Oldham, 78
Oliver, Denis Frank, 94, 153
Olympia, 201
Orr, Captain, 57
Osmer, William, 23
Oxenford, John de 50, 181
Oxford, 162
Oxford Street, 74
Oxon, John de, 4

Pagan, Anthony Hugh, 202
Pagan, Mrs. Diana, 62, 200
Palgrave, Sir Francis, 162, 163
Park Lane, 20
Parker, Benjamin, 183
Parkinson, George Westhead, 202
Parris, Matthew, 40
Parseley, John, 190, 191
Pavilion Road, London, 47
Paxman, Edward Philip, 46, 51, 73, 102
Pendley Manor, Tring, 47, 89, 201
Perthshire, 90
Philip, HRH Prince, Duke of Edinburgh,
  209, 212, 215
Phillips, Captain Mark, 84, 87, 211, 212,
  213, 217
Phillips, Peter Mark Andrew, 217
Phillips, Stanley, 103
Pickwick, Samuel, 201
Pitt, William, Earl of Chatham, 216
Pliny, 226
Plummer, Sir Desmond, 149
Poitiers, Battle of, 223
Pollen, A.F. 202
Poole, James, 107, 194
Poole, John, 107
Poole, William, 194
Popham, Benjamin, 68, 185
Potter, Thomas, 158
Poulden, Rev. Preb. F.A., 63, 73, 95, 189
Poultry, 12
Prince, John, 24
Prince, Rev. John, 24
Prince of Wales (Edward VII), 35
Prince, Leslie Barnett (Author), 9, 11, 16,
  17, 46, 57, 60, 63, 64, 67, 70, 72, 73, 76,
  82, 83, 85, 88, 94, 103, 105, 107, 108,

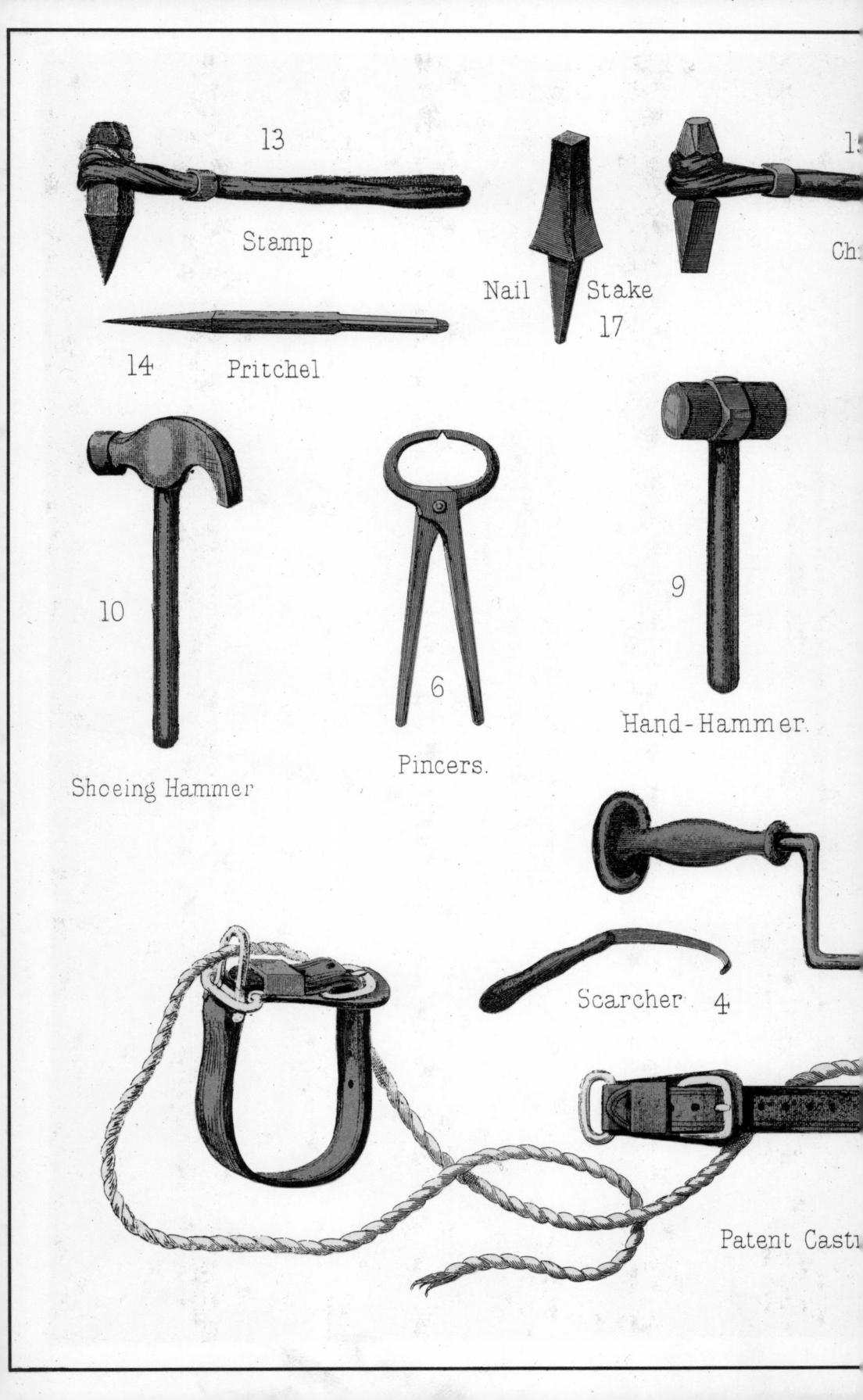

13

Stamp

Nail   Stake
17

1...

Ch...

14   Pritchel

10

Shoeing Hammer

6

Pincers.

9

Hand-Hammer

Scarcher   4

Patent Cast...